T0210893

Lecture Notes
in Business Information Processing   **213**

More information about this series at http://www.springer.com/series/7911

Marten van Sinderen · Vincent Chapurlat (Eds.)

Enterprise Interoperability

6th International IFIP Working Conference, IWEI 2015
Nîmes, France, May 28–29, 2015
Proceedings

Editors

Marten van Sinderen
University of Twente
Enschede
The Netherlands

Vincent Chapurlat
École des Mines d'Alès
Nîmes
France

ISSN 1865-1348   ISSN 1865-1356   (electronic)
Lecture Notes in Business Information Processing
ISBN 978-3-662-47156-2   ISBN 978-3-662-47157-9   (eBook)
DOI 10.1007/978-3-662-47157-9

Library of Congress Control Number: 2015937531

Springer Heidelberg New York Dordrecht London

Printed on acid-free paper

Springer-Verlag GmbH Berlin Heidelberg is part of Springer Science+Business Media
(www.springer.com)

Preface

Enterprise interoperability is a key factor for the success of collaborative organizations. It determines to what extent companies can make use of each other's unique capabilities and so create added business value through synergetic effects. It also determines the agility of a company in that it enables the company to leave or change an existing collaboration structure and establish collaboration with new partners efficiently.

Enterprise interoperability transcends different functional levels and has many concerns that need to be considered. Moreover, all phases of the enterprise interoperability lifecycle must be anticipated, supported, and maintained by business partners in order to be able to fully exploit the potential of collaboration. Enterprise interoperability is thus an essential requirement for companies, but because of its scope and complexity, it is not easily achieved.

The design and engineering of enterprise interoperability is challenging in an increasingly interoperation-demanding economy and society. Enterprises operate in dynamic contexts with changing demands, market opportunities, business partners, and technology solutions. Enterprise interoperability therefore cannot be solved alone by developing and adopting a static set of standards. Enterprise interoperability solutions for future enterprise networks should be able to negotiate standards and standard options, have built-in mechanisms to cope with changing partners, aligning interoperability settings with partners' business goals, and be context-aware and self-adaptive in case of long-running enterprise interoperations. Enterprise interoperability engineering addresses these issues, starting from existing definitions and frameworks that have been developed and tested in previous research and projects.

IWEI is an International IFIP Working Conference covering all aspects of enterprise interoperability with the purpose of achieving flexible cross-organizational collaboration through integrated support at organizational, business, and technical levels. It provides a forum for discussing ideas and results among both researchers and practitioners. Contributions to the following areas are highlighted: scientific foundations for specifying, analyzing, and validating interoperability solutions; architectural frameworks for addressing interoperability challenges from different viewpoints and at different levels of abstraction; maturity models to evaluate and rank interoperability solutions with respect to distinguished quality criteria; and practical solutions and tools that can be applied to interoperability problems to date.

This year's IWEI – IWEI 2015 – was held during May 28–29, 2015, in Nîmes, France, following previous events in Enschede, The Netherlands (2013), Harbin, China (2012), Stockholm, Sweden (2011), Valencia, Spain (2009), and Munich, Germany (2008). The theme of IWEI 2015 is *"From Enterprise Interoperability Modelling and Analysis to Enterprise Interoperability Engineering,"* thus especially soliciting submissions and discussions related to enterprise interoperability engineering issues in dynamic enterprise networks.

IWEI 2015 was organized by the IFIP Working Group 5.8 on Enterprise Interoperability in cooperation with INTEROP-VLab and PGSO (Pole Grand sud-Ouest) from INTEROP-Vlab. The objective of IFIP WG5.8 is to advance and disseminate research and development results in the area of enterprise interoperability. IWEI provides an excellent platform to discuss the ideas that have emerged from IFIP WG5.8 meetings, and, reversely, to transfer issues identified at the conference to the IFIP community for further contemplation and investigation.

The proceedings of IWEI 2015 are contained in this volume. Out of 20 submissions, a total of 9 full research papers, 4 short papers, and 2 industrial papers were selected for oral presentation and publication. The selection was based on a thorough review process, in which each paper was reviewed by three experts in the field. The papers are representative of the current research activities in the area of enterprise interoperability. They cover a wide spectrum of enterprise interoperability issues, ranging from foundational theories, frameworks, architectures, methods and guidelines to applications and case studies.

Two keynotes were given by Dr. Sergio Gusmeroli, Research and Innovation Director of TXT in Italy, and Prof. Henrique Martins, CEO of SMMS – Shared Services of the Ministry of Health in Portugal. Dr. Gusmeroli addressed the application of enterprise interoperability methods and tools to manufacturing service ecosystems. Professor Martins talked about the phenomenon of information explosion and the challenge it brings to enterprise interoperability. He discussed the European eHealth Network and its associated eHealth Interoperability Framework.

We would like to take this opportunity to express our gratitude to all those who contributed to the IWEI 2015 working conference. We thank the authors for submitting content, which resulted in valuable information exchange and stimulating discussions; we thank the reviewers for providing useful feedback to the submitted content, which undoubtedly helped the authors to improve their work; and we thank the attendants for expressing interest in the content and initiating relevant discussions. We are indebted to IFIP TC5 as well as INTEROP-VLab for recognizing the importance of enterprise interoperability as a research area with high economic impact, and acting accordingly with the establishment of WG5.8. Finally, we are grateful to the École des Mines d'Alès (EMA) for hosting the working conference.

March 2015   Marten van Sinderen
                                                    Vincent Chapurlat

Organization

IWEI 2015 was organized by IFIP Working Group 5.8 on Enterprise Interoperability, in cooperation with INTEROP-VLab and PGSO (Pôle Grand Sud-Ouest) of INTEROP-VLab.

General Chair

Vincent Chapurlat   École des Mines d'Alès, France

Program Chair

Marten van Sinderen   University of Twente, The Netherlands

Workshop Chair

Martin Zelm   INTEROP-VLab, Germany

IFIP Liaison

Guy Doumeingts   INTEROP-VLab/Université de Bordeaux, France

Local Arrangements Chairs

Nicolas Daclin   École des Mines d'Alès, France
Valérie Roman   École des Mines d'Alès, France

International Program Committee

João Paulo A. Almeida   Federal University of Espírito Santo, Brazil
Bernard Archimede   ENIT Tarbes, France
Frédérick Bénaben   EMAC, France
Khalid Benali   LORIA – Nancy Université, France
Alain Bernard   Centrale Nantes, France
Peter Bernus   Griffith University, Australia
Xavier Boucher   EMSE, France
Ricardo Chalmeta   University of Jaume I, Spain
Vincent Chapurlat   École des Mines d'Alès, France
David Chen   Université de Bordeaux, France
Eng Chew   University of Technology, Sydney, Australia
Nicolas Daclin   École des Mines d'Alès, France
Antonio De Nicola   ENEA, Italy
Alexandre Dolgui   EMSE, France
Guy Doumeingts   INTEROP-VLab/Université de Bordeaux, France

Yves Ducq	Université de Bordeaux, France
Ip-Shing Fan	Cranfield University, UK
Luís Ferreira Pires	University of Twente, The Netherlands
Erwin Folmer	Kadaster/University of Twente, The Netherlands
Ricardo Goncalves	New University of Lisbon, UNINOVA, Portugal
Ted Goranson	Sirius-Beta, USA
Maria Iacob	University of Twente, The Netherlands
Pontus Johnson	KTH, Sweden
Leonid Kalinichenko	Russian Academy of Sciences, Russian Federation
Stephan Kassel	Westsächsische Hochschule Zwickau, Germany
Kurt Kosanke	CIMOSA Association e.V., Germany
Lea Kutvonen	University of Helsinki, Finland
Elyes Lamine	Université Jean-François Champollion, France
Robert Meersman	Free University of Brussels, Belgium
Kai Mertins	Knowledge Raven Management GmbH, Germany
Zoran Milosevic	Deontik Pty Ltd., Australia
Andreas Opdahl	University of Bergen, Norway
Angel Ortiz	Polytechnic University of Valencia, Spain
Hervé Panetto	Université Henri Poincaré Nancy I, France
Raul Poler	Universitat Politècnica de València, Spain
Manfred Reichert	University of Ulm, Germany
Pierre-Yves Schobbens	Facultés Universitaires Notre-Dame de la Paix, Belgium
Ahm Shamsuzzoha	University of Vaasa, Finland
Marten van Sinderen	University of Twente, The Netherlands
Bruno Vallespir	Université de Bordeaux, France
François Vernadat	ECA Europe, Luxembourg
Georg Weichhart	University of Linz, Austria
Milan Zdravkovic	University of Niš, Serbia

Additional Reviewers

Mario Lezoche   Université Henri Poincaré Nancy I, France

Sponsoring Organizations

IFIP TC5, www.ifip.org
INTEROP-VLab, www.interop-vlab.eu
PGSO Pôle Grand Sud-Ouest INTEROP-VLab,
   https://extranet.ims-bordeaux.fr/External/PGSO/
OMG, www.omg.org
ERCIS, www.ercis.org
École des Mines d'Alès (EMA), mines-ales.fr

Contents

Short and Position Papers

Industrial Papers

Full Papers

Semantic Interoperability in Astrophysics for Workflows Extraction from Heterogeneous Services

Thierry Louge[1](✉), Mohamed Hedi Karray[2], Bernard Archimède[2], and Jürgen Knödlseder[3]

[1] Institut de Recherche en Astrophysique et Planétologie,
Université de Toulouse - UPS, 57 Avenue d'Azereix,
65000 Tarbes, France
thierry.louge@irap.omp.eu
[2] Ecole Nationale d'Ingénieurs de Tarbes ENIT, Université de Toulouse,
47 Avenue d'Azereix, BP1629, 65016 Tarbes Cedex, France
[3] Institut de Recherche en Astrophysique et Planétologie, CNRS,
9 Avenue du Colonel Roche, BP 44346,
31028 Toulouse Cedex 4, France

Abstract. Modern instruments in astrophysics lead to a growing amount of data and more and more specific observations, among which scientists must be able to identify and retrieve useful information for their own specific research. The Virtual Observatory (http://www.ivoa.net/deployers/intro_to_vo_concepts. html) architecture has been designed to achieve this goal. It allows the joint use of data taken from different instruments. Retrieving and cross-matching those data is in progress, but it's impossible today to find a sequence resolving a given science case needing a combination of existing services of whom the user doesn't knows the specifications. The goal of this work is to propose the basis of an architecture leading to automatic composition of workflows that implement scientific use cases.

Keywords: Interoperability · Ontologies · Virtual observatory · Astrophysics

1 Introduction

In view of the ever-growing quantity of scientific data provided by modern astrophysics, the community of universe sciences built a system of "virtual" observatories, allowing to express metadata in a shared format (VOTable[1] being the most widely used) and offering a set of protocols and services to access the data. The goal of the associated architecture is allowing the share of scientific data produced by instruments from all fields of universe sciences, from astrophysics to geophysics through planetology, heliophysics, etc. The global goal is very well shared by everyone involved but many specific needs occurred, sometimes leading to specific developments ending with the emergence of several VO "branches", guided by different organizations such as IVOA

---

[1] http://www.ivoa.net/documents/VOTable/.

© IFIP International Federation for Information Processing 2015
M. van Sinderen and V. Chapurlat (Eds.): IWEI 2015, LNBIP 213, pp. 3–15, 2015.
DOI: 10.1007/978-3-662-47157-9_1

(International Virtual Observatory Alliance) for astrophysics, VAMDC (Virtual Atomic and Molecular Data Center) for astrochemistry, IPDA (International Planetary Data Alliance) for planetology, etc. Furthermore, the volume of data increases in every science field and the needs for common protocols and formats are shared outside of astrophysics. In this context, Research Data Alliance[2] deals with the same kind of challenges than the VO, in order to organize every science field around the same concepts and software architecture. Expressing data and services in a shared format should lead to an easier way to find and combine appropriate services for scientific uses.

In the field of services computing research, a common way used to find web services is to use Service Oriented Access Protocol (SOAP), in conjunction with Web Services Definition Language (WSDL) services descriptions and Universal Description Discovery and Integration (UDDI) registries [15] to locate appropriate services. This approach is expected to reach a new level of effectiveness with the emergence of semantic web principles [14], and the use of ontologies describing knowledge under the form of metadata with concepts, relationships and objects.

We present in this work an architecture combining the methods used on service discovery and contributions of the VO in astrophysics. This architecture allows a VO transparency enhancement by performing the matching and selection of services automatically, from the description of a scientific use-case. We should be able to combine in our workflows VO and non VO-related services alike, providing that they are correctly described in the ontology and detected as relevant for the given use-case. Generated workflows will be presented to the user who'll be able to closely inspect every single step to evaluate the results, judge the accuracy and annotate them to provide enhancements for future or immediate re-runs. In this paper, we'll briefly expose the state of the art concerning web services composition and VO capabilities, then suggest an architecture to allow automation of workflows composition and the first test results we get.

2   State of the Art

2.1   Web Services Composition

A way to resolve web services composition is to query a UDDI services registry, select appropriate services based on their WSDL description and query them with SOAP protocol. "WSDL is the emerging language for describing the present web service technology and presents the syntactic description of the web services. It only present the structure of the data sent and received through the web, but is unable to present the meaning of the data" [17]. Such a description, focusing on the semantics of data rather than their technical representation may be obtained using ontologies.

Ontologies may be used as interoperability layer between services, to ensure that skills of one service corresponds to the needs of another one [16]. More specifically, ontologies are used to describe services, the way they operate and the data they need to be used. One of the purposes is to increase the effectiveness of interoperability,

---

[2] https://rd-alliance.org.

selection and composition of services by describing them in one common ontology, which is very close to what we would like to realize with astrophysics services and that we present in Sect. 4.

Semantic web makes software agents regular web users as are humans, and enhance web services composition thanks to the new reasoning possibilities offered, as exposed in [18]. In this paper, authors expose several existing approaches dealing with services composition and conclude that inputs and outputs of services are not enough to get an appropriate composition. In order to enhance composition performance, one has to specify the services pre/post conditions. The pre-condition prescribes what is necessary to hold before the Web service can be executed and the post-condition prescribes what holds after the service execution [18]. This combination of compatibilities, pre-execution conditions to match and post-execution results to achieve is completed with the notion of Quality of Service (QoS) describing how non-functional requirements have been judged during the execution of the service (response time, availability…).

Then authors review several approaches for web composition, like using Knowledge Interchange Format (KIF) rules to express user constraints to match with an ontology for services (OWL-S), which is the closest one to the architecture that we present in this work.

2.2   Virtual Observatory (VO) in Astrophysics

VO is a software construction very tied to its application domain that allows to express observed and theoretical data with a common description, and the building of services based on the same formats and protocols. Interoperability, which is the core concern of this architecture is reached through definite descriptive fields and software tools able to understand the VO formats, datamodels and protocols. Nevertheless, difficulties still exist because of the multiple different ways to adapt the datamodels, imposed by the great amount of specific definitions tied to specific observations and their diversity. Even if the VO is nowadays a reality and a success, its everyday use is frequently restricted by not providing enough ease-of-use, because of a too weak transparency for the end user that has to deal with thousands of services with little support or poor descriptions.

Datamodels: The Description. Querying a VO service returns an XML document, which is called "datamodel" (DM), and defines the mandatory information so that the answers of a service can be used by VO-compliant software, and optional information completing the minimal required description. Datamodels can be used by different protocols and share some vocabulary to interoperate.

Software querying the VO must, to be able to properly use the data, understand every DM.

Protocols: Data Access. As shown in Fig. 1,[3] IVOA data access layer is composed of several protocols, each of them being dedicated to a service category such as Simple Spectral Access (SSA) for spectra, Table Access Protocol (TAP) for catalogs of

---

[3] http://www.ivoa.net/documents/DALI/20131129/REC-DALI-1.0-20131129.html.

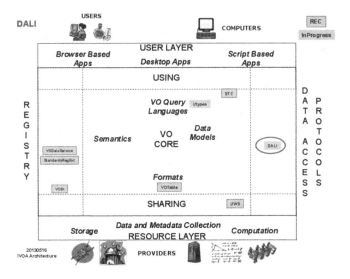

Fig. 1. Data access layer (DAL) in the overall IVOA architecture

observations or direct access to database tables, etc. Generally, protocols are not tied to specific DMs, with the exception of SSA which relates to the spectra DM.

An example is the ConeSearch protocol, which is rather widely used and implemented by a large number of services, and which allows to search for an observation in the very general term, being a spectra, an image or anything else, real or theoretical around a reference point in the sky. As ConeSearch allows to describe data in a very general way it allows to retrieve any kind of observation and so any kind of scientific results. Today, more than ten thousand different services are registered serving this ConeSearch protocol, and the diversity of their results and specificities is a burden for an effective interoperability.

Semantic Interoperability in IVOA: UTypes, UCDs, VOUnits. Data description in the DM use a defined ensemble of symbols (UTypes) referencing information that can be found inside the structure of the given DM, coupled with a more generic vocabulary allowing the user to get some details about the given information: the UCDs (Universal Content Descriptors).

IVOA data description is completed by another recommendation (VOUnits), listing every unit understandable by VO-compliant tools, and suggests to simply put non-listed units between single-quotes.

This can be illustrated with an example coming from Photometry DM: we find UTYPe "photDM: PhotometryFilter.spectralLocation.unit.expression" designing "Unit of the spectral axis used to characterize the spectral coordinate of the zero point" associated with the ucd "meta.unit" designing the unit. In an SSA answer from a service we could find: "ucd = "instr.bandwidth" utype = "SSA:Char.SpectralAxis.Coverage.Bounds.Extent" unit = "angstrom"", for the meaning of the information (ucd), its role in the DM (utype) and its unit (unit). Despite all those possibilities, some specific data are not taken into account by the DM definitions, hence some information is lost as there is no equivalent VO representation, and the corresponding services can not be used in an interoperable way. An example are polarized spectra: while spectra can be described using the spectrum DM, there exists no description for the polarization information, neither at the DM level or the service description, which stronly limits the usage of the data.

Also, we frequently find services with only partial use, or non-standard use of the DMs (one frequent case is to meet ucd = "POS_EQ_RA" for pos.eq.ra which is the correct ucd) as the data provided are not systematically checked.

All these reasons call for the addition of an interoperability layer, as implemented for example in the IRIS framework [10], allowing to attach supplementary information to VO services.

Software Tools. Dedicated software[4] exists allowing the query of VO registries and retrieval and understanding of data. Sometimes very general as Aladin, or more specialized ("Montage" for images mosaïc visualization, "CASSIS" for the vizualisation of spectra, just to cite those ones), they are the interface between users and the mechanisms described above. Sometimes, they only serve a predefined ensemble of services,[5] for which their performances are optimized and the precise data description known beyond the DM content. Software development, specific to a certain kind of data categories are regularly appearing, such as photometry in the Vizier catalogs [1].

Another kind of tools that exist are the workflows planners. They offer an automation of workflows composed of queries to predefined VO services and scientific processing. The principle is that the user defines a solution to the problem, builds a workflow by specifying what services are to query and how data are to be processed with which tools. The workflows can be executed as often as required, for example with different input parameters, and they can be publicly shared with the scientific community (e.g. http://www.myexperiment.org). Taverna is one of those tools and integrated in some of the HELIO (heliophysics-oriented VO) services to provide the user direct description of HELIO services inside Taverna quickly and easily [2].

These considerations on data discovery were met again concerning the scientific software and lead to the idea of having an application registry that would allow to access directly the tools that fit the user needs. Initiatives such as Astrophysics Source Code Library (ASCL), which development is still on progress [13] aims at providing such a registry. One of the main difficulties for the users today is indeed to locate and learn to use the appropriate tool for a scientific use-case, and to put it in relation with other software tools if needed.

3 Practical Use of the VO

3.1 Using the VO: Overview

The data models used by IVOA are both flexible and heterogeneous. Mandatory keywords are limited, but necessarily imprecise to allow adaption to a large variety of

---

[4] http://www.ivoa.net/astronomers/applications.html.

[5] http://www.usvao.org/science-tools-services/time-series-search-tool/.

data or different origins. Each service can enrich the description according to the defined format, yet there is no guarantee that all services will implement the same extensions. For some areas of research (e.g., gamma-ray astronomy), the possibilities for describing observations are limited. Therefore initiatives as HELIO [2] to helio-physics appear, trying to provide a more accurate description of specific data. Another problem is the knowledge of the existence of services. Current registries provide a list of services and their characteristics, but this list may be very long, making it difficult for a user to identify the most adapted service for a given use-case.

Even in the case of two services offering the same type of data (spectra, for example) and in the same wavelength band, there is nothing to put both in relation, and a user accessing one of the services will not be informed about the existence of the second. These concerns are taken into account by the IVOA, which works on the development of a protocol called "DataLink".[6] Once established, DataLink will allow a data provider to specify other data in relation to those it provides. However, this link will be established based on knowledge of a data provider and according to the capacity of each organization to provide this protocol, to maintain and update its content from the emergence of new data and/or new services.

So it is the user's responsibility to make a selection and ensure the joint use of data, which can be a complex operation due to the large amounts of data and data sources that exist. This large number of possibilities involves treatment "a priori" by the user, which lead primarily to already known services, and can not sort of the more than 10,000 service offering for example the protocol "Cone Search" what are those likely to provide useful information to its study. The concrete and systematic use of the Virtual Observatory remains complicated even for an informed user due to differences between the technical sales descriptions of services and their multiplicity.

3.2 Use-Case: Analysis of the Crab Nebula

Let us consider a specific use-case for reference: an astrophysicist wants to produce a multi-wavelength analysis of the Crab Nebula. This case study is similar to a case described in an article in the SF2A (French Society of Astronomy and Astrophysics) [3], which searches for the same type of analysis on two services, HESS and Fermi-LAT.

How to get there with current software? The first step consists of using a tool that queries OV services to identify those that provide spectra. Spectral data can be provided by services satisfying the ConeSearch and the SSA protocols. Both protocols need to be examined. For services satisfying the ConeSearch protocol those have to be identified which according to the provided UCDs actually provide spectral information. From the resulting list of services, a detailed analysis of the service description needs to be made to identify the services that are relevant to the problem (e.g. which are the data of highest quality, which data are obsolete, which data are inaccurate, etc.). Also, the services need to be identified that provide data in a format and in units that are exploitable by the tools at hand. Doing so on hundreds or thousands of services is

---

[6] http://www.ivoa.net/documents/DataLink/20140930/PR-DataLink-1.0-20140930.html.

impossible without automation, and we likely will choose the first we meet and seem to agree about. Then, the user can recover the data provided that the server is not down, and provided that the actual source of interest (here the Crab Nebula) has actually been observed. Eventually at this step, alternative services need to be considered.

4 Proposed Solution

4.1 Design of an Astrophysics Services Ontology

As we have seen, the VO covers multiple aspects and although we took the IVOA as an example of architecture, yet not all astrophysical information and services do comply to VO standards. Our goal is to develop a solution that uses the Virtual Observatory as transparent as possible so that an end user would not be concerned about data query and reading, service identification, and mixing VO and non-VO services. In the world of bioinformatics, a similar problem of interoperability is addressed by the SADI project [6], a web service description model based on Ontology Web Language (OWL) for particular services to interface with Taverna. Our approach has many similarities with this work, extending its principle to the workflows OWL description and to place the OWL representation services outside of the services themselves, to allow existing models to continue to operate without changes and to integrate into the system.

The overall architecture of our system is illustrated in Fig. 2. The ontology that we will produce will be updated by different sources, OVs and autonomous services alike. It will generate a knowledge base within which the reasoning will take place.

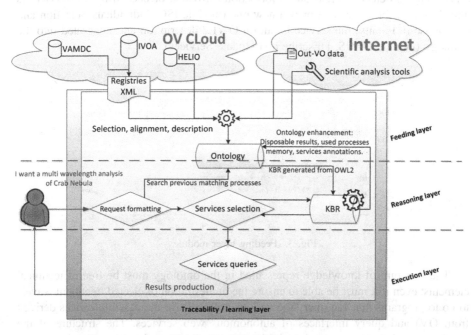

Fig. 2. Overall architecture

The results of our work are intended to be used as a web service to various input levels:

- The standard user, who will provide scientific cases for which we propose processing streams available.
- Second level of the user wish to consult the knowledge at his disposal by visualizing ontology and performing queries on its structure.
- The third level of user, who can enter the description of a service in the ontology, to see it incorporated into the range of opportunities available.
- The administrator, who will update the ontology with new treatment libraries or tools at large installed on the physical server and use program, and descriptions from the third level user alike.

The ontology will be used through a web interface, and updated by the administrator of the system based on suggestions from the users concerning service or workflow comments and annotations, or new services candidates to be part of the system.

4.2   Structure and Ontology Filling

Figure 3 focuses on the main source of knowledge in the ontology, which are the description of the skills of web services. They are either collected through XML descriptions issued from registries (IVOA organization) by the module "ASTRO1" or through other available documents (WSDL-like descriptions, and the system will also provide a specific interface dedicated to descriptions of new services). After being collected, the description is analyzed to gather information concerning the skills of the service and to detect whereas and information (provided or needed by the service) is already known in the system or is a new one (module ISC, Individuals Selection and Comparison). Finally, the service is put on OWL2 description and integrated into the ontology (module DEUS, DEscribe and Update Services).

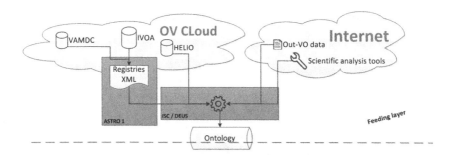

Fig. 3. Feeding layer modules

The structure of knowledge represented in the ontology must be free of technical elements, even if it must be able to ensure the orchestration of elected treatment waves, to go to programs that can query the various protocols (in the case of services derived from OV) and query interfaces of autonomous web services. The structure of the ontology used to represent domain knowledge, support for both the description

contained in the existing data models and skills of available services. The workflows generated by the system will also be included in this structure. Services and workflows are described with the same semantic metadata, which support interoperability between the collected data.

Matching the Information. A more detailed description on the ASTRO1, ISC and DEUS modules is shown in Fig. 4. When an existing service provides new or updated information, or when a new service becomes available the ontology needs to be updated. This implies matching the new information with any existing information to identify to what class the new information belongs, or if an updated information needs to be merged with some already existing information. This identification of ontology elements to link with new sources of information is an important aspect for the sustainability and genericity of our system. Our design will rely on the principles of finding alignments between concepts based on their descriptions and mapping semantic models, learning from them to best understand furthers ones that have been outlined in references [7, 8].

4.3   Reasoning with the Ontology

Request Representation. The questioning of this service go through the interpretation of the requests made by the user to understand the elements of the system. The reconciliation between the expression of the case by the user and the concepts and relations of the ontology will be managed by assistance to the collection and use of key words recognition techniques based on parsing the natural language [11]. In addition with the natural expression, an interface-driven query construction will help the user to describe the use-case he wants the system to solve.

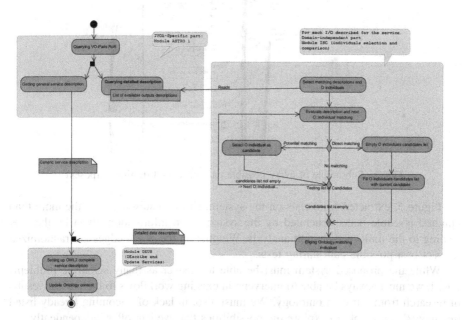

Fig. 4. Information matching detection

For the use case exposed in 3.2, the user may give the request through natural language, e.g. "Multiwavelength analysis of Crab nebula", and give the system some more information by using a web interface to specify some more information, as coordinates of the target, specific wavelengths to ignore or to prioritize, etc. Combination of natural language description and web interface specifications will lead to a request representation allowing to query the system to get every possible workflow and choose the more appropriate.

We'll illustrate our system with this use case, saying that the user gives the system starting information: target name (Crab nebula) and a radius (tolerance factor applied to object coordinates), and wants multiwavelength analysis. The request representation matches those given informations with internal representation, being "multilambda" for result of multiwavelength analysis, "radius" and "target_name" for given object name and runs the system based on those requirements.

Generating a Graph of Possible Workflows. During the step of generating all paths, we will examine a basic workflows to determine if partial results are already available in previous compositions, and to determine their reusability, their enrichment and the necessary adaptations. We will use current methods of isomorphism search graph or subgraphs [4, 5], aiming at extracting workflows service states to reuse in a similar context, we will have to bring our own knowledge base in order to best use them. Among these works, those studying the structure of workflows from Taverna [9] will be of great support.

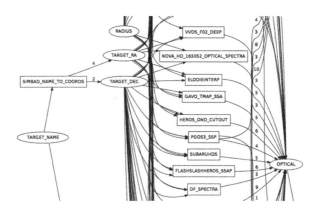

Fig. 5. Subsample of every possible path generated (testing purposes)

Figure 5, extracted from tests on the system, shows a subsample of the more than hundred possible paths generated by the system from information given by the user leading to the multi-wavelength analysis. Weights on the graph edges are randomized to elect best possible path during tests.

While the proposed system must be able to answer as many scientific problems posed, we must always be able to intervene in existing workflows to include the results of research from our own ontology. We must also, in lack of oncoming already listed treatments, being able to explore the possibilities that we can offer independently.

4.4   Selecting One Workflow

Multiple workflows will be identified that lead to an answer of the user request, and a method is needed to identify the best workflow to choose. This requires information beyond the description of the problem, and may include past experience, preferred services, or preferred data sources. Any constraints or choices will be indicated explicitly to the user at all stages of the processing flow, and the user can modify these parameters to adapt the workflow selection.

Figure 6 illustrates best possible choice, based on random weights on services to obtain every information needed to go from information given by the user to the result.

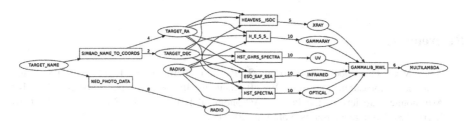

Fig. 6. One given path (generated for testing purposes)

The given information are used by the system that elect services (in squares) to provide information (in rounds) to come to the final information, multi-wavelength analysis.

5   Conclusion and Future Work

We propose to describe astrophysical data and services using an ontology that connects these resources for arbitrary scientific workflows. Our system will rely on the Virtual Observatory initiative to ensure the interoperability of services although we also envision inclusion of non-VO services in our system. This work heavily relies on the use of ontological description of astrophysical quantities and services to cross-match generic, user-based descriptions of data and services with a structured knowledge of the domain. A few VO services use ontological description which matches with the notion of "Astroinformatics" [12]. This notion is related to the expanding number of data available and the need to provide useful and efficient tools to extract knowledge and sleeping science from this big data source. In our knowledge, nothing has been tried in this field using an ontological representation of knowledge as a base for automated service workflow discovery and composition from the description of a scientific use-case.

The challenge is to provide a good enough information recognition between services and requests from many different sources. It will allow the discovery of relevant services, and then organize them in order to produce results. Also, it allows to compare those results with other sources; as well as giving the possibility to the user to provide feedback and modify the entire workflow to fit very specific needs.

We still have to take into account some internal specificities of the services to be able to get a fully usable workflow and obtain complete results (corresponding to "execution layer" in Fig. 2). Hence, we have to look at the need for services to obtain subset of information they need through one service alone. There are cases when some subset of input information (or all information) for one service need to result of a unique source, others where such subsets may come from different sources and our system must be able to handle every case. Also, it will be necessary to work on the user-guided interface to express queries semantically understandable by the system. Actually, the use of randomize weights hasn't to be considered as the final goal. In our future works, we'll try to apply a more sophisticated method to choose accurate paths for every step of the flows.

References

1. Allen, M.G., Ochsenbein, F., Derrière, S., Boch, T., Fernique, P., Landais, G.: Extracting photometry measurements from VizieR catalogs. In: Manset, N., Forshay, P. (eds.) Astronomical Society of the Pacific. Astronomical Data Analysis Software and Systems XXIII ASP Conference Series, vol. 485 (2014)
2. Bentley, R., Brooke, J., Csillaghy, A., Fellows, D., Le Blanc, A., Messerotti, M., Pérez-Suarez, D., Pierantoni, G., Soldati, M.: HELIO: discovery and analysis of data in heliophysics. In: 2011 Seventh IEEE International Conference on eScience (2011)
3. Derrière, S., Goosmann, R.W., Bot, C., Bonnarel, F.: Using the virtual observatory: multi-instrument, multi-wavelength study of high-energy sources. In: SF2A 2014 (2014)
4. Missier, P., Paton, N.W., Belhajjame, K.: Fine-grained and efficient lineage querying of collection-based workflow provenance. In: 13th International Conference on Extending Database Technology (EDBT) (2010)
5. Grigori, D., Corrales, J.C., Bouzeghoub, M., Gater, A.: Ranking BPEL processes for service discovery. IEEE Trans. Serv. Comput. 3(3), 178–192 (2010)
6. Wilkinson, M.D., Vandervalk, B., McCarthy, L.: The semantic automated discovery and integration (SADI) web service design-pattern, API and reference implementation. J. Biomed. Semant. 2(1), 5–23 (2011)
7. Taheriyan, M., Knoblock, C.A., Szekely, P., Ambite J.L.: A scalable approach to learn semantic models of structured sources. In: Proceedings of the 8th IEEE International Conference on Semantic Computing (2014)
8. Parundekar, R., Knoblock, C., Ambite, J.: Discovering concept coverings in ontologies of linked data sources. In: Cudré-Mauroux, P., Heflin, J., Sirin, E., Tudorache, T., Euzenat, J., Hauswirth, M., Parreira, J.X., Hendler, J., Schreiber, G., Bernstein, A., Blomqvist, E. (eds.) ISWC 2012, Part I. LNCS, vol. 7649, pp. 427–443. Springer, Heidelberg (2012)
9. Chen, J.: Designing scientific workflows following a structure and provenance-aware strategy. Thèse de doctorat Université Paris Sud (2013)
10. Laurino, O., Budynkiewicz, J., D'Abrusco, R., Bonaventura, N., Busko, I., Cresitello-Dittmar, M., Doe, S., Ebert, R., Evans, J., Norris, P., Pevunova, O., Refsdal, B., Thomas, B., Thompson, R.: Iris: an extensible application for building and analyzing spectral energy distributions. Astron. Comput. 7–8, 81–94 (2014). doi:10.1016/j.ascom.2014.07.004
11. Fuqi, S.: Contribution of ontology alignment to enterprise interoperability. Thèse de doctorat Université Bordeaux1 (2013)

12. Longo, G., Brescia, M., Djorgovski, S.G., Cavuoti, S., Donalek, C.: Data-driven discovery in astrophysics, astro-Ph.IM, 21 Oct 2014
13. Alice Allen and Judy Schmidt. Looking before leaping: Creating a software registry. Technical report 1407.5378, arXiv (2014). http://arxiv.org/abs/1407.5378
14. Berners-Lee, T., Hendler, J., Lassila, O.: The semantic web a new form of web content that is meaningful to computers will unleash a revolution of new possibilities. Sci. Am. **284**, 34–43 (2001)
15. Rao, J., Su, X.: A survey of automated web service composition methods. In: Cardoso, J., Sheth, A.P. (eds.) SWSWPC 2004. LNCS, vol. 3387, pp. 43–54. Springer, Heidelberg (2005)
16. Benatallah, B., Hacid, M., Rey, C., Toumani, F.: Semantic reasoning for web services discovery. In: Proceedings of World Wide Web (WWW) Workshop E-Services and the Semantic Web (2003)
17. Zeshan, F., Mohamad, R.: Semantic web service composition approaches: overview and limitations. Int. J. New Comput. Archit. Their Appl. **1**, 640–651 (2011)
18. Bartalos, P., Bieliková, M.: Automatic dynamic web service composition: a survey and problem formalization. Comput. Inf. **30**, 793–827 (2011)

A General Model Transformation Methodology to Serve Enterprise Interoperability Data Sharing Problem

Tiexin Wang[✉], Sebastien Truptil, and Frederick Benaben

Centre Génie Industriel, Université de Toulouse - Mines Albi,
Campus Jarlard, 81000 Albi, France
{tiexin.wang,sebastien.truptil,
frederick.benaben}@mines-albi.fr

Abstract. Interoperability, as one of the key competition factors for modern enterprises, describes the ability to establish partnership activities in an environment of unstable market. In some terms, interoperability determines the future of enterprises; so, improving enterprises' interoperability turns to be a research focus. "Sharing data among heterogeneous partners" is one of the most basic common interoperability problems, which requires a general methodology to serve. Model transformation, which plays a key role in model-driven engineering, provides a possible solution to data sharing problem. A general model transformation methodology, which could shield traditional model transformation practices' weaknesses: low reusability, contains repetitive tasks, involves huge manual effort, etc., is an ideal solution to data sharing problem. This paper presents a general model transformation methodology "combining semantic check measurement and syntactic check measurement into refined model transformation processes" and the mechanism of using it to serve interoperability's data sharing issue.

Keywords: Interoperability · Model-driven engineering · Model transformation · Semantic check · Syntactic check

1 Introduction

Nowadays, the world is becoming smaller and smaller. With the advancements of science and technology, more and more collaborations among countries, companies and persons are appeared. Such collaborations appear and disappear within specific periods, with achieving or failing of their goals. Based on this fact, the ability of cooperating with different partners becomes crucial to modern systems and organizations. Furthermore, "interoperability" is proposed specially to describe such ability. There are several definitions for interoperability; one of the initial definitions of interoperability could be referred in [1]. Another two definitions are listed here: as defined in [2], "interoperability is the ability of a system or a product to work with other systems or products without special effort from the user"; a similar definition of interoperability is stated in [3], interoperability is "a measure of the degree to which diverse systems, organizations, and/or individuals are able to work together to achieve

© IFIP International Federation for Information Processing 2015
M. van Sinderen and V. Chapurlat (Eds.): IWEI 2015, LNBIP 213, pp. 16–29, 2015.
DOI: 10.1007/978-3-662-47157-9_2

a common goal. For computer systems, interoperability is typically defined in terms of syntactic interoperability and semantic interoperability". Two key issues that stated in the two definitions are: "cooperate without special users' effort" and "semantic and syntactic" aspects. Although in different domains and from different views of one domain, the definitions of interoperability might be slightly different, the essence reflected by these definitions is similar. Figure 1 shows the interoperability issue and the data sharing problem of it.

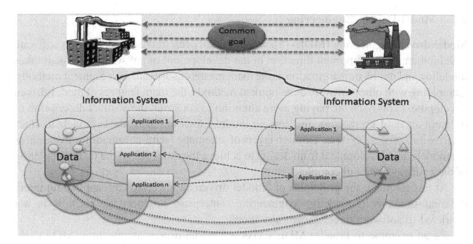

Fig. 1. An illustration of interoperability issue

Figure 1 shows a collaboration situation between two companies. Modern companies use information systems to manage their business; in some aspects, the cooperation among companies depends on the merge of their information systems. Furthermore, merging information systems relies on the interactions of their applications. So, sharing data among these applications (both within one system and from different systems) is important for enterprise cooperation. However, generally the structures of data are designed for specific applications used by particular enterprises; it is difficult to share data among different applications. Model transformation provides a possible solution to data sharing issue.

"Enterprise Interoperability Framework (EIF)" [4] shows a possible way of combining formally enterprise interoperability and model-driven engineering (especially the model transformation part). However, traditional model transformation practices have their own weakness: low reusability, repetitive tasks, huge manual effort, etc. In order to apply model transformation to solve interoperability problems, a general model transformation methodology (shield these weaknesses) is required. This paper presents such a general model transformation methodology.

This paper is divided into five sections. In the second section, the basic principles of model-driven engineering (MDE) and model transformation are presented. The third section describes the overview of the general methodology. The detail of syntactic and semantic checking measurements is illustrated in the fourth section. Finally, the conclusion is proposed in the fifth section.

2   Basic Background Theories

In this section, the basic background theories of this general model transformation methodology (GMTM) are presented. These theories are divided into two group:theories owned by MDE domain and theories belonging specially to model transformation domain.

2.1   Model-Driven Engineering

Model-driven engineering (MDE) [5], which initially referred as model-driven software development, is an important direction in the development of software process. It takes modeling and model transformation as the main means of software development methods. Comparing with other software development methods, the main features of model-driven development approach are paying more attention to construct the abstract description of different areas of knowledge: the domain models; then based on these models to characterize the software system. Through layers of automatic (semi-automatic) conversion of the models, the development from design to achieve the transition to the final completion of the entire system will complete.

At this moment, the principles of "model driven engineering" are applied on many different domains (knowledge engineering, enterprise engineering, etc.); it is not restricted to software development any more.

As an example to broader MDE's vision, "model-driven architecture (MDA)" [6] was launched in 2001 by the Object Management Group (OMG). Figure 2 shows the basic principles of MDA.

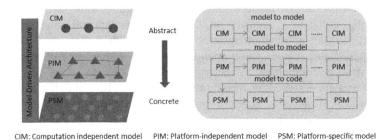

CIM: Computation independent model   PIM: Platform-independent model   PSM: Platform-specific model

Fig. 2. Simple illustration of MDA

In MDA, models could be divided into three groups: "CIM", "PIM" and "PSM". In each of the three groups, large number of models could be built to reflect the characteristics, which based on different point of views, of one system. Models in PIM layer should be generated by transforming the models from CIM layer; the mechanism of building PSM layer's models follows the same principle (generated by transforming models from PIM layer).

In MDE context, everything could be regarded as a model or could be modeled. In simple words, MDE uses models to describe the reality (concerns the modeling techniques)

and uses model transformations to solve conversion problems. Modeling, as one key role of MDE, means the activities of building models; model transformation, as another key role of MDE, means the process of taking the source model to generate the target model.

2.2   Model and Meta-model

Model and meta-model are two basic concepts in MDE; Fig. 3 shows the relation between them.

Fig. 3. Relation between model and meta-model

As defined in [7], model is "a simplification of the subject and its purpose is to answer some particular questions aimed towards the subject". Models are built to represent the characteristics of real systems based on specific point views. Meta-models are a specific kind of model; they make statements about what can be expressed in valid models. Meta-models could have several layers; meta-model defines building rules for models that conform to it.

2.3   Model Transformation

Model transformation plays a key role in MDE; it is the nexus among heterogeneous models. With the extensive usage of MDE theory, more and more theories, techniques and tools of model transformation have been created. Large amount of model transformation practices have been developed to serve some specific domain problems using these theories, techniques and tools; two examples are stated in [8, 9].

In general, according to [10], there are two main kinds of model transformation approaches. They are: model-to-code approaches and model-to-model approaches. For model-to-code approaches (PIM to PSM), there are two categories: "Visitor-based approaches" and "Template-based approaches". For the model-to-model approaches, there are five categories:

- Direct-dManipulation Approaches: offering an internal model representation plus some API to manipulate this model
- Relational Approaches: grouping declarative approaches where the main concept is mathematical relations
- Graph-Transformation-Based Approaches: e.g., VIATRA, ATOM and GreAT
- Structure-Driven Approaches: an example is "OptimalJ" model transformation
- Hybrid Approaches: combining different techniques from the previous categories

The detail of these approaches (their applicable situations, working mechanism, etc.) could be consulted in [10].

However, as mentioned above, traditional model transformation practices have internal weaknesses; these weaknesses limit the scope of model transformation usage. As the inner characteristics and requirement of modern enterprise interoperability (e.g. agility, transient, heterogeneity, complexity), traditional model transformation practices are not a good choice to serve it. So, a general model transformation methodology is required.

3   Overview of the General Methodology

This section presents the detail of GMTM. The main objective of GMTM is "overcoming the shortcomings of traditional model transformation practices and serving to enterprise interoperability". "General" means the use of this methodology is widely, not limited to a specific domain. In order to be general, the process of defining model transformation mappings should be automatic. To achieve this goal, semantic and syntactic checking (S&S) measurements are combined into the traditional model transformation process.

3.1   Theoretical Main Framework of the General Methodology

GMTM is created on the basis of a theoretical main framework, which is based on [11], and shown in Fig. 4.

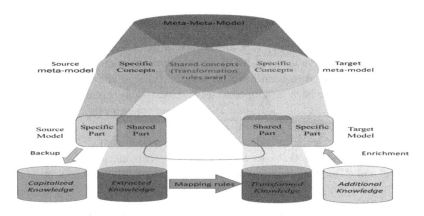

Fig. 4. Theoretical main framework

Figure 4 illustrates the theoretical basis of GMTM. The significance of doing model transformation could be "sharing knowledge", "exchanging information", etc. The purpose of model transformation practice is: generate the target model based on the source model.

The necessary condition of doing model transformation between two models is: the source model and target model should have some potential common items (to be detected and found). For the reason "models are built based on the rules defined in their meta-models", the potential common items could be traced on meta-model layer.

The source MM shares part of its concepts with the target MM. As a consequence, the source model embeds a shared part and a specific part. The shared part provides the extracted knowledge, which may be used for the model transformation, while the specific part should be saved as capitalized knowledge in order not to be lost. Then, mapping rules (built based on the overlapping conceptual area between MMs) can be applied on the extracted knowledge. The transformed knowledge and an additional knowledge (to fill the lack of knowledge concerning the non-shared part of concepts into the target MM) may be finally used to create the shared part and the specific part of the target model.

3.2 The Meta-meta-model Within Main Framework

According to [12], in order to apply semantic checking measurements in the process of defining model transformation mapping rules, some principles should be obeyed. In this GMTM, the mechanism of applying S&S in model transformation process is defined in a meta-meta-model (MMM), which is shown at the top of Fig. 4.

There are several meta-modelling architectures, for example "MOF: Meta-Object Facility" [13]. These architectures define their own semantic and syntax. For GMTM these existing meta-modelling architectures are complex to use. So, based on the context of model transformation, we adapt the idea stated in MOF and generate this MMM. Figure 5 shows the content of this MMM.

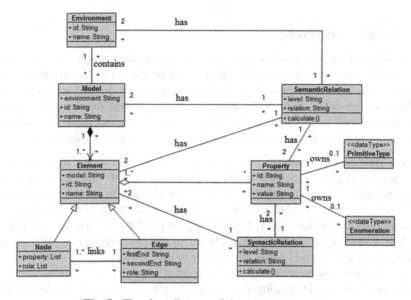

Fig. 5. The class diagram of the meta-meta-model

For GMTM, this MMM works on the top abstract level of all the other models. As this MMM is defined as a common criterion, the meta-models (for both source models and target models) could be built or transformed to the versions that conform to it.

As shown in Fig. 5, there are ten core elements in this meta-meta-model. As models may come from various domains or systems, a class named "Environment" is defined to stand for these domains. All the model instances are standed by the class "Model", every model belongs to a specific "Environment". "Model" is made of "Element", which has two inheritances: "Node" and "Edge". "Node" are linked by "Edge" based on their "roles". "Element" has a group of "Property", the "Property" could identify and explain the "Element". "Property" has a data type: "Primitive Type" or "Enumeration"; to a certain extend, data type could differentiate "Property".

All these items (with the relationships among them), illustrated above, present the standard requirement on specific meta-models. Another two key items shown in Fig. 5 are: "Semantic Relation" and "Syntactic Relation". They exist on different kinds of items (e.g. between a pair of elements). Model transformation rules are generated based on these two relations.

Generally, model transformation mappings are defined on the element level (node and edge); the mapping rules are usually generated by domain experts. However, applying model transformation practices to serve enterprise interoperability requires model transformation practices to be more flexible and easier (faster) to integration. So, semantic checking and syntactic checking that focused on element and property levels, are introduced to automatically define the mappings (replacing manual efforts). Also, in the MMM, the property and its dada type are highlighted; both of them are used to deduce semantic relation on element level. Furthermore, the inner attribute of element and property: their names, have also been used to define semantic and syntactic relations.

3.3   Matching Mechanism

In GMTM, model transformation is regarded as an iterative process: a target model (generated by one transformation iteration) could be the source model for the next iteration. In each iteration phase, transformation process is divided into three steps: matching on element level (coarse-grained matching), hybrid matching (fine-grained matching) and auxiliary matching (specific parts matching). All these three steps are supported by software tool; experts may only be involved in the validating process.

Iterative Matching Mechanism. According to the theoretical main framework, model transformation mappings are built on the potential shared parts between source model and target model. During the transformation process: the specific part of source model is saved as capitalized knowledge and the specific part of target model should be enriched with additional knowledge. So, a question may be put forward: how to deal with the capitalized knowledge and where the additional knowledge comes from? The "iterative matching mechanism" gives a possible answer to this question.

Figure 6 shows the general idea of this iterative matching mechanism.

One complete model transformation process may involve several iterations; each of iterations is an independent model transformation instance. An intermediate model is both the target model of the former iteration and source model of the latter iteration. All the specific parts (unmatched items: properties and elements) from source models are saved into ontology as capitalized knowledge, and the specific parts of target models

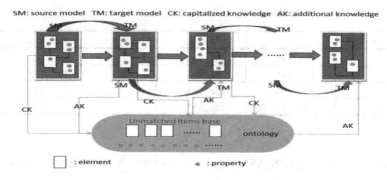

Fig. 6. Overview of iterative matching mechanism

are enriched with additional knowledge (capitalized knowledge from former iterations) that extracted from the same ontology.

Matching on Element Level. Generally, model transformation mappings are defined on element level (nodes and edges); if two elements (come from source model and target model, respectively) stand for the same concept (shared concept between two models), a mapping should be built. As stated above, semantic and syntactic checking measurements are applied on a pair of elements to detect the relation between them.

The mechanism of defining matches on element level is illustrated by an example shown in Fig. 7.

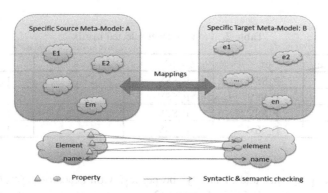

Fig. 7. Example of making matching on element level

The two specific meta-models (marked as A and B) are supposed to be conformed to the MMM. Model A has "m" elements and model B has "n" elements; the mappings should be built within the "m*n" element's pairs. Table 1 shows this comparison matrix. This matrix is built automatically by software tool; based on different inputs (model instances), similar matrix would be generated automatically.

Within each element's pair, there exists an "Ele_SSV" value. "Ele_SSV" stands for "element's semantic and syntactic value"; it is calculated based on the elements' names and their properties. Formula (1) is defined to calculate "Ele_SSV" value.

Table 1. Element level selected matrix

A⟍B	e1	e2	......	en
E1	Ele_SSV	Ele_SSV	......	Ele_SSV
E2	Ele_SSV	Ele_SSV	......	Ele_SSV
......	Ele_SSV	Ele_SSV	......	Ele_SSV
Em	Ele_SSV	Ele_SSV	......	Ele_SSV

$$\text{Ele\_SSV} = \text{name\_weight}^* \text{S\_SSV} + \text{property\_weight}^* \left(\sum\nolimits_{i=1}^{x} \text{Max(P\_SSVi)} \right) / x \quad (1)$$

In (1), "name_weight" and "property_weight" are two impact factors for the parameters elements' names and elements' properties, respectively. Both the values of "name_weight" and "property_weight" are between 0 and 1; the sum of them is 1. "S_SSV" stands for "string semantic and syntactic value; it is calculated based on the words (element's name is a word). "P_SSV" stands for "semantic and syntactic value between a pair of properties"; another example which shown below, is used to calculate "P_SSV". "x" stands for the number of properties of a specific element from source meta-model (e.g. element E1).

The example shown below is used to generate the "Ele_SSV" value within the element's pair of E1 and e1 (focuses on their properties' group); Table 2 is created for this example. This kind of tables is also built automatically (for different comparing elements' pairs) by software tool.

Table 2. Property level selected matrix

E1⟍e1	p1	p2	......	py
P1	P_SSV	P_SSV	......	P_SSV
P2	P_SSV	P_SSV	......	P_SSV
......	P_SSV	P_SSV	......	P_SSV
Px	P_SSV	P_SSV	......	P_SSV

E1 has "x" properties and e1 has "y" properties; within each of the "x*y" pairs of properties, there exists a "P_SSV". Formula (2) shows the calculating rule of "P_SSV".

$$\text{P\_SSV} = \text{pn\_weight}^* \text{S\_SSV} + \text{pt\_weight}^* \text{id\_type} \quad (2)$$

In (2), "pn_weight" and "pt_weight" are two impact factors for the parameters properties' names and properties' types, respectively. The sum of "pn_weight" and "pt_weight" is 1. "S_SSV" is the same as stated in (1); this time, it stands for the semantic and syntactic value between two properties' names. "id_type" stands for "identify properties type". If two properties have the same type, this value is 1; otherwise, this value is 0.

With the help of Table 2 (also needs the "S_SSV" between E1's name and e1's name), the "Ele_SSV" between element "E1" and "e1" could be calculated. In this way, Table 1 could be fulfilled with calculated values. For each element (E1, E2...) of the source model A, it has a maximum "Ele_SSV" value with a specific target model element (e1, e2...); if this value exceeds a predefined threshold value (e.g. 0.5), a match is built between the two elements. Moreover, making matching between two elements requires building mappings among their properties; Table 2 provides necessary and sufficient information to build mappings on property level. The rule of choosing property matching pairs is same of choosing element matching pairs (set another threshold value). In this way, both on element and property levels, the matches are: "one to one" and "many to one".

At this moment, the impact factors and selecting threshold values are assigned directly by experience.

Hybrid Matching. After first matching step, some of the elements (both belonging to source and target meta-models) are still unmatched; even the matched elements, some of their properties are still unmatched. The hybrid matching step focuses on these unmatched items.

This matching step works on property level, all the matching pairs would be built among properties (come from both the unmatched and matched elements).

All the unmatched properties from source model will be compared with all the properties from target model. A comparison matrix (similar to Table 2) is created to help complete this step. The mechanism of building such matching pairs is also depending on semantic and syntactic checking measurements (based on properties' names and types).

In hybrid matching step, all the matching pairs are built on property's level. This step breaks the constraint: property matching pairs only exists within matched element's pairs; this constraint is the main granularity issue involved in model transformation process. However, it is also necessary to consider about the influence from element's level when building mappings in hybrid matching step. The matching mechanism of this step shows in (3).

$$HM\_P\_SSV = el\_weight^*S\_SSV + pl\_weight^*P\_SSV \qquad (3)$$

In (3), "HM_P_SSV" stands for "hybrid matching property semantic and syntactic value". "el_weight" and "pl_weight" are two impact factors for the parameters "element level" and "property level", respectively. The sum of "el_weight" and "pl_weight" is 1. "S_SSV" is calculated between two elements' names (for source property and target property, respectively). "P_SSV", as stated in (2), calculates the syntactic and semantic relation between two properties based on their names and types.

This step achieves "one to many" matching mechanism on element's level, and on property level matching breaks the matched elements' constraint: properties from one source element could be matched to properties that from several target elements.

Auxiliary Matching. After the first and second matching steps, all the shared parts (presented in the theoretical main framework) between source model and target model are regarded to be found. However, according to the iterative model transformation process mentioned at the beginning of this subsection, there are still some specific parts that should be stored as capitalized knowledge or enriched as additional knowledge. Auxiliary matching step focuses on the mechanism of storing and reusing these specific parts from both source and target models.

All the unmatched items from source model, which regarded as specific parts, are stored in ontology (which is called "AMTM_O" within this project). AMTM_O designed with the same structure as MMM that shown as Fig. 5.

The syntactic and semantic checking measurements that involved in these three matching steps will be explained in detail respectively in the following section.

4 Syntactic and Semantic Checking Measurements

GMTM requires defining automatically the model transformation mapping rules. So, semantic and syntactic checking measurements (executed by software tool) are involved. As shown in (4), the "S_SSV" stands for the semantic and syntactic value between two strings.

$$S\_SSV = sem\_weight^*S\_SeV + syn\_weight^*S\_SyV \qquad (4)$$

"Sem_weight" and "syn_weight" are two impact factors for the parameters semantic value and syntactic value; the sum of them is 1. The two following subsections illustrate the way to calculate "S_SeV" and "S_SyV", respectively.

4.1 Syntactic Checking Measurement

Syntactic checking measurement is used to calculate the syntactic similarity between two words (elements' and properties' names in our case). There exists several syntactic checking methods; majority of them use classic similarity metrics to calculate the syntactic relations. Some of examples could be referred in [14].

The syntactic checking measurement in GMTM could be divided into two phases:

1. Pretreatment: focuses on finding if two words that in different forms (e.g. tense, morphology, gender) stand for the same word.
2. "Levenshtein Distances" algorithm [15]: calculates the syntactic similarity between two words.

"Levenshtein distances" is equal to the number of operations needed to transform one string to another. There are three kinds of operations: insertions, deletions and substitutions. Formula (5) shows the calculation of syntactic relation between two words: word1 and word2 based on "Levenshtein distances".

$$S\_SyV = 1 - LD/Max(word1.length, word2.length) \qquad (5)$$

In (5), "S_SyV" stands for the syntactic similarity value between "word1" and "word2"; "LD" stands for the "Levenshtein distances" between them. The value of "S_SyV" is between 0 and 1; the higher of this value means the higher syntactic similarity.

4.2   Semantic Checking Measurement

Contrast to syntactic checking measurement (rely just on comparing the two words); semantic checking measurement should rely upon a huge semantic thesaurus which contains large amount of words, their semantic meanings and semantic relations among them. A specific semantic thesaurus has been created for GMTM, and it is based on the basis of "WordNet" [16]. Figure 8 shows the structure of this semantic thesaurus.

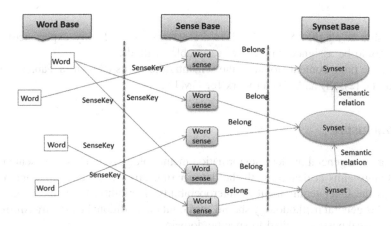

Fig. 8. Structure of the semantic thesaurus

Figure 8 shows three kinds of elements stored in the semantic thesaurus.

- Word base: normal English words (nouns, verbs and adjectives) are stored here.
- Sense base: contains all the word senses; a word could have "one or several" senses. E.g., word "star": it has six senses (four as a noun and two as a verb).
- "Synset" base: synonym groups; the word senses are divided into different synonyms groups. Semantic relations are built among different synsets.

Table 3 shows the content stored in this semantic thesaurus and the numbers of each kind of items.

Table 3. Content in semantic thesaurus

Items	Number
Words	147306
Word senses	206941
Synsets	114038

There are five kinds of semantic relations defined among synsets: "synonym", "hypernym", "iterative hypernym", "similar-to" and "antonym". For each of the semantic relations, a specific value (between 0 and 1) is assigned to it. Table 4 shows these "value and semantic relation" pairs.

Table 4. Relations and values pairs

Semantic relation	S_SeV	Remark
Synonym	0.9	Words from the same synset
Hypernym	0.8	Two synsets have this relation
Similar-to	0.85	Only between two adjectives
Antonym	0.2	Words have opposite meanings
Iterative hypernym	0.8^n	Inheritance hypernym relation

In Table 4, all the "S_SeV" values are assigned directly (by experience); these values should be assigned with more reasonable methods.

With the huge content stored in the semantic thesaurus (shown in Tables 3 and 4, formula (1), (2), (3) and (4) can work for GMTM.

5   Conclusion

In this paper, a general model transformation methodology (GMTM) is presented. This methodology aims at dealing with the data sharing problem of enterprise interoperability. As the inner requirement of interoperability: flexibility, faster exchange information, this general methodology should surmount the traditional model transformation practices' weaknesses (limited to specific domains).

Some points, which need to be improved in the future, are listed below:

- The impact factors such as: "sem_weight" and "pn_weight" and threshold values: the better way of assigning them is by using some mathematic strategy ("choquet" integral?).
- Semantic checking measurement: only formal English words are stored in the semantic thesaurus with semantic meanings; not for words (in specific cases).
- The S_SeV values that defined in Table 4: more test cases are needed to modify these values into reasonable scope.

The usage of GMTM is not limited to the interoperability domain; GMTM allows MDE theories to serve other engineering domains too.

Fig. 9. Position of GMTM usage

Figure 9 shows the general contribution of GMTM: converting rough data to information. With rules that defined in specific domains, such information could be transformed to knowledge which serves to domain specific problems.

By combining semantic and syntactic checking measurements into model transformation process, an efficient general model transformation methodology is created.

With the improvement on some of the details that involved in this GMTM, this methodology may serve to a large number of domains.

References

1. AMICE: CIMOSA: CIM Open System Architecture, 2nd edn. Springer, Berlin (1993)
2. Konstantas, D., Bourrières, J.P., Léonard, M., Boudjlida, N.: Interoperability of Enterprise Software and Applications, IESA 2005. Springer, London (2005)
3. Ide, N., Pustejovsky, J.: What does interoperability mean, anyway? toward an operational definition of interoperability. In: Proceedings of the Second International Conference on Global Interoperability for Language Resources (ICGL 2010) (2010)
4. Chen, D., Dassisti, M., Elvesæter, B.: Enterprise Interoperability Framework and Knowledge Corpus - Final report Annex: Knowledge Pieces, Contract no.: IST508 011, Deliverable DI.3 Annex, 21 May 2007
5. Schmidt, D.C.: Model-driven engineering. IEEE Comput. **39**(2), 25–31 (2006)
6. Soley, R., OMG staff: Model-Driven Architecture, OMG Document, November 2000. http://www.omg.org/mda
7. Bézivin, J.: Model driven engineering: an emerging technical space. In: Lämmel, R., Saraiva, J., Visser, J. (eds.) GTTSE 2005. LNCS, vol. 4143, pp. 36–64. Springer, Heidelberg (2006)
8. Castro, D.V., Maros, E., Vara, J.M.: Applying CIM-to-PIM model transformations for the service-oriented development of information systems. Inf. Softw. Technol. **53**(1), 87–105 (2011)
9. Grange, R., Bigand, M., Bourey, J.P.: Transformation of decisional models into UML: application to GRAI grids. Int. J. Comput. Integr. Manuf. **23**(7), 655–672 (2010)
10. Czarnecki, K., Helsen, S.: Classification of model transformation approaches. In: OOPSLA 2003 Workshop on Generative Techniques in the Context of Model-Driven Architecture (2003)
11. Bénaben, F., Mu, W., Truptil, S., Pingaud, H.: Information systems design for emerging ecosystems. In: 4th IEEE International Conference on Digital Ecosystems and Technologies (DEST 2010) (2010)
12. Fabro, D., Bézivin, M.D., J., Jouault, F., Breton, E.: AMW: a generic model weaver. In: 1ère Journées sur l'Ingénierie Dirigée par les Modèles, Paris (2005)
13. Object Management Group: MOF 2.0 Query/Views/Transformations RFP. OMG Document (2002)
14. William, W. C., Pradeep, R., Stephen, E. F.: A comparison of string metrics for matching names and records. In: KDD Workshop on Data Cleaning and Object Consolidation, vol. 3 (2003)
15. Wilbert, H.: Measuring Dialect Pronunciation Differences using Levenshtein Distance. Ph.D. thesis, Rijksuniversiteit Groningen (2004)
16. Huang, X., Zhou, C.: An OWL-based wordnet lexical ontology. J. Zhejiang Univ. **8**(6), 864–870 (2007)

An Ontology for Interoperability: Modeling of Composite Services in the Smart Home Environment

Manja Görner$^{(\boxtimes)}$, Thomas Göschel, Stephan Kassel, Sabrina Sander, and Thomas Klein

Westsächsische Hochschule Zwickau - University of Applied Sciences, Dr.-Friedrichs-Ring 2A, 08056 Zwickau, Germany
{Manja.Goerner,Thomas.Goeschel,Stephan.Kassel, Sabrina.Sander,Thomas.Klein}@fh-zwickau.de

Abstract. A developed service for smart home environments controls and coordinates a variety of appliances to influence physical environmental parameters selectively and to create a pleasant and activity appropriated room atmosphere. In the meaning of this paper this kind of service is defined as a composite service. There are several approaches to map services in ontologies. But these ontologies are not able to map composite services as they are introduced here. In this paper a possibility for mapping composite services with an ontology is presented. The composite services are defined on a devices landscape, with devices using exclusively DC voltage. The mapping of the composite services is done to promote compatibility to other systems. The paper's scope is to show recent research activities and their partial results. Because the work is still in process final results are outstanding.

Keywords: Composite services · Interoperability · Ontology · Smart home

1   Introduction

In the field of smart home, it is a general goal to bring more intelligence to the automation systems. [1] Moreover, the efficiency in using energy should be increased. One approach is using photovoltaic systems (PV systems). With these systems the consumer can generate his or her own power. The generated electricity is fed into the own and surpluses in the public network. Currently, the DC voltage (direct current) generated by a PV system is alternately directed into AC voltage (alternating current). But many appliances in households based on DC voltage. So AC voltage is rectified back in the device's power supply. These inverter and rectifiers create significant energy losses. In this respect, the direct use of DC voltage in the power grid is interesting.

In the project EGNIAS at the University of Applied Sciences Zwickau the potentials of using DC voltage in the smart home (SH) environment were examined. Therefore appliances, which are used in SHs and based on DC voltage, have been identified. On this device landscape services have been defined. These services are

© IFIP International Federation for Information Processing 2015
M. van Sinderen and V. Chapurlat (Eds.): IWEI 2015, LNBIP 213, pp. 30–38, 2015.
DOI: 10.1007/978-3-662-47157-9_3

"composite services", which can directly influence physical environmental parameters. The focus in this paper is, how these services can be represented in an ontology and thus made available to other processes. For this, firstly the concept of a "composite service" is presented. Then the existing research contributions and ontology approaches are shown. From the results of this inspection, the need to conceive an own ontology for the "composite services" is demonstrated. The developed concept will be presented and applied for a specific service.

2 Composite Services

First, it is necessary to identify appliances which can be operated with DC voltage. It turns out that these can be found mainly in the field of low voltage. According to the Energy Information Agency (EIA), the fastest growing portion of residential electricity use is consumer electronics and small appliances [2]. Therefore, the selection of the units has focused on this sector. Exceptions are the selected lamps. LED lamps are also suitable for the project, which is why they were included. So among other things the device landscape contains a phone, a tablet PC, a radio and a variety of LED lamps. On this basis the "composite services" were defined. The aim is that the room can be set to different use alternatives. Special attention must be set to the subjectivity of human perception assets. For example, a person's perception of the same light intensity is different in various situations. This contrasts with the system's objectivity that is controlled with absolute values. Therefore, the user needs must be analyzed, interpreted and integrated accordingly in the services. For example, the illumination of room areas can be differentiated. In this regard manual changes of the user are stored and used as a standard for the next application. Thus, the services are customizable.

A composite service is defined as a process to influence physical environmental parameters selectively to create a pleasant and activity appropriated room atmosphere. So with a composite service not a single device is controlled but a variety of devices is coordinated. The services are therefore not fine-grained, which represents a new approach in building automation.

The services will now be displayed in such a way that it is compatible with existing approaches. The design of the defined services shall be formally mapped. This promotes compatibility in such a way, that the composite services can also be integrated into other room control systems.

3 Related Literature

In the topic smart home there exist a number of research activities, which are focused on services.[1]

---

[1] As in the project EGNIAS energy efficiency plays a big role in the smart home environment. For example in [3] an empirical study which deals with this issue and which is based on an analysis of user activities is presented.

Moji Wei et al. [4] present an "Ontology Based Home Service Model". That is a model to retrieve and invoke services according to user's needs automatically. But firstly needs must be determined. The contribution mainly deals with how these needs can be determined. The services, which are retrieved, include the retrieval of a single device. However, the here defined composite services do not meet this fine-grained structure and thus they represent a continuation of the approach of Moji Wei et al.

Mobility and heterogeneity are characteristics of many devices in the SH. In order to manage these devices efficiently, the system CASSF (Context-Aware Service Scheduling Framework) [5] filters out and offers suitable services. This is done according to the task requirements (TR) and serves an improved user experience and content adaptation. Therefore the devices and their functions were mapped in an ontology, a context-sensitive service selection program was developed and a method for content adaptation was proposed. This shall achieve an enhanced user satisfaction. In CASSF functions are derived from the user's needs. This is the basis for the services. The analysis of the needs was based on Maslow's hierarchy of needs [6]. The needs are interpreted with the aim of providing an appropriate service. But in the here presented concept it is the point that the user tells the system his planned activities and expected that the room sets on it, for example, by an appropriate lighting scenario. Which scenario is to provide in a situation was indicated to the system within the customizing. So in the concept the analysis of needs is not done by the system. This distinguishes the CASSF approach from the shown one. However, considering that at the same time there could be several people in a room, which have different requirements, these requirements have to be reconciled and the related services have to be combined. For this service combination CASSF could provide a solution approach.

The approach presented by Yung-Wei Kao and Shyan-Ming Yuan [7] is based on the theory that a user in a smart home thinks semantically. His request to the system might be: "I want to turn off all the lights on the second floor." To illustrate this in an ontology USHA (User-configurable Semantic Home Automation System) and a self-defined markup language SHPL (Semantic Home Process Language) were developed. SHPL is able to semantically link the information "all" or "none" and the concept of belonging [7]. Thus "I want to turn off all the lights on the second floor" can be implemented.

The presented approach goes on one step further in this relationship. The user does not need to selectively turn on or off the lights and appliances. Instead, he tells the system only, which is his planned activity and the room sets on it automatically. Therefore the devices are addressed differentiated. For example, all the lamps of a region are turned on, but only with a power of 25 %, except lamp XY, which is turned on with full power. With our approach this central aim of context-aware systems is achieved. Even the following circumstance is feasible: If the environment due to external influences is already so bright that the full power of lamp XY does no longer increase this brightness, the lamp does not need to be turned on or only with a lower power.

4 Basic Ontologies

The conception of the defined composite services shall be formally mapped. This is to promote compatibility in such a way that the design can also be integrated into other systems than the control room of the project. For such a mapping ontologies are very useful. There are a number of different ontologies. But all were situated within a particular context. In this chapter two ontologies are presented, whose contexts have a high degree of relationship to the described developed services in the smart home environment. The aim is to illustrate the ontology's contribution to map the presented composite services.

Using DogOnt [8], modeling an intelligent, automated environment with the devices, their status, functions and messages, as well as the architecture is possible (Fig. 1).

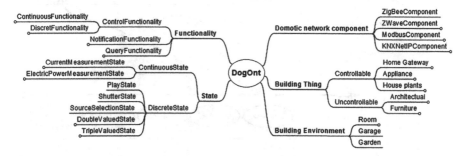

Fig. 1. Overview of the DogOnt ontology (source: based on [5] p. 794)

It seems to be the most complete ontology for modeling building components. It includes a wide taxonomical organization of controllable devices (appliances, home plants and home gateways), including their functions (control, notification and query) and notifications. However, no description of hardware features of the devices is possible. This is important for example to determine the quality of the offered service [9]. In addition DogOnt is not able to map composite services, as here defined. Although it contains commands by which the command to individual devices can be mapped. But composite services include a variety of commands to a variety of devices. The ability to map this instruction bundle, which is furthermore derived from corresponding input factors, is missing in DogOnt.

Instead Owl-S [10] is able to describe scenarios and services. It makes possible to discover, invoke, compose, and monitor Web resources to offer particular services and supports to do it with a high degree of automation. In OWL-S services with an input and an output are defined (Fig. 2).

This approach is picked up by Davy Preuveneers and Yolande Berbers [11]. They developed the ontology CODAMOS. They use this ontology in service-oriented computing context. But web services do not include the functionalities which comprise the here defined composite services. However, they provided a decisive approach to the development of an ontology which is able to map these composite services.

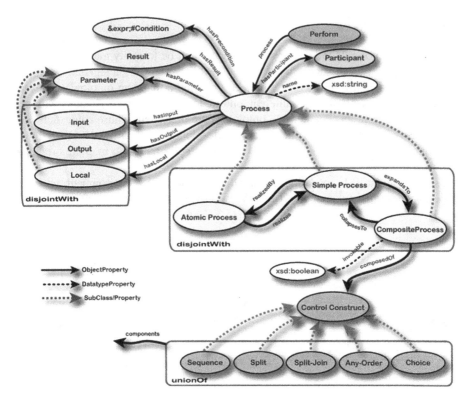

Fig. 2. The process ontology of OWL-S3 (source: http://www.w3.org/Submission/2004/
SUBM-OWL-S-20041122/)

5 Research Contribution

The representation of something real in the meaning of ontologies includes a conceptual layer and identities layer. In the conceptual layer the general construct with corresponding relations is shown. The identities-layer is a parallel level to the conceptual layer. In the world of ontologies identities are the specific properties of the object. Therefore in the identities layer the real objects, based on the structure of the conceptual layer, can be mapped.

The following part shows how a non-fine-grained composite service can be mapped in ontologies. Therefore a concrete example of a composite service is presented. Subsequently, the conceptual layer is explained, therewith such a non-fine-grained service can be mapped. Finally, the presented service example is mapped on the identity layer.

In Fig. 3 there is to see a schematic representation of the model room, which is constructed by us. The lamps are controlled directly and the devices by means of the sockets. Based on this devices landscape the services have been defined.

As an example the welcome_service shall be mapped. The welcome_service is the basic service of the control. The aim of this service is to illuminate brightly the entire

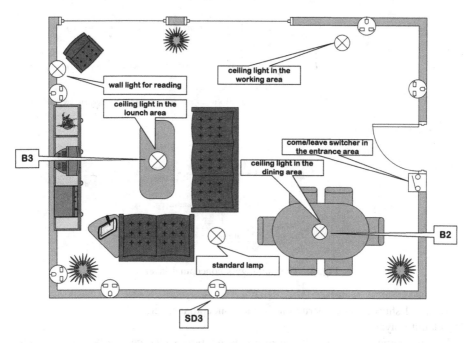

Fig. 3. The model room

room. Therefore the dimmable lamps over the dining table (B2) and over the lounch table (B3) are switched on with full power. The floor lamp next to the couch is also turned on. This is connected to a socket (SD3), which must be activated.

Because DogOnt is basically able to represent the devices and components in a SH, it makes sense to extend this ontology. To incorporate the notion of a process, the process design of OWL-S can be taken up. For the input and output of the services DogOnt provides its own relevant states and commands.

The conceptual layer:

A service is a subclass of a process. A process has an input and an output. The input consists of the room_usage_type, the light_intensity_state and a bright-ness_reference_state. The room_usage_type and brightness_reference_state are a discrete_state. The various room-usage-types in the EGNIAS- project are "welcome", "dining", "working", "reading", "music" and "tv". These are variables of the room control. With them the planned activities of the user are stored in the system. The brightness_reference_state is a parameter which is required for room control. A brightness_reference_value is associated with it. The light_intensity_state is already defined in DogOnt.

A process generates commands. Thus commands are the output of a process. Commands are also defined in DogOnt. A subclass is added here: the *step_up/down_command*. This compares a *controllable_building_thing*'s s*tate_value* with a *reference_value* and adjusts the *state_value* to the *reference_value*.

The commands affect an object of *controllable_building_thing*, which is represented by the property *for*.

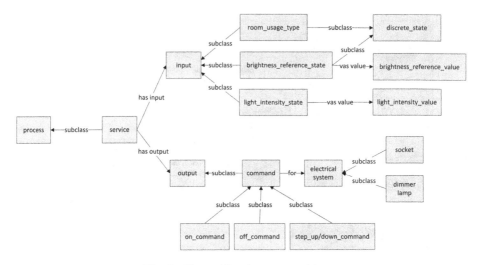

Fig. 4. The ontology's conceptual layer

Figure 4 shows this construction in the conceptual layer.
The identity layer:

The welcome_service needs the room_usage_type welcome, the brightness_reference_state for the dining area (brightness_reference_state_dining_area) and the lounch area (brightness_reference_state_lounch_area) with the value 100 (percent) as well as the light_intensity_state for these areas (light_intensity_state_lounch_area, light_intensity_state_lounch_area) as input. The values of these last two states are provided by brightness sensors. The welcome_service's output contains of an on_command for the socket (on_command_SD3), step_up/down_commands for the dimmer lamps (stept_up/down_command_B2, step_up/down_command_B3) as well as off_commands for all other sockets and lamps. Fig. 5 shows the identity layer for the welcome_service.

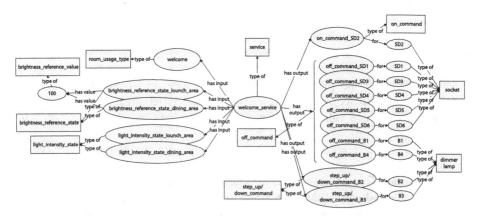

Fig. 5. The ontology's identity layer

6 Conclusion and Further Work

The starting points of this paper are two general goals: more intelligence and more energy efficiency in the Smart Home. In the project EGNIAS these aspects were picked up and linked. The result of the project activity is a model room. This model room is equipped with appliances whose functionality is based on DC voltage. A power grid was implemented, which supplies the appliances directly with the appropriate DC voltage. On this device landscape composite services were set up. A composite service is defined as a process to influence physical environmental parameters. By choosing a room usage type (dining, reading, working …) the room shall create a pleasant room atmosphere that is appropriate to the user's planned activity. So composite services are not fine-grained, because a variety of devices is coordinated to each other.

To make the whole system compatible to other systems the composite services were mapped in an ontology. It was realized by picking parts of DogOnt and OWL-S. The reuse of existing ontologies reflects the desire for compatibility. In DogOnt the concept of a smart home is mapped extensively. OWL-S provides the design of a process, but relates to computing services. Therefore, the concept of a service in OWL-S has to be adapted to the concept of a composite service. It also was combined with elements of DogOnt. So these two ontologies have been linked and a composite service can be mapped.

Because the device landscape's control is not yet flexibly variable, the current implementation of services can be classified as static. Each device has to be introduced manually to the system. This still does not meet the dynamism with which a user is acting in his apartment and within he should be supported. Further research activities will therefore deal with the problem, how new devices can be dynamically inserted into the system. A solution could be a communication via UPnP. The devices' required information could be stored in the cloud and loaded from there as needed in the system. Furthermore, a possibility to accordingly extending of existing services or to defining new services has to be found.

References

1. Bregman, D.: Smart home intelligence - the eHome that learns. Int. J. Smart Home 4(4), 35–46 (2010)
2. http://smartgrid.ieee.org/june-2013/881-is-dc-s-place-in-the-home
3. Nguyen, T., Aiello, M.: Energy intelligent buildings based on user activity: a survey. Energy Build. 56, 244–257 (2013)
4. Wei, M., Xu, J., Yun, H., Xu, L.: Ontology-based home service model. ComSIS 9(2), 813–838 (2012)
5. Liang, Y., Zhou, X., Yu, Z., Wang, H., Guo, B.: A context-aware multimedia service scheduling framework in smart homes. EURASIP J. Wirel. Commun. Netw. 2012, 67 (2012). http://jwcn.eurasipjournals.com/content/2012/1/67
6. Maslow, A.H.: A theory of human motivation. Psychol. Rev. 50(4), 370–396 (1943)
7. Kao, Y.-W., Yuan, S.-M.: User-configurable semantic home automation. Comput. Stan. Interfaces 34, 171–188 (2012)

8. Bonino, D., Corno, F.: DogOnt - ontology modeling for intelligent domotic environments. In: Sheth, A.P., Staab, S., Dean, M., Paolucci, M., Maynard, D., Finin, T., Thirunarayan, K. (eds.) ISWC 2008. LNCS, vol. 5318, pp. 790–803. Springer, Heidelberg (2008)

9. Grassi, M., Nucci, M., Piazza, F.: Ontologies for smart homes and energy management: an implementation-driven survey. In: Proceedings of the IEEE Workshop on Modeling and Simulation of Cyber-Physical Energy Systems MSCPES (2013)

10. Martin, D. et al.: OWL-S: Semantic Markup for Web Services. W3CMember Submission, 22 November 2004. http://www.w3.org/Submission/OWL-S/

11. Preuveneers, D., Berbers, Y.: Automated context-driven composition of pervasive services to alleviate non-functional concerns. Int. J. Comput. Inf. Sci. 3(2), 19–28 (2005)

Validation and Verification of Interoperability Requirements

Mamadou Samba Camara[1]([✉]), Rémy Dupas[2], and Yves Ducq[2]

[1] ESP, Université Cheikh Anta Diop, Génie Informatique,
dakar-fann, BP: 5085 Dakar, Senegal
mamadou.camara@ucad.edu.sn
[2] Université de Bordeaux IMS, UMR 5218,
33400 Talence, France

Abstract. The research objective of this work is to develop an approach
to reach inter-enterprise interoperability and to test its achievement using
practices from the software engineering process. Four fundamental activities are identified in the software process: software specification, software
development, software validation and software evolution [1]. In this work,
the interoperability requirements specification is based on measurable
and non-measurable quality characteristics. It is also demonstrated that
the improvement proposed in software specification activity will have
positive impact on the software development activity. For the validation activity, the definition of a interoperability testing sub-process is
made through a two-step decomposition: one step to verify measurable
requirements and another to validate non-measurable ones.

Keywords: Enterprise interoperability · Software specification · Software validation · Service Oriented Architectures · Business Process Modeling

1 Introduction

Interoperability is defined by the ALCTS[1] [2] as the ability of two or more systems
or components to exchange information and use the exchanged information without special effort by either system. Improving interoperability depends largely
on the implementation of a Collaborative Information System(CIS) by means of
a software engineering process. In this work, the interoperability requirements
specification is based on measurable and non-measurable quality characteristics.
It is also demonstrated that the improvement proposed in software specification
activity will have positive impact on the software development activity. For the
validation activity, the definition of a interoperability testing sub-process is made.
The next three sections presents respectively the literature reviews of requirements specification, interoperability in relation to the software process and business process performance. The two following sections are dedicated to the research
design and the application respectively.

---

[1] The Association for Library Collections and Technical Services.

© IFIP International Federation for Information Processing 2015
M. van Sinderen and V. Chapurlat (Eds.): IWEI 2015, LNBIP 213, pp. 39–52, 2015.
DOI: 10.1007/978-3-662-47157-9_4

2   Literature of Software Requirements Verification and Validation

After the validation activity, the software system is delivered to the customer and is installed and put into practical use. When the validation activity reveals problems, this means that the system is not good enough for use, then further development is required to fix the identified problems [1]. Software system requirements are often classified as functional and non-functional requirements [1]. Software validation or, more generally, verification and validation is intended to show that a system both conforms to its specification and that it meets the expectations of the system customer [1,3]. Except for small programs, systems could not be tested as a single, monolithic unit. The testing process is made up of three stages, Development testing, System testing and Acceptance testing, in which system components are tested then the integrated system is tested and finally, the system is tested on customer's data [1]. The aim of verification is to check that the software meets its stated functional and non functional requirements [1,3,4]. The aim of validation is to ensure that the software meets the customer's expectations (i.e. expectations of the organization that commissioned the system) [1,3]. Properties expressed as quantitative measures can be naturally verified [5]. Properties that refer to subjective feeling can be difficult to verify and are a natural target for validation [5].

3   Interoperability Literature Review

A review of the literature conducted to analyze how the activities of software specification, software development and software validation [1] were carried out in the interoperability domain.

3.1   Interoperability Requirements

Approaches used to represent interoperability requirements, in the literature can be summarized as following with their limitations:

1. The maturity models [6–8]: Repetition, Ambiguity, Imprecision and incoherence because the needs are expressed in natural language [9].
2. Formal representation of interoperability requirements [9,10]: the implementation of this approach may experiment scalability problems [11].
3. Interoperability requirements as problems.
   (a) Requirements are specified by the mean of collaboration processes models: the requirements are disconnected from existing systems and also to the interoperability problems to solve.
   (b) The interoperability matrix [12,13]: do not provide a structured set of requirements [14].

3.2 Collaborative Information System (CIS) Architecture

A CIS aims at supporting "Information Systems (IS) Interoperability", that is to say, to satisfy requirements such as data conversion, application sharing and process management [15]. The CIS should then include two different parts: connectors to be plugged into partners information systems and the concrete entity managing the collaboration: an intermediate information system. Several research works were conducted in order to find logical and technical solutions for the CIS. Approaches proposed in these works can be categorized in two groups: Model-Driven Interoperability (MDI) approaches [16,17] and Business Process Lifecycle (BPL) based approaches [18]. It can be noticed that, in all approaches for CIS development, the proposed platforms are based on Service Oriented Architectures (SOA) [19]. Requirements specification proposed in the approaches for the development of CIS does not provide sufficient information to describe interoperability problems and then facilitate the software development activity.

3.3 SOA Testing

Since our problem is related to the verification and the validation of interoperability, we will focus primarily on testing approaches and techniques for service-based systems. For the testing of SOA applications, [20] identified four distinct testing layers: Unit testing, Service testing, Integration testing and System testing. References [21,22] advocated for the realization of system testing at process level. The first limitation of this work [21], is the fact that the business process performance metrics used in the test process are not defined. In our opinion, although interoperability implementation is generally based on SOA, the testing approaches proposed for service-based systems are not suitable for testing inter-enterprise interoperability achievement. Indeed, these approaches [20–22] do not reference interoperability problems, which makes them useless for verifying the elimination of the latter.

4 Business Process Performance Indicators Calculation from Event Logs

The Business Process represents a chain of interrelated activities that normally must be connected with the customer requirements [23]. Process models are built in the design phase and are later used to implement the information system. Process performance measurement is an important aspect of Business Process Management (BPM). In this research, the considered process PIs are the average elapsed time, average cost and percentage of failure at the process level and represent the aggregation of the PIs for the activities [24,25]. This choice relies on the assumption that these characteristics encompass all other types of dynamic properties of business processes [11].

An "event log" is defined as "a chronological record of computer system activities" which are saved to a file on the system [26]. Any information system using transactional systems will provide workflow information in some form and to some extent, such as tasks available, their events and the details of these events like starting/ending timestamp [27,28]. The main data source that can be used for the calculation process PIs in the verification of interoperability requirements are the integrated event logs which are widely used in the fied of cross-organizational process mining. Cross-organizational workflow is usually distributed on different servers owned by different partners or different organizations [29,30]. Cross-organizational workfows are enabled by web-services technology [31]. A Framework for workflow integration based on process mining is proposed in [30]. The integrated log results from the integration between the running logs of two or more organizations. In the running log collected from each organization, an event record is an 8-tuples containing Case(Id), Activity (Name), Start time, end time, Required resources, Released resources, Messages received, Messages sent. The data integrated between the running logs contains an additional column labeled "Organization".

5   Research Design and Hypothesis

The present research work aims at developing an approach to reach inter–enterprise interoperability and to test its achievement using practices from the software engineering process. In the approach proposed in [32], interoperability requirements are specified by representing interoperability problems directly on business process models. The testing sub-process defined in this work [32] was limited to the validation of interoperability requirements but did not enable the verification because of the nature of these requirements. Four fundamental activities are identified in software process: software specification, software development, software validation and software evolution [1]. For each of the first three activities, our approach proposes to define a sub-goal and determines how to achieve it:

1. **Software Specification.** Interoperability requirements specification ensures certain characteristics: requirements are structured (i.e. understandable and identifiable) and testable.
2. **Software Development.** The structured nature of interoperability requirements will ease the logical and technical architecture definition.
3. **Software Validation.** The testability of interoperability requirements facilitates the definition of a method that enables testing the level of achievement of interoperability improvement. The objective will be to prove that the implementation of the CIS has improved the interoperability up to the desired level.

We propose a framework for the definition of a Performance Measurement System (PMS) (Fig. 1) made up, in its complete version, of cost, time and quality PIs for all the processes impacted by the implementation of the CIS. To have a comprehensive verification process, interoperability measures defined at process level will be used. Indeed, as it is explained in [11], defining measures at activity level will produce too numerous indicators and increase the PMS complexity. The framework should be understood as road-map where each state represents additional process PIs on which the verification step of the interoperability testing sub-process (Sect. 5.3) is applied using approaches defined in process mining. We assume that the PMS is constructed through a series of states where S_i denotes the set of indicators in the $state_i$

- the difference $S_i - S_{i-1}$ represents additional indicators defined in order to take into account new concerns defined in S_i. Therefor S_{i-1} is always included in S_i
- the directed arcs from S_{i-1} to S_i represents the influence of S_{i-1} to $S_i - S_{i-1}$ that is also a part of S_i.

The four states as well as their influence relationships are defined as following:

1. State1. The first state concerns time PIs for process instances excluding those containing loops. A loop causes a task to be executed multiple times for a given case [28,33]. According to [34], if the maximum number of loops is high then the number of loops can greatly differs from instance to instance. In other words, the presence of loops will results in variability in the time and other process PIs between different instances of a given process. In our opinion, the origin of this variability is the random nature of reasons why process or task can fail.

2. State2. In the second state, the new concern is the measurement of loops in business processes. Traditional workflow systems define loops for repeating parts of the process. Tasks or sets of tasks are iterated for multiple reasons:
   - they have not yielded an expected result [35].
   - the workfow management system is configured to act automatically (i.e. pass the case back to the last performer) after a long passivity of performers [31]. Therefore, we can conclude that the time PIs of the state1 influence the failure (or loop) PIs added in state2.

3. State3. The process PIs added in state3 are related to time but the difference with the ones defined in state1 is the fact that they also measure the variability of time caused by loops. The group of indicators in state3 are influenced by the indicators defined in state2 because, according to [36], the quality of the process expressed in the number of failures or loops is an indicator for necessary rework. More generally, it is safe to say that quality characteristics of business process influence time (and cost).

4. State4. The new process PIs included in state4 are related to cost. These measures receive impact of time and failure.

The rest of this paper represents the first state of the framework, the scope of the verification step is then limited to process PIs of $state_1$ (i.e. time process PIs). Process mining techniques enable to automatically mines upper bounds for different key performance indicators (like waiting times, execution times etc.) of a process by taking into account both the timestamps of tasks in a log and the overall structure of the process model given as input [33,37,38].

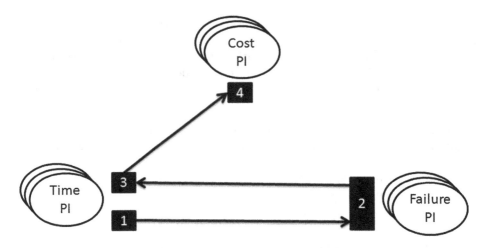

Fig. 1. Framework for the definition of the PMS

5.1   Improving the Interoperability Requirements Specification

The interoperability requirements specification proposed in this work results in the definition of two categories of requirements:

1. **Measurable Interoperability Requirements.** This category concerns measurable interoperability requirements that can be verified in the testing activity. Indeed, according to [1], non-functional requirements should be written quantitatively, whenever possible, so that they can be objectively tested. The measurable interoperability requirements are metrics representing the desired interoperability level for each business process as a result of the implementation of the CIS. These measurable requirements are related three process PIs considered as sufficient to measure interoperability by [11]: the average elapsed time, average cost and percentage of failure. As explained in the beginning of Sect. 5, this study uses only the average elapsed time and will measure this indicator for all business processes impacted by the implementation of the CIS.

2. **Non-measurable Interoperability Requirements.** This category contains interoperability requirements that can be validated in the testing activity but not verified because of to their non-measurable nature. For this category, the requirements specification consists in representing directly interoperability problems in business process models, mainly in "As-is" ones. The adopted representation is based on a principle that consists of distinguishing between business activities and Non-Value-Added (NVA) activities, mainly inspired by the work done in [11]. Business activities create value in a business process. The NVA activities are defined as the components of business processes that represent efforts between partners to achieve interoperability in information exchange. According to [39], Non-value-adding work, creates no value for customer but is required in order to get the value-adding work done.

One the most important principles of Business Process Reengineering (BPR) is the value-focus principle. The value-focus principle states that [40], NVA activities must be targeted for elimination in order to save time and/or money. Interoperability problems are depicted in BPMN (Business Process Model and Notation) [41] business process models. The stereotypes [42], generally used for the UML language, will be used to differentiate NVA to business activities in the BPMN process models. BPMN is more suitable for modeling collaborative processes because it helps situate the boundaries of the collaborating companies using pools. The proposed representation technique enables to overcome limitation presented in the Sect. 3.1, since the requirements will relate interoperability problems to target elements such as people, organization units and material resources which are clearly identifiable in the collaborating enterprises.

Interoperability requirements are part of non-functional requirements. Both measurable and non-measurable requirements defined in this research work are considered as non-functional requirements because of their relation to interoperability. Indeed, according to [1], non-functional requirements arise through user needs, because of budget constraints, organizational policies or the need for interoperability with other software or hardware systems.

5.2 Ease Architecture Definition

Software development is the activity where the software is designed and programmed. The requirements specification results are inputs of the design and implementation processes [1]. In order to develop solution for interoperability problems, the interoperability matrix utilizes the concepts of solution space [12,13]. The solution space is composed of the three dimensions of the INTEROP framework. The cross of an interoperability barrier, an interoperability concern and an interoperability approach includes the set of solutions to breakdown a same interoperability barrier for a same concern and using a same approach. In order to determine correctly the solution (third dimension), there must be sufficient information to describe interoperability problems (two first dimensions). The requirements representation in process models contains the following information: tasks where interoperability problems arise and the resources (human and non-human) involved in the interoperability problems. This set of information will facilitate the design process and then improve the software development activity.

5.3 Adapt Validation Activity

In the SE process, the validation activity can be considered as a test process that can be divided into a set of test sub-processes defined to perform a specific test level (e.g. system testing, acceptance testing) or test type (e.g. usability testing, performance testing) within the context of an overall test process for a test project [43]. A test type is a group of testing activities that are focused on specific quality characteristics [43]. In the validation activity of software process, the improvements will consist on considering interoperability as a quality characteristic and developing the interoperability test type. On the basis of the recommendations given in the literature of service-based systems testing, the interoperability testing sub-process will be executed at system testing level using business process models (Sect. 3.3). The interoperability testing sub-process is divided into two steps: Verification and Validation of interoperability requirements.

Verification of Interoperability Requirements. The first step of the interoperability testing sub-process is the verification of measurable interoperability requirements. Each business process in the scope of the project must be executed several times to calculate its average elapsed time. As mentioned in Sect. 4, information needed for the computation of this process PI average elapsed time are the probability related to the different path and the average elapsed time of the activities in the process model. In the context of inter-enterprise collaboration these information can be obtained using the cross-organizational workflow model and the integrated event log. Applying the Framework for workflow integration based on process mining described in Sect. 4 will help to get the cross-organizational workflow model and the integrated event log. The events log analysis enable calculating process PIs that represent measurable interoperability requirements. The goal of this step is to verify if the level of interoperability is improved at the level expected from the implementation of the CIS as determined in the software specification activity. When the percentage of interoperability improvement is judged unsatisfactory then the validation step is launched in order to identify, understand and possibly resolve interoperability problems.

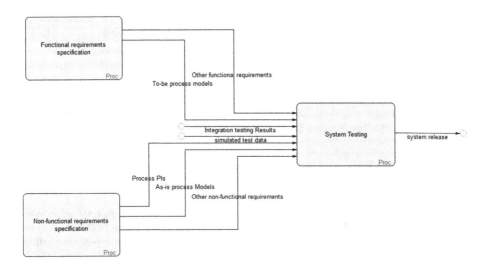

Fig. 2. The interoperability testing sub-process

Validation of Interoperability Requirements. The second step of the interoperability testing sub-process is the validation of non-measurable interoperability requirements. The main input of this step (Fig. 2) is the "As-is" business process models which contain the interoperability requirements specification (Sect. 5.1). The validation is carried out by executing each process in order to verify if all the NVA activities it contains in its "As-is" version are effectively eliminated by the implementation of the CIS. The execution of a business process may reveal the presence of NVA activities. In this situation, the "As-is" business process model gives sufficient information about the interoperability problems related to the concerned NVA activities. The information will be used to fix the interoperability problems.

6 Application

The illustrative example used to demonstrate the applicability of the methodology involves a supply chain in which an interoperability investment is used to improve the quality of the collaboration. The partners involved in this collaboration are a customer (an e-commerce company), a stockist (a warehouse owner), a customs agent and the customs administration. The goal of the interoperability investment is to allow the customers to be quickly connected at a low cost and with flexibility to their partners and to the customs administration using an interoperable information system.

6.1 Interoperability Requirements Specification

The specification of both measurable and non-measurable interoperability requirements is illustrated through a goods entry (collaboration) process in which all four partners concerned by the investment participate. The goods entry process begins when the customer places an order and terminates when the stockist updates the material accounting and informs the customer that it can begin to distribute and sell the goods. For this process, the specification of the non-measurable requirements consist in representing NVA activities in the "As-is" version of the model using stereotypes (Fig. 3).

The specification of the measurable interoperability requirements for the goods entry process consist in calculating the percentage of improvement in the average elapsed time PI between "As-is" and "To-be" situations. The partners in the illustrative example provide the average elapsed time for each activity in the goods entry business process, which allows the calculation of the average elapsed time process PI of 183 min for the "As-is" situation. The "To-be" process models essentially depends on the number of identified barriers that the solution is intended to remove. In the illustrative example, the SOA-based solution was expected to remove all of the identified barriers. Therefore, to arrive at the "To-be" process model, the NVA activities are simply removed from the "As-is" model (Fig. 3). Simulation of the "To-be" process models can be used to estimate the average elapsed time process PI which has a value of 152 min. The value of

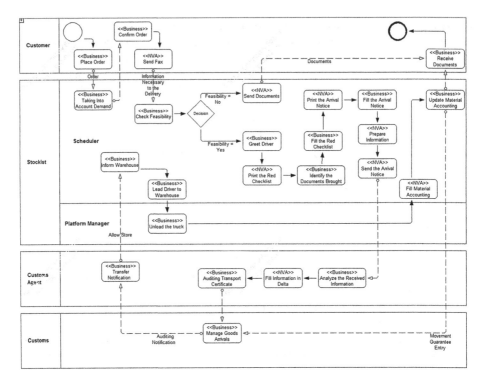

Fig. 3. Goods entry process- "As-is" version

the metrics representing this interoperability requirement is −17, meaning that the decrease of average elapsed time between the "As-is" and "To-be" situations for the goods entry process is expected to be of 17 percent.

6.2 Software Architecture Definition and Implementation

Consider the following activities of the goods entry process: "Transfer notification"(1), "Inform warehouse"(2), "Lead driver to warehouse"(3), "Unload the truck"(4), "Fill Material Accounting"(5), "Update Material Accounting"(6). All these activities are business ones except "Fill Material Accounting" which is a NVA activity representing a non-measurable interoperability requirement and it is hypothesized that an interoperability barrier existing somewhere in the process. Identifying software systems supporting the activities connected to the NVA activity will help in determining technological barriers between (e.g. 1 is executed using Delta which is non-inter-operable with Sage used for 5 and 6). Understanding why these systems are not inter-operable will facilitate finding solutions. Web services are an industry effort to provide platform-independent SOA using interoperable interface descriptions, protocols, and data communication [44]. In the software development activity, the decision was made to use web services architecture to implement the CIS. The main reason is that web services architecture can support the business activities while removing NVA activities identified in all the "As-is" business process models obtained in the requirements specification. The software development activity was realized using .NET Web Services implemented using the Microsoft .NET platform [45].

6.3 Interoperability Testing Sub-process Application

The interoperability testing sub-process is executed in the system testing phase after the testing of the functional requirements. The functional requirements testing allowed verifying that the implemented CIS supports the business process as described in the "To-be" models. For the goods entry process, the verification of interoperability requirements shown a reduction of 20 percent in average elapsed time, a value greater than the threshold set in the requirements specification. The validation of interoperability requirements conducted reveals that all the NVA activities identified in the "As-is" goods entry process models were removed in the implementation of the CIS. The results of verification and validation steps allow us to assert that the interoperability problems in the goods entry process were fully eliminated.

7 Conclusion

This work was aimed to improve software specification, development and validation activities of software process in projects related to interoperability. The interoperability requirements specification is based on measurable and non-measurable quality characteristics. Non-measurable requirements are defined as interoperability problems directly depicted in business process models using the concept of NVA activity. The average elapsed time process PI is used for the development of measurable interoperability requirements. It has been then demonstrated that the proposed form of interoperability requirement specification can positively impact the software development and the software validation activities. For the validation activity, the definition of a interoperability testing sub-process is made through a two-step decomposition: one step to verify measurable requirements and another to validate non-measurable ones. A perspective of this work will consist in extending the verification step to the remaining process PIs defined in [11]: average cost and percentage of failure.

References

1. Sommerville, I.: Software Engineering. Addison-Wesley, Reading (2011)
2. ALCTS: Description and access task force on metadata (2010)
3. Boehm, B.W.: Software engineering: Rd trends and defense needs. In: Wegner, P. (ed.) Research Directions in Software Technology. MIT Press, Cambridge (1979)

4. Chapurlat, V., Braesch, C.: Verification, validation, qualification and certification of enterprise models: Statements and opportunities. Comput. Indus. **59**(7), 711–721 (2008)
5. Baresi, L., Pezze, M.: An introduction to software testing. Electron. Notes Theor. Comput. Sci. **148**(1), 89–111 (2006)
6. Tolk, A., Muguira, J.: The levels of conceptual interoperability model (2003)
7. Morris, E., Levine, L., Meyers, C., Place, P., Plakosh, D.: System of systems interoperability (sosi): Final report. Technical report, Carnegie Mellon University (2004)
8. Kingston, G., Fewell, S., Richer, W.: An organizational interoperability agility model. Technical report, DSTO Fern Hill, Department of defence, Canberra ACT 2600, Australia (2005)
9. Mallek, S., Daclin, N., Chapurlat, V.: The application of interoperability requirement specification and verification to collaborative processes in industry. Comput. Ind. **63**(7), 643–658 (2012)
10. Cornu, C., Chapurlat, V., Quiot, J.M., Irigoin, F.: Customizable interoperability assessment methodology to support technical processes deployment in large companies. Ann. Rev. Control **36**(2), 300–308 (2012)
11. Camara, M., Ducq, Y., Dupas, R.: A methodology for the evaluation of interoperability improvements in inter-enterprises collaboration based on causal performance measurement models. Int. J. Comput. Integr. Manuf. **27**(2), 103–119 (2014)
12. Chen, D., Doumeings, G., Vernadat, F.: Architectures for enterprise integration and interoperability:past, present and future. Comput. Ind. **59**(7), 647–659 (2008)
13. Ducq, Y., Chen, D., Doumeings, G.: A contribution of system theory to sustainable enterprise interoperability science base. Comput. Ind. **63**(8), 844–857 (2012)
14. INCOSE: Guide for writing requirements. Technical report, INCOSE (2012)
15. Touzi, J., Lorr, J.P., Bnaben, F., Pingaud, H.: Interoperability through model-based generation: the case of the collaborative information system (cis). In: Gonalves, R.J., Müller, J.P., Mertins, K., Zelm, M. (eds.) Enterprise Interoperability New Challenges and Approaches. Springer, London (2007)
16. Chungoora, N., Young, R.I., Gunendran, G., Palmer, C., Usman, Z., Anjum, N.A., Cutting-Decelle, A.F., Harding, J.A., Case, K.: A model-driven ontology approach for manufacturing system interoperability and knowledge sharing. Comput. Ind. **64**(4), 392–401 (2013)
17. Khadka, R., Sapkota, B., Pires, L.F., van Sinderen, M., Jansen, S.: Model-driven approach to enterprise interoperability at the technical service level. Comput. Ind. **64**(8), 951–965 (2013)
18. Franco, R.D., De Juan-Marn, R., Rodrguez-Merino, C., Martnez, J.L.: Colnet platform: Resilient collaborative networks through interoperability. In: Poler, R., Doumeings, G., Katzy, B., Chalmeta, R. (eds.) Enterprise Interoperability V: Shaping Enterprise. Springer, London (2012)
19. Pessoa, R.M., Silva, E., van Sinderen, M., Quartel, D.A.C., Pires, L.F.: Enterprise interoperability with soa: a survey of service composition approaches. In: Enterprise Distributed Object Computing Conference Workshops. IEEE (2008)
20. Wieczorek, S., Stefanescu, A.: Improving testing of enterprise systems by model-based testing on graphical user interfaces. In: 17th IEEE International Conference and Workshops on Engineering of Computer-Based Systems. IEEE (2010)
21. Lee, Y.: Event-driven soa test framework based on bpa-simulation. In: First International Conference on Networked Digital Technologies (NDT 2009). IEEE (2009)

22. Vieira, M., Leduc, J., Hasling, B., Subramanyan, R., Kazmeier, J.: Automation of gui testing using a model-driven approach. In: The 2006 International Workshop on Automation of Software Test. ACM (2006)

23. Doumeingts, G., Ducq, Y., Vallespir, B., Kleinhans, S.: Production management and enterprise modelling. Comput. Ind. **42**(2–3), 245–263 (2000)

24. Yaxiong, T., Zhen, X., Huibin, X.: Bpm exception monitoring based on process knowledge. In: Proceedings of IEEE Conference on Cybernetics and Intelligent Systems (CIS), IEEE Xplore Digital Library, Singapore, 28–30 June 2010

25. IBM: Websphere business modeler: Process cost analysis (2014)

26. Jans, M., Alles, M., Vasarhelyi, M.: The case for process mining in auditing: sources of value added and areas of application. Int. J. Account. Inform. Syst. **14**(1), 1–20 (2013)

27. Liu, Y., Zhang, H., Li, C., Jianxin Jiao, R.: Workflow simulation for operational decision support using event graph through process mining. Decis. Support Syst. Ind. **52**(3), 685–697 (2012)

28. van der Aalst, W., van Dongen, B.F., Herbst, J., Maruster, L., Schimm, G.W.A.: Workflow mining: a survey of issues and approaches. Data Knowl. Eng. **47**(2), 237–267 (2003)

29. van der Aalst, W.M.P.: Configurable services in the cloud: supporting variability while enabling cross-organizational process mining. In: Meersman, R., Dillon, T.S., Herrero, P. (eds.) OTM 2010. LNCS, vol. 6426, pp. 8–25. Springer, Heidelberg (2010)

30. Zeng, Q., Sun, H.X., Duan, H., Liu, C., Wang, H.: Cross-organizational collaborative workflow mining from a multi-source log. Decis. Support Syst. **54**(3), 1280–1301 (2013)

31. van der Aalst, W.M.P., Reijers, H.A., Weijters, A., van Dongen, B., Alves de Medeiros, A., Song, M., Verbeek, H.: Business process mining: an industrial application. Inf. Syst. **32**(5), 713–732 (2007)

32. Samba Camara, M., Dupas, R., Ducq, Y., Mané, B.: Interoperability improvement in inter-enterprises collaboration: a software engineering approach. In: Mertins, K., Bénaben, F., Poler, R., Bourrières, J.-P. (eds.) Enterprise Interoperability VI: Interoperability for Agility, Resilience and Plasticity of Collaborations. Springer, Switzerland (2014)

33. van der Aalst, W.M.P., Weijters, A.: Process mining: a research agenda. Comput. Ind. **53**(3), 231–244 (2004)

34. Grigori, D., Casati, F., Castellanos, M., Dayal, U., Sayal, M., Shan, M.C.: Business process intelligence. Comput. Ind. **53**(3), 321–343 (2004)

35. Gunther, C.: Process Mining in Flexible Environments. Ph.D. thesis, Technische Universiteit Eindhoven, Eindhoven, The Netherlands (2009)

36. Muehlen, M.Z., Rosemann, M.: Workflow-based process monitoring and controlling-technical and organizational issues. In: Proceedings of the 33rd Annual Hawaii International Conference on System Sciences, IEEE Xplore Digital Library, 4–7 Jan 2000

37. Business process intelligence. In: Handbook of Research on Business Process Modeling. IGI Global (2009)

38. Rozinat, A., Mans, R., Song, M., van der Aalst, W.M.P.: Discovering simulation models. Inf. Syst. **34**(3), 305–327 (2009)

39. Hammer, M.: Beyond Reengineering. HarperBusiness (1996)

40. Hammer, M., Champy, J.: Reengineering the Corporation: A Manifesto for Business Revolution. HarperBusiness, New York (1993)

41. OMG: Business process model and notation (bpmn). version 2.0 (2011)
42. Frankel, D.S.: Model Driven Architecture: Applying MDA to Enterprise Computing. Wiley, New York (2003)
43. ISO/IEC/IEEE: 29119-2-software and systems engineering. software testing (2013)
44. Chappell, D.: Enterprise Service Bus. O'Reilly Media, New York (2004)
45. Ferrara, A., MacDonald, M.: Programming .NET Web Services. O'Reilly Media, Inc., USA (2002)

Interoperability as a Key Concept for the Control and Evolution of the System of Systems (SoS)

Stéphane Billaud[(⊠)], Nicolas Daclin, and Vincent Chapurlat

LGI2P, Ecole des Mines d'Alès, Parc Scientifique G. Besse,
30035 Nîmes Cedex 1, France
{stephane.billaud,nicolas.daclin,
vincent.chapurlat}@mines-ales.fr

Abstract. A coalition of enterprises wanting to collaborate, and more generally a Collaborative Network of Organizations (CNO), can conceptually be assimilated as a System of Systems (SoS) presenting a number of characteristics to respect all over its life cycle. Interoperability is one of these characteristics (both functional and non-functional), which is from our point of view, essential in order to guarantee the control of the SoS, its behavior and the fulfillment of its mission(s). Moreover, it ensures the reaction of the SoS to deal with some risky situations and with potential local or global deficits during its functioning. In this paper, we propose to determine the relation between the current level of interoperability of the SoS and its functioning whatever may be its situation. A matrix shows how this relation evolves taking into account several characteristics of the SoS, particularly its capacity to respect interoperability requirements (Compatibility, Interoperation, Autonomy and Reversibility) and the so-called analysis perspectives of the SoS: Performance, Integrity and Stability. This relation is requested in order to permit and to guide SoS behavioral simulation currently in development. Thus, a set of indicators is derived and formalized.

Keywords: Interoperability · System of Systems (SoS) · System of Systems Engineering (SoSE) · Performance · Stability · Integrity · Adaptability

1 Introduction

The following definition seems to adequately encapsulate the multiple definitions that have been given to the concept of System of Systems and will be useful for the remainder of this paper. A System of Systems (SoS) is a set of **heterogeneous** and existing subsystems assembled together to achieve a global mission that a system alone cannot fulfil, while maintaining the **operational** and **managerial independency** (**autonomy**) of each of the subsystems. These subsystems have then to be able to **communicate** and to **work harmoniously** together or to **adapt** their behavior and functioning locally when facing any **evolution** of the environment of the SoS [1–5]. It is admitted that the SoS Engineering (SoSE) activities carefully focus on choosing and assembling these subsystems as well as designing appropriate interfaces to facilitate this assembling [6]. Subsystems are selected and involved according to their potential roles, available

© IFIP International Federation for Information Processing 2015
M. van Sinderen and V. Chapurlat (Eds.): IWEI 2015, LNBIP 213, pp. 53–63, 2015.
DOI: 10.1007/978-3-662-47157-9_5

resources, competences and know-how that can be shared in order to fulfil the SoS mission. Particular attention is given to some constraints that have to be also considered especially the capacity of subsystems of being interoperable. Indeed, for instance DoDAF [7] and System Engineering [8, 9] claim that interoperability is required to coordinate and make efficient such large multi-disciplinary and heterogeneous coalition of subsystems. Therefore, interoperability has to be fully considered when the chosen subsystems are assembled for a more or less short period during which they will have to work together, share flows, data and resources in order to build their SoS.

Moreover, a strong linkage exists between the interoperability and the so-called analysis perspectives namely Stability, Integrity and Performance [6]. Therefore, and to address this challenge, the original aim of this paper is to investigate the impact of the interoperability on the so-called analysis perspectives by proposing an impact matrix and by defining a set of indicators that characterizes and helps to understand this impact. With respect to the state-of-the-art and to the best of our knowledge, the requested interoperability of heterogeneous subsystems has not been yet handled before and this paper characterizes the novelty of the approach. It is evidently a new challenging area and there are research directions towards discovering it [10].

This paper focuses first on the reasons behind considering the interoperability as a crucial characteristic of the SoS in order to control it and to help it achieving its mission throughout its evolution and in various situations that might take risky aspects. Afterwards, we define a set of requirements that allow us characterizing the requested subsystems' interoperability. Moreover, relationship between subsystems' interoperability and SoS' analysis perspectives is presented. The first result is a matrix aiming to assist the engineers, designers and managers involved in SoSE process in choosing their subsystems prior the assembling and understanding the impact of the interoperability over the SoS analysis perspectives all over its life cycle. This will be done by evaluating this impact through a simulation technique not described here. Therefore, a set of indicators is defined in order to concretize the existing relationship between the interoperability and the SoS analysis perspectives. These indicators are not exhaustive but in our point of view, the selected ones are complete and enough to allow the evaluation of the impact of interoperability on the SoS analysis perspectives.

2 Interoperability

2.1 Interoperability *vs.* SoS Characteristics

Interoperability is defined recurrently in the literature in a way to provide a better understanding of its various aspects and levels [11]. Thus, our attention is directed to define interoperability as the ability of **connected**, **autonomous**, "**loosely coupled**" and possibly **heterogeneous** systems to coexist, to **interoperate** and to exchange flows (data and services, material or energy) to/from other systems while continuing their own logic of operation preserving their autonomy.

In essence, this definition reveals various characteristics, which are consistent with the SoS expected characteristics. The autonomy of a subsystem i.e. the possibility to continue to act and make decisions, in order to ensure its own mission independently of other subsystems, is consistent with the expected managerial independency of the subsystems. The reversibility of a relation between two subsystems that allows a subsystem to achieve its mission, after breaking an alliance with other subsystems composing the same SoS, is coherent with the requested operational independency of the subsystems. The subsystems are seen as "loosely coupled". On the one hand, this kind of coupling enhances the connectivity which characterizes a SoS, where subsystems are capable of building links among their interfaces and destroying them dynamically [12] and on the other hand, it enhances the evolutionary development of the SoS [3] when it becomes possible to easily remove, modify or add subsystems from the SoS. The heterogeneity of the subsystems is essential for the SoS since it can only achieve its global mission by leveraging the diversity of its subsystems [12].

Thus, maintaining a sufficient level of interoperability of each subsystem helps the preservation of these SoS characteristics (constituent subsystems autonomy, enriched connectivity and commitment to diversity of subsystems) and the SoS behavior.

Last, SoS passes through various stages in its life cycle (See Fig. 1) during which these characteristics may evolve but have to be maintained in an acceptable range.

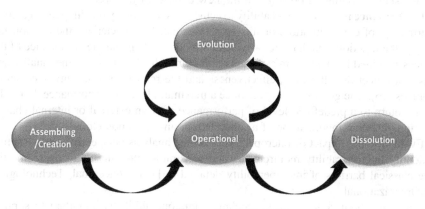

Fig. 1. Life cycle of a SoS [6]

2.2   Interoperability *vs.* SoS Analysis Perspectives

Beyond the classical System Engineering approach, System of Systems Engineering (SoSE) puts emphasis on the selection of relevant subsystems taking into consideration the necessity of staying interoperable in order to participate efficiently in the global mission of the SoS.

In this way, it is required to formalize the design of a SoS by taking into consideration the relationships between subsystems' interoperability and some functional characteristics as non-functional of a SoS. We focus here on the impact of subsystems interoperability on non-functional characteristics namely analysis perspectives Stability, Integrity and Performance) as demonstrated hereafter.

Stability reflects the ability of a SoS to maintain its viability and to adapt (e.g. its structure or its behavior i.e. this requests generally adaptation of concerned subsystems) to any change in its environment [6, 13]. It characterizes the cohesive relationship that should exist between the system structure and its activities or programs which define what the system should do. The stability level of the SoS must evolve when subsystems have to deal with some risky and/or unexpected situations whether they are due to internal or external events. Stability has six basic concepts which are generic for any SoS: Constancy, Resilience, Persistence, Resistance, Elasticity, and Domain of attraction [14]. Currently, none of the existing approaches (known as architectural styles of self-adaptation) enables a SoS to reason about itself and adapt to achieve particular stability, performance or quality objectives in the face of uncertainties and changes. The only existing architectural style of self-adaptation handles the stability from a local point of view of the subsystems without taking into consideration the subsystems interoperability that can impact positively or negatively the stability [15].

Integrity reflects the ability of a SoS to return to a known functioning and operating mode in case of any local change in its existing configuration (e.g. loss of one or more resources, or non-expected or even emergent situation due to subsystems interactions). When one or more subsystems of the SoS leaves the SoS, these subsystems have to continue to maintain their own operations and the remaining group of subsystems should continue to operate in the new context of the SoS.

Performance reflects the SoS ability to achieve its mission by reaching its objectives in terms e.g. of costs, duration, quality of service etc. It characterizes the relationship between the functions that have to be executed by the system and the compliance of the services provided by the resources for example, through indicators of time, quality and costs that reflect the efficiency, effectiveness and the relevance of the involved set of resources [16]. The goal is not to guarantee a maximum level of performance, but to be able to return to a predefined level of performance after an external or internal change (addition, deletion, modification of a subsystem or an interaction etc.).

Evaluating the impact of interoperability on the analysis perspectives requests first to identify interoperability requirements and constraints allowing us to overcome the three classical barriers of interoperability detailed in [17]: Conceptual, Technological and Organizational.

Improving both conceptual and technical interoperability is important to support organizational interoperability. These barriers take place in four areas of concerns of the SoS: flows (carrying out data, material or energy), services, processes and business. It is important to consider the three barriers to draw the interoperability requirements in order to allow proactive anomaly detection at the three levels (conceptual, technical and organizational).

The first basic interoperability requirement concerns the subsystems compatibility. The **compatibility** refers here to the interfaces imposed by the interactions between the subsystems. Interfaces can be technical, organizational, HMI or logical at high level of abstraction. Imposing standards interfaces or well-defined interfaces and common integration mechanisms are not always the solution in dynamic environment that can be considered as a SoS [18, 19].

The second basic interoperability requirement concerns the subsystems' **autonomy**. A subsystem must effectively respects the expected objectives, stakeholders' requirements and constraints defined for the SoS (e.g. cost, delay, quality) but meanwhile, it should respect its own requirements.

During the operational phase of the SoS, subsystems' **interoperation** appears as another interoperability requirement. It concerns, the ability of a collection of subsystems to share or exchange specified information/energy/material in order to achieve a specified purpose/mission in a given context.

In the dissolution phase of the SoS, the inter subsystems' relations (**reversibility**) is an important interoperability requirement. For instance, once a set of subsystems break the alliance with each other, each subsystem must be able to return to a state in which it reaches at least its original level of performance while executing its usual operations and consequently it respects its own requirements.

Last, interoperability requirements vary from one SoS type to another. For instance Directed SoS is considered here whereas the SoS requires to have an authority and a management role over its group of subsystems while preserving their ability to operate independently.

2.3   Interoperability Measurement

Interoperability has been studied in multiple fields [20, 21] and various approaches have been proposed to measure and evaluate the interoperability level of a system whatever may be its nature and sometimes its complexity. These approaches are mainly based on maturity measurement. A recent survey presented fourteen interoperability models used to measure the interoperability [11]: Spectrum of Interoperability Model (SoIM) [22], Quantification of Interoperability Methodology (QoIM) [23], Military Communications and Information Systems Interoperability (MCISI) [24], Levels of Information System Interoperability Model (LISI) [25] (this model is similar to SoIM, it is suited and adapted for measuring information systems interoperability), Interoperability Assessment Methodology (IAM) [26] (this model is similar to QoIM), Organizational Interoperability Maturity Model for C2 (OIM) [27] (This model is an extension of the LISI model), Stoplight [28], Levels of Conceptual Interoperability Model (LCIM) [29] (this model is similar to LISI and OIM, however it is used in the conceptual design to prove if meaningful interoperability between the systems is possible), Layers of Coalition Interoperability (LCI) [30], NATO C3 Technical Architecture Reference Model for Interoperability (NMI) [31], System-of-Systems Interoperability Model (SoSI) [32] (SoSI was proposed to support the Software Engineeringùùù* Institutes SoS interoperability research. However, it does not contain specific metrics to quantify interoperability within a SoS), Non-Technical Interoperability Framework (NTI) [33] (this model is based on the OIM organizational model), Organizational Interoperability Agility Model (OIAM) [34] (it builds upon the OIM organizational model), The Layered Interoperability Score (i-Score) [35] (This model is a mathematical method made in order to measure the interoperability of all types of systems for a very specific operational scenario/thread).

After presenting the approaches mentioned previously, we realize that all of them focus on a specific application domain (the interoperability of information systems) and only few approaches integrate the organizational aspects of interoperability. Moreover, none of these interoperability measurement approaches has been presented or tested in large systems or organizations like the SoS and [11] did not present any evidence of that. Therefore, the approach presented in the next section, offers an evaluation matrix that allows measuring the interoperability impacts, in a large and complex context (SoS), on the SoS analysis perspectives.

3   Interoperability Impact Matrix

The impact matrix aims to present a new approach of the interoperability-impact analysis which combines the interoperability sub requirements and their impact on the SoS analysis perspectives. Therefore, it is divided into two main axes: (I) the interoperability (**Compatibility, Interoperation, Autonomy and Reversibility**) and (II) the SoS analysis perspectives (**Performance and Adaptability**). The integrity and stability of the SoS are combined into one characteristic that we call: the SoS' **adaptability**. It is the ability of a SoS to adapt to any new situation or change and to return to a known operating or functioning mode whatever the changes result from internal (integrity) or external (stability) causes. It will be evaluated based on its six concepts: Constancy, Resilience, Persistence, Resistance, Elasticity, and Domain of attraction mentioned in Sect. 2.2.

Mainly, two subsystems inside a SoS are at a high level of interoperability if and only if they are at a high level of Compatibility, Interoperation, Autonomy and Reversibility.

Compatibility. Compatibility means to harmonize subsystems in order to be ready to collaborate. Compatibility focuses on a static point of view of the collaboration and remains insufficient to determine if the subsystems are interoperable during the SoS life cycle. It is necessary to consider the evolution of the context and of the situation of each subsystem. A set of indicators is required to analyze the impact of the compatibility between the subsystems on the performance of the SoS. They are divided into subgroups according to the kind of compatibility.

1. Organizational and conceptual compatibility indicators: **syntax** (the information to be exchanged is expressed with the same syntax?), **preparedness** (the data are well defined and documented?), **Understanding** (communication and shared information rate), **Command style** (are authorities/responsibilities are clearly defined?) and **trust.**
2. Technical compatibility indicators: **Common Operating Environments**, **Standard procedures and training**, **standard complaint**, **Basic data format** (Information exchange is restricted to homogeneous data exchange), **Media format, Applications, security profile** (a security profile contains information that governs at what security level(s) a system may operate), **Media exchange procedures, System services**, **data**, **Heterogeneous information** (This form of information represents data repositories that contain more than one data format) and **Information space.**
3. Operational and behavioral compatibility indicators: compatibility with **prior experience**, compatibility with **existing work practices** and compatibility with **preferred work style**.
4. Functional compatibility: **response** and **execution time**.

In this case, compatibility impacts each perspective as follows:

Compatibility → Performance: The compatibility between subsystems impacts the SoS performance. In the absence of compatibility of interfaces for example, it becomes impossible for interactions to take place, therefore the system will be unable to fulfill its mission(s) and by consequence unable to reach its performance's objectives. Furthermore, a low level of compatibility implies a limited interaction which will induce a lower performance.

On the one hand, an increase in the compatibility between the subsystems imposes sometimes constraints to respect. These constraints imply a decrease in the performance of the SoS. On the other hand, an increase in the compatibility might be useless if the subsystems reached already a sufficient level of compatibility to guarantee the predefined level of performance for the SoS. In this case, the performance will not vary with the increase of the compatibility.

A decrease in the compatibility between the subsystems prevents or limits the exchange of data/material/energy etc., this induces a decrease in the performance of the SoS. However, if the subsystems need a level of compatibility less than the actual one in order to perform perfectly, then a decrease of the compatibility will have no impact on the level of the predefined performance since their level of compatibility was higher than requested and they can absorb a decrease in the compatibility on condition that it remains sufficient to keep the necessary level to perform adequately.

Compatibility → Adaptability: An increase or decrease in the compatibility following an add, remove or modification of a subsystem or an interaction between the subsystems might induce a decrease in the performance of the SoS since the subsystems take a certain time to reach again an accepted level of compatibility necessary to get to the predefined level of performance. The level of performance might stay stable if the subsystems are able to adapt rapidly.

Interoperation, is the ability of a collection of communicating systems to share or exchange specified information/energy/material in order to achieve a specified purpose/mission in a given context. It is measured through a set of indicators which seem to be only adequate to a specific types of telecommunication SoS. However, these indicators can be applied to any kind of SoS since the flow between subsystems can be data, information, material or energy. Therefore, these indicators are not limited to the domain of telecommunication:

1. **Time of interoperation:** The time of interoperation corresponds to the duration between the date when information is requested and the date when the requested information is used.
2. **Quality of interoperation:** The quality of interoperation takes in consideration three kinds of quality: (1) the quality of exchange (The quality of exchange draws up if the exchange is correctly performed), (2) the quality of use (The quality of use represents the number of information received by a partner in comparison with the number of information requested.) and, (3) the quality of conformity (The quality of conformity corresponds to the exploitation of the information).
3. **Capacity:** is the rate at which data may be passed over time.

4. **System overload:** when more data must be exchanged than the system is able to transmit.
5. **Underutilization:** when the system data rate/message load is less than its full capacity but messages are waiting in queues to be transmitted.
6. **Under capacity:** when messages remain in queues and the system data rate is at the maximum.
7. **Data latency:** is the elapsed time from the transmission to the reception.

Then, interoperation impacts each perspective as follows:

Interoperation → Performance: The interoperation between the subsystems impacts the SoS performance. In the absence of the interoperation, the subsystems are no longer able to exchange data/material/energy etc. therefore the SoS cannot achieve its mission (s) neither its performance's objectives. Moreover, a subsystem with a very low capacity limits the interoperation with another subsystem with higher capacity; therefore the performance of the overall system (SoS) will be impacted.

An increase or decrease in the interoperation between the subsystems might have three different impacts on the performance of the SoS. It decreases the SoS performance if we exceed the capacity of the subsystems to absorb the high rates of interoperation. However, it increases the SoS performance if the subsystems are able to interoperate with the new imposed rates with higher performance.

Interoperation → Adaptability: An increase in the interoperation might induce an increase in the adaptability if and only if the subsystems are capable to operate with the new imposed rates, otherwise it implies a decrease in that adaptability and the SoS is not able to return to its predefined level of performance since the new interoperation indicators are not adequate to the new local or external changes. A decrease in the interoperation induces an increase in the SoS adaptability since the restrictions on the subsystems in terms of interoperation indicators are less significant.

The autonomy of the subsystems is the fact to be free to pursue its purpose. That freedom is limited by some constraints. However, those constraints cannot be allowed to overwhelm or violate its capacity or nature to perform. The autonomy is measured based on the classical performance indicators of each subsystem. Autonomy impacts the SoS analysis perspectives as follows:

Autonomy → Performance: Each subsystem of the SoS has its own mission(s) to fulfill independently from the overall mission of the SoS. However, if the autonomy of the subsystems increases, its participation in the SoS can be lower which implies a decrease in the SoS performance. Conversely, a decrease in the autonomy of a subsystem makes its participation in the SoS global mission less restrictive.

Autonomy → Adaptability: An increase in the subsystems' autonomy imposes more restrictions that prevent the new changes to be absorbed. Therefore, a decrease in the adaptability takes place. However, a decrease in the subsystems' autonomy implies more freedom to react to any changes and to return rapidly to the predefined level of performance, therefore an increase in the adaptability takes place.

Last, the reversibility means that a subsystem may maintain or retrieve easily its autonomy and performance (including positive and/or negative variations that are accepted) at the end of any collaboration. Reversibility has no impact on the analysis perspectives of the SoS, once a subsystem leaves the SoS, it continues its life cycle independently from the System of Systems. However, the requirements related to each subsystem have to be verified.

Table 1 shows how the variation in the interoperability requirements level (inducing then measurement of the respect of the requirement by suing one or several of the methods presented before) impacts the analysis perspectives of the SoS.

Table 1. Matrix of the subsystems interoperability's impact on the SoS analysis perspectives (S: Stable, I: Increase, D: Decrease).

Interoperability	Analysis perspectives	
	Performance	Adaptability
Compatibility	S/D	S/D
Interoperation	D/S/I	D/S/I
	D/S/I	I
Autonomy	S/D	D
	S/I	S/I
Reversibility	None	None

4   Conclusions and Perspectives

This paper illustrated the importance of the interoperability of the subsystems in the control and evolution of the System of Systems. After careful analysis, we realized that there exists a strong linkage between the interoperability and the SoS characteristics and between the interoperability and some other non-functional characteristics of the SoS (analysis perspectives).

The significance of this paper lies in its ability awareness about the need to consider the interoperability prior the assembling of the subsystems. An impact matrix of the interoperability on the analysis perspectives has been proposed, it is a first crucial step towards an effective System of Systems Engineering. It permits the correct control and evolution of the SoS inside uncertain and unknowable environment in which it must operate.

The proposed matrix will serve to allow the evaluation of the impact of the interoperability on the analysis perspectives. This evaluation will be achieved through the simulation which is currently under development.

References

1. Boardman, J., Sauser, B.: System of Systems - the meaning of Of. In: IEEE/SMC International Conference on System of Systems Engineering, pp. 118–123 (2006)

2. Jamshidi, M.: System of Systems Engineering: Innovations for the Twenty-First Century. Wiley, Hoboken (2011)
3. Maier, M.W.: Architecting principles for systems-of-systems. Syst. Eng. **1**, 267–284 (1998)
4. Ackoff, R.L.: Towards a System of Systems concepts. Manage. Sci. **17**, 661–671 (1971)
5. Carney, D., Fisher, D., Place, P.: Topics in Interoperability: System-of-Systems Evolution. Software Engineering Institute, Carnegie Mellon University, Pittsburgh, PA (2005)
6. Bilal, M., Daclin, N., Chapurlat, V.: Collaborative networked organizations as system of systems: a model-based engineering approach. In: Camarinha-Matos, L., Afsarmanesh, H. (eds.) Collaborative Systems for Smart Networked Environments. IFIP AICT, vol. 434, pp. 227–234. Springer, Heidelberg (2014)
7. Departement of Defense: DoD Architecture Framework, vol. 1, Definitions and Guidelines, Architecture, pp. 1–46 (2007)
8. R.D. Adcock (EIC). Hoboken, N.T.T. of the S.I. of T.: The Guide to the Systems Engineering Body of Knowledge (SEBoK), v. 1.3. http://www.sebokwiki.org/. Last visited 17 July 2014
9. International Council on Systems Engineering (INCOSE): INCOSE Systems Engineering Handbook v. 3.2.2. SE Handb. Work. Gr. 1306 (2011)
10. Camarinha-matos, L.M.: Collaborative networks: a mechanism for enterprise agility and resilience. In: Enterprise Interoperability VI, pp. 1–8 (2014)
11. Ford, TC., Colombi, J.M., Graham, S.R., Jacques, D.R.: A survey on interoperability measurement. In: Twelfth International Command and Control Research and Technology Symposium (2007)
12. Stevens Intitute Of Technology: Castle Point On Hudson, Hoboken, N. 07030: Report On System Of Systems Engineering (2006)
13. Pénalva, J.M., Page, E.: SAGACE: la modélisation des systèmes dont la maîtrise est complexe. In: ILCE (1990)
14. Grimm, V., Wissel, C.: Babel, or the ecological stability discussions: an inventory and analysis of terminology and a guide for avoiding confusion. Oecologia **109**, 323–334 (1997)
15. Weyns, D., Andersson, J.: On the challenges of self-adaptation in systems of systems. In: International Workshop on Software Engineering for Systems-of-Systems, SESoS 2013, pp. 47–51 (2013)
16. Bonnefous, C., Courtois, A.: Indicateurs de performance (2001)
17. Interop: Enterprise Interoperability-Framework and knowledge corpus - Final report. INTEROP NoE, FP6 - Contract n° 508011, Deliv. DI.3. 1, pp. 1–44 (2004)
18. Kasunic, M.: Measuring Systems Interoperability: Challenges and opportunities. Technical Note C. 2004 TN 003 Carnegie-Mellon Univiversity, Software Engineering Institute INST, Pittsburgh, PA (2004)
19. Panetto, H.: Meta-modèles et modèles pour l'intégration et l'interopérabilité des applications d'entreprises de production. Dr. Diss University, Université Henri Poincaré-Nancy I (2006)
20. Truptil, S.: Collaborative process design for mediation information system engineering. In: 6th International Conference on Information Systems for Crisis Response and Management (2009)
21. Ruggaber, R.: ATHENA - advanced technologies for interoperability of heterogeneous enterprise networks and their applications. In: Konstantas, D., Bourrières, J.-P., Léonard, M., Boudjlida, N. (eds.) Interoperability of Enterprise Software and Applications, pp. 459–460. Springer, London (2006)
22. Lavean, G.: Interoperability in defense communications. Commun. IEEE Trans. **28**, 1445–1455 (1980)
23. Mensh, D., Kite, R., Darby, P.: A methodology for quantifying interoperability. Nav. Eng. J. **101**(3), 251 (1989)

24. Amanowicz, M., Gajewski, P.: Military communications and information systems interoperability. In: 1996 Proceedings of the IEEE Military Communications Conference, MILCOM 1996, vol. 1, pp. 280–283. IEEE (1996)
25. Defense, D.: Of: C4ISR Architecture Working Group Final Report - Levels of Information System Interoperability (LISI). Washington, DC OSD(ASD(C3I)) C4ISR AWG (1998)
26. Leite, M.J.: Interoperability assessment. In: Proceedings of the 66th Military Operations Research. Society Symposium, Monterey, CA (1998)
27. Clark, T., Jones, R.: Organisational interoperability maturity model for C2. In: Proceedings of the 1999 Command and Control Research and Technology Symposium (1999)
28. Hamilton, J., John, A., Rosen, J.D., Summers, P.A.: An interoperability road map for C4ISR legacy systems. Acquis. Rev. Q. **28**, 17–31 (2002). Winter
29. Andreas, T., Muguira, J.A.: The levels of conceptual interoperability model. In: Proceedings of the 2003 Fall Simulation Interoperability Work, vol. 7 (2003)
30. Tolk, A.: Beyond technical interoperability-introducing a reference model for measures of merit for coalition interoperability. Old Dom, UNIV, Norfolk (2003)
31. NATO: NATO Allied Data Publication 34: NATO C3 Technical Architecture. Nato, Belgium. vol. 2 (2003)
32. Morris, E., Levine, L., Meyers, C., Place, P., Plakosh, D.: System of Systems Interoperability (SOSI): final report (No. CMU/SEI-2004-TR-004). Carnegie-Mellon University, Software Engineering Institute INST, Pittsburgh, PA (2004)
33. Stewart, K., Clarke, H., Goillau, P., Verrall, N., Widdowson, M.: Non-technical interoperability in multinational forces. In: 9th International Command and Control Research and Technology. Symposium (2004)
34. Kingston, G., Fewell, S., Richer, W.: An organisational interoperability agility model. Defence Science Technology Organ, Canberra (2005)
35. Ford, T., Colombi, J., Graham, S., Jacques, D.: The interoperability score. In: Proceedings of the Fifth Annual Conference on System Engineering Research, pp. 1–10 (2007)

Towards an Agile and Collaborative Platform for Managing Supply Chain Uncertainties

Matthieu Lauras[1]([⊠]), Jacques Lamothe[1], Frederick Benaben[1],
Beatriz Andres[2], and Raul Poler[2]

[1] Université Toulouse, Mines Albi, Campus Jarlard, Route de Teillet,
81000 Albi, France
{lauras,lamothe,benaben}@mines-albi.fr
[2] Universitat Politecnica de Valencia, Camino de Vera s/n,
46022 Valencia, Spain
{bandres,rpoler}@cigip.upv.es

Abstract. Nowadays, one of the main challenges for Supply Chains is the management of disruptions and uncertainties. Turbulence and instability have now to be considered as the 'normal' situation. Future Supply Chains should be able to cope with this new context to stay competitive. To solve this issue, new approaches and technologies have to be designed in order to improve the agility capability of supply networks. To contribute to this new problem statement, as a part of the H2020 C2NET research project, this paper proposes a concrete research framework. The research aim consists in defining precise research orientations in one hand, and structuring a set of technical tasks able to result in an agile and collaborative platform on the other hand. Basically, the main components of the research framework are presented and the expected impacts are discussed.

Keywords: Supply Chain · Uncertainty · Collaborative platform · Agility · Research framework

1 Introduction

Modern Supply Chains are continuously challenged by unexpected disruptive events that are increasing in their frequency and effects: supply failures, demand changes, internal disruptions, etc. In this context, turbulence and instability can be no longer considered as an episodic crisis, rather the "norm" or the default status. The question is then to know how the Supply Chains can strive and gain in such disruptive environments and which supportive roles can the technology play. Current IT and decision-making systems are designed to run in more or less "stable" environment. Disturbances are captured by exception handling mechanisms. Thus, calling for a new perspective in Supply Chains design and engineering. While current Supply Chains are tempting to be robust, tomorrow's Supply Chains need to become agile.

The current research work proposes to develop some innovative solutions to bridge this gap. This research project is a sub-part of the C2NET H2020 project (2015–2018) that covets leveraging the potential of Cloud technologies providing a manufacturing

© IFIP International Federation for Information Processing 2015
M. van Sinderen and V. Chapurlat (Eds.): IWEI 2015, LNBIP 213, pp. 64–72, 2015.
DOI: 10.1007/978-3-662-47157-9_6

infrastructure for a real-time knowledge of different supply chain components such as manufacturing assets status, inventory levels or current demand at consumption points. By providing specific tools for optimization and collaboration in the cloud, companies involved in a Supply Chain will be able to increase their agility to respond quickly, flexibly and efficiently to changes in demand and unexpected events that have place during products supply. C2NET is providing a technological infrastructure that will enable a continuous data collection in real time from manufacturing processes that take place within a plant including logistics operations intra-plants, as well as from products, which are being processing along the whole supply chain. C2NET will facilitate its adaptation to actual manufacturing chains allowing data collection from a wide range of different information sources such as legacy systems (Enterprise Resources Planning, Manufacturing Execution Systems, Business Intelligence...), industrial control systems or directly from devices with different levels of intelligence built into machines and products such as smart sensors, embedded systems or Radio Frequency Identification. Collaboration throughout the Supply Chain using cloud-based tools and solutions is the main concept on which C2NET platform is based. This cloud platform is articulated around three main components as described in Fig. 1:

- The C2NET Data Collection Framework (DCF) that collects in real-time information from processes and products within the supply chain;
- The C2NET Optimizer (OPT) that allows providing production plans and decisions to all concerned supply chain partners;
- The C2NET Collaboration Tools (COT) that proposes a set of services able to facilitate the achievement of agreements and drastically reduce response time and cost of decision-making processes.

In this paper we focus only on the collaboration tools (C2NET-COT). The problem statement of this set of tools is to develop a new approach for facilitating collaborative demand, production and delivery plans along the supply network. Basically, the technical ambition is to design a modular architecture for interoperability of intra plant and extra plant processes in conjunction with mobile, collaborative tools for data sharing, data analytics and knowledge-based systems, at factory and at supply network level.

The paper is split up into three main sections. First a literature selection will propose to underline the concepts of "Agile Supply Chains" and "Collaborative networks". On this basis, we will propose in a second part a research framework able to structure the future developments on this subject. Then, a third part will discuss the main impacts that should be obtained at the end of this research project.

2 Literature Selection

Many companies have not fully recognized the nature of systemic supply chain risk and have continued to focus on seeking efficiency improvements (Christopher and Peck 2004). These authors argue that a new priority consist in searching for supply chain strategies that embody a significantly higher degree of resilience. Resilience implies

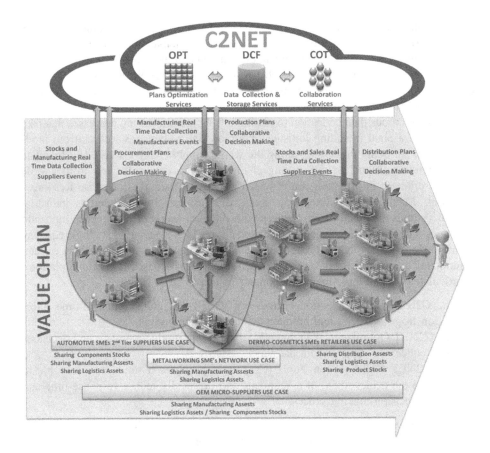

Fig. 1. Overview of the C2NET Project (platform and use cases).

flexibility and agility. Its implications extend beyond process redesign to fundamental decisions on sourcing and the establishment of more collaborative supply chain relationships based on far greater transparency of information (Christopher and Peck 2004).

2.1   Agile Supply Chains

According to Lee (2004), an agile supply chain is a set of partners responding quickly to short-term changes in demand (or supply) and handling external disruptions smoothly. Sometimes agility can be mistaken for other similar but different concepts such as adaptability, resilience and virtuality. Researchers also had interest on the capabilities that are required to access agility. Charles et al. (2010) justifies that agility requires the combination of:

– Effectiveness: ability to satisfy the customer demand;
– Completeness: ability to satisfy totally the customer demand;

- Reliability: ability to respect the customer delivery lead time;
- Responsiveness: ability to respond quickly which requires to: (i) detect quickly changes [Visibility], (ii) decide quickly on the adaptation to make using flexibility [Reactivity], and (iii) implement quickly the decisions [Velocity].

Another definition has been proposed by (Benaben 2012):
Agility = (Detection + Adaptation) × (Effectiveness + Responsiveness)

In the following we will keep this definition. Recently various initiatives have appeared for analyzing and supporting the deployment of agility in supply chain. Such initiatives are SOA and WebService based (Ahn et al. 2012; Ameri and Patil 2012; Zhang et al. 2012). Accorsi (2011) describes notably a specific SaaS, the Business Process as a Service (BPaaS). Ahn et al. (2012) discuss moreover the slow adoption of XML standards such as ebXML and RosettaNet in agile supply chains and identifies three pitfalls: (i) these standards are presently not adapted to agile supply chains which constrained by high market volatility and short customer lead times; (ii) lack of stringent, vendor-independent business process standards that create a barrier to achieving the high level alignment and flexibility; (iii) technologies for the management of online relationships are hardly accessible to SMEs because of a wide variety of partnering options that might be required, a large number of trading partners, product diversity, and strategic diversity. (Benaben 2012) proposes a framework for differentiating the various strategies of workflow agility:

- Delayed choice: the process is partially defined during the design time and finalized at the execution. In this approach, the implementation of some sub-processes is chosen within a predefined list at the moment of the process execution. This approach is implemented in the YAWL system (Adams et al. 2005).
- Delayed design: the process is partially defined, but some sub-processes are not identified during the design. This approach suggests to come back to a specific design time when required during the execution.
- Risks management: various alternative paths are identified during the design time in order to adapt to risks, threats or opportunities. One path is finally chosen during each execution of the process. With this approach the number of paths to be identified can be too important in practice.
- AdHoc design: this approach extends the concept of delayed design. The sequence of activities can be changed, some tasks can be added or cancelled or repeated. It is the more common approach (Adams et al. 2005).

The C2NET Collaborative Platform will propose a concrete support able to manage the agility of the collaborative situation, especially in manufacturing network environment. The main contribution of the C2NET Project regarding extent literature on this point consists in making agile Supply Chains concrete. Specific objectives will include the design and the implementation of an integrated system able to supervise, detect, adapt and assess the collaborative situation.

2.2 Collaborative Networks

The way how manufacturing and service industries manage their businesses is changing due to the emerging new competitive environments. According to (Camarinha-Matos and Afsarmanesh 2005) the enterprises' success in the new dynamic environments is associated to the improved competencies in terms of new business models, strategies, governance principles, processes and technological capabilities of manufacturing enterprises of 2020. Moreover, especially for SMEs, the participation in collaborative networks is also a key issue for any enterprise that is willing to achieve differentiated and competitive strengths. Consequently, establishing collaborative relationships becomes an important issue to deal with customer needs, through sharing competencies and resources. Collaborative Networks consist of a variety of heterogeneous autonomous entities, geographically distributed, in which participants collaborate to achieve a common goal and base their interactions through computer networks. SMEs are characterized by limited capabilities and resources; therefore, in order to overcome possible barriers that can appear when establishing collaboration, joint efforts must be performed to achieve the desired collaborative scenarios. When establishing collaboration, networked partners share information, resources and responsibilities to jointly plan, implement, and evaluate a program of activities to reach a common goal and therefore jointly generate value. Thus, establish collaborative relationships imply sharing risks, resources, responsibilities, losses, rewards and trust. Collaborative networks manifest in a large variety of forms, such as virtual organizations, virtual enterprises, dynamic supply chains, professional virtual communities, collaborative virtual laboratories (Camarinha-Matos and Afsarmanesh 2005) and collaborative non-hierarchical networks (Poler et al. 2013). The main challenges for creating collaborative networks are presented in VOmap and are divided into five focus areas (i) socio economic, (ii) VO management, (iii) ITC support services, (iv) ICT Infrastructures and (v) formal models and theories.

Based on this background, the C2NET project will focus on the research and technical development to overcome possible barriers encountered when enterprises participate in collaborative networks characterized by distributed partners with decentralized information. The C2NET project will allow exploiting enterprises' capabilities and resources to efficiently succeed on the participation in collaborative networks. Specific objectives will include the design of cloud computing ICT, due to the advantages encountered for manufacturing and service industry networks, and the development of an integrated framework, consisting of models, methodologies and tools, to support enterprises in dealing with decentralized decision making within collaborative networks.

3 Research Framework

Our research project aims at providing a Collaborative Manufacturing Network Platform with a set of tools in charge of managing the agility of the collaborative situation. These tools are specifically in charge of exploiting the gathered data in order to formalize a clear vision of the collaborative situation and to propose dynamic adjustments. The following specific objectives are targeted in this research framework:

- Supervision: Define and implement the exploitation mechanisms to use collected data (from IoT, from monitoring or any other means) in order to maintain models of the collaborative situation.
- Detection: Define and implement the exploitation mechanisms of the situation models in order to diagnose any source of divergence of the collaboration with regard to the expected situation.
- Adaptation: Define and implement the reaction mechanisms to deduce from the analysis of the situation models, the appropriate adjustments to propose to the running collaborative situation.
- Assessment: Define, deploy, measure and exploit Key Performance Indicators (KPI) to ensure the relevant evaluation of the consequences of the adaptation actions

This part of the research work will improve the C2NET platform by providing it with five components dedicated to meet the four objectives previously described. These five components will be: (i) a knowledge base dedicated to store the collected data as exploitable models, (ii) a first service in charge of interpreting the collected data or reference KPI to feed the knowledge base, (iii) a second service in charge of watching the knowledge base in order to detect any divergence requiring adaptation measures, (iv) a third service in charge of exploiting the knowledge base and the detection reports to deduce and define the relevant adaptation actions, and (v) a fourth service in charge of continuous assessment of the agility actions in order to evaluate the taken measures and to provide a second order of agility by allowing thus the potential improvement of the three other services. Consequently, our research framework is structured according to these five elements (a knowledge base and four services). The Fig. 2 describes this research framework.

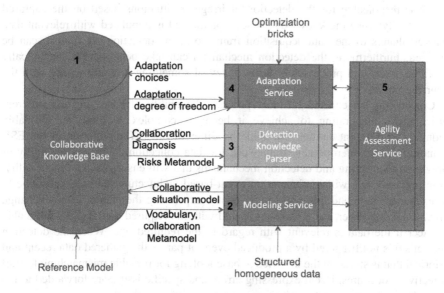

Fig. 2. Research framework proposal.

Hereafter, we give some requirements regarding tasks that have to be done to develop the previously discussed elements.

3.1 The Knowledge Base

Based on both a state-of-the-art on collaborative knowledge bases (domain ontologies vs. collaborative situation ontologies) and the reference models, this first design aims at defining and implementing an exploitable knowledge base about collaborative situations. This knowledge base should be compliant with any collaborative situation concerned by the C2NET project in terms of concerned business domain and concerned collaborative structure. The obtain knowledge base should be open and usable by the four agility services.

3.2 The Modeling Service

This second design aims at defining and implementing the first agility service. This task should define the translation mechanisms that could allow to update the knowledge base according to the continuously gathered data. This task includes a strong work on data format interpretation (syntactic view) and also on data content interpretation (semantic view).

3.3 The Detection Service

This third design aims at defining and implementing the second agility service. This service is responsible for the detection of irregular situations based on the captured data. Actually, once the knowledge base implemented is populated with relevant data gathered thanks to the data acquisition framework, the detection mechanism can be triggered. Furthermore, the detection mechanism can take benefit from semantically described assets and processes in order to reveal something is going wrong with the occurring process.

Considering an enacted business process, the ability of surveying the different participants collaborating to achieve it becomes complex as these are probably belonging to different entities and abide by different rules. The adoption of the ESB technology as an interoperable framework for data collection augments the ability of applying a monitoring and detection mechanisms that will ensure such a functionality. More precisely, we will implement an event-based architecture that will subscribe to the exchanges data and that will trigger events expressing the nature of the exchange (time, sender, receiver, etc.). Once compared with the required pattern we will be able to detect if the data is relevant with regard to the required one. When the detection mechanism is not triggered by a produced event, it parses the gathered data recent and historical that is stored in the knowledge base looking for possible mismatching to start corrective procedures. Event expressing errors and specific issues are forwarded to the adaptation and assessment services.

3.4 The Adaptation Service

This fourth design aims at defining and implementing the third agility service. This service should use the analysis of the detection service, as well as the full knowledge base to deduce and suggest adaptation measures that could fit with the current situation and prevent its actual divergence.

3.5 The Assessment Service

This fifth design aims at defining and implementing the fourth agility service. This service is in charge of agility assessment (to bring agility to the agility tools). This task should define relevant KPI and also the way to improve or change the rules and mechanisms of detection and adaptation services.

4 Expected Impacts

By implementing the research framework previously described, this research work should be able to propose a concrete solution to support the collaborative value chain by facilitating the diagnosis of any source of divergence of the collaboration with regard to expected situation. Moreover the project will be able to support the adaptation of the stakeholders' behaviors by implementing reaction mechanisms based on global and local optimization algorithms. The research work will facilitate the coordination between stakeholders by connecting them efficiently. Particularly, this will eliminate superfluous, inaccurate or irrelevant information regarding the monitoring of the current situation. It will also automate some analysis or actions based on pre-defined business rules in order to support local or global decisions.

The results of the C2NET project will mainly apply to both large enterprises and SMEs in Industry and Non-financial services. Practically, such a contribution should allow increasing drastically the competitiveness of Supply Chains by improving: Consumers' On Time Delivery, Total Lead-Time, Time-to-Market, Inventories, Carbon footprint, Profitability ratio, Efficiency ratio...

Acknowledgement. The research leading to these results has received funding from European Community's H2020 Programme (H2020/2014-2020) under grant agreement n°636909, "Cloud Collaborative Manufacturing Networks (C2NET)".

References

Accorsi, R.: Business process as a service: chances for remote auditing. In: 2011 IEEE 35th Annual Computer Software and Applications Conference Workshops (COMPSACW), pp. 398–403. IEEE, July 2011

Adams, M., ter Hofstede, A.H.M., Edmond, D., van der Aalst, W.M.P.: In: Proceedings of the 17th Conference on Advanced Information Systems Engineering Forum (CAiSE 2005 Forum), Porto, Portugal, June 2005

Ahn, H.J., Childerhouse, P., Vossen, G., Lee, H.: Rethinking XML-enabled agile supply chains. Int. J. Inf. Manage. **32**(1), 17–23 (2012)

Ameri, F., Patil, L.: Digital manufacturing market: a semantic web-based framework for agile supply chain deployment. J. Intell. Manuf. **23**(5), 1817–1832 (2012)

Benaben, F.: Conception de systèmes d'information de médiation pour la prise en charge de l'interopérabilité dans les collaborations d'organisations, Habilitation à Diriger des Recherches, INP Toulouse (2012)

Camarinha-Matos, L.M., Afsarmanesh, H.: Collaborative networks: a new scientific discipline. J. Intell. Manuf. **16**(4–5), 439–452 (2005)

Charles, A., Lauras, M., Van Wassenhove, L.: A model to define and assess the agility of supply chains: building on humanitarian experience. Int. J. Phys. Distrib. Logistics Manage. **40**(8/9), 722–741 (2010)

Christopher, M., Peck, H.: Building the resilient supply chain. Int. J. Logistics Manage. **15**(2), 1–14 (2004)

Lee, H.L.: The triple-A supply chain. Harvard Bus. Rev. **82**(10), 102–113 (2004)

Poler, R., Carneiro, L.M., Jasinski, T., Zolghadri, M., Pedrazzoli, P.: Intelligent Non-hierarchical Manufacturing Networks. Wiley, Hoboken (2013)

Zhang, W., Xu, Y., Dong, X.F.: Design and implementation of the agile supply chain information sharing platform in steel industry based on service-oriented architecture and Web service. Adv. Mater. Res. **505**, 75–81 (2012)

Towards a Sustainable Implementation of Interoperability Solutions: Bridging the Gap Between Interoperability Requirements and Solutions

Nicolas Daclin[(⊠)] and Sihem Mallek-Daclin

LGI2P, Parc scientifique G. Besse – école des mines d'Alès,
30035 Nîmes cedex, France
{nicolas.daclin,sihem.mallek}@mines-ales.fr

Abstract. The main objective of this communication is to present and discuss the need, for partners, to suitable interoperability solution according to their expectations. First, the problematic of the selection of a solution is presented and the stakeholders' needs to tackle this statement are highlighted. Then, existing works related to interoperability requirements and interoperability solutions are briefly presented and discussed. Finally, criteria - and associated examples - that guide stakeholders in their selection are presented.

Keywords: Enterprise interoperability engineering · Verification · Interoperability requirements · Interoperability solutions

1 Introduction

The concept of interoperability [1] is now considered as a crucial issue and a key factor of success for such enterprises that share and exchange processes, services data, enterprise applications [2]… in a collaborative context. Numerous works has been led to characterize [3], implement [4, 5] and improve [6, 7] this aspect of a partnership. Originally coming from the computer science and Information and Communication Technologies (ICT) fields [8] and, exclusively considered as a technical problem, interoperability has expanded, since, and considers now other less technical aspects. Also, in addition to technical aspects, interoperability can includes organisational aspects (for instance, who does what, how, when and who is responsible for what?…) as well as conceptual aspects (for instance, does the data to be exchanged use a data model?…) [9–11]. Similarly, if interoperability was seen only as an ability that enables and improves the sharing and the exchange of data, it now considers other fields such as the interoperability of processes (synchronization/coordination of activities, mutual adjustment [12]). Finally, as a simple matter of interfacing issue, the development of interoperability takes also an interest in other aspects of a collaboration that can affect either a given partner or the partnership itself. In that sense, it takes, for instance, an interest in the preservation of the autonomy of each partner involved into the collaboration [13].

© IFIP International Federation for Information Processing 2015
M. van Sinderen and V. Chapurlat (Eds.): IWEI 2015, LNBIP 213, pp. 73–82, 2015.
DOI: 10.1007/978-3-662-47157-9_7

As we may have noticed, interoperability has become an important expected capability – in other word a requirement (especially a non-functional requirement – NFR [14]) – for enterprises that want to establish and maintain an effective partnership in terms of exchange and sharing of their information, products and resources (material as human)... but also that want to align and, further, if requested, to orchestrate their process commonly or else, that want to work together at an higher level in term of decision or policies. However, with a better understanding and definition of interoperability, also appeared a greater complexity in its implementation, monitoring and control and improvement. Naturally, interoperability solutions - that cover the set of interoperability aspects - are developed to satisfy the needs of interoperability for partners that collaborate. In this context it is important to allow partners to select solutions that meet - at best – all their expectations in term of interoperability. Although the space of problems of interoperability is clearly identified on one hand, and the space of interoperability solutions is clearly defined on the other hand, the link between both is not clearly established and formalized. This statement may lead partners to select their interoperability solutions in a hazardous way and without knowing the potential impacts of the implementation of a given interoperability solution onto other aspects (*e.g.* other requirements, performance of the collaboration...) of the partnership. As a consequence the here presented research attempts to clarify the link between interoperability requirements and interoperability solutions and to enable partners to select solutions fully adapted to their needs and in a proper way.

This paper is structured as follow. After this brief introduction, the problem and expected results of this research are presented. The research works related to the fields of this research is given and discussed in Sect. 3. Section 4 presents the foundations of the proposed reference model to define and select accurate interoperability solutions regarding the dimensions that has to consider. To illustrate the first proposition to implement and to use the proposed model, a case study is made available to the readers and shows it into the overall context of interoperability within a collaborative process. The final section presents the conclusions and the prospects of this research.

2   Problem and Expected Outcomes

In enterprise collaboration engineering context as in any other domains (system engineering, Information System, mechatronic...), it is difficult for stakeholders to have and to select a solution that satisfies all their expectations initially expressed. Indeed, it is not enough to have a jumbled and unconnected list of solutions if it is not consistently and precisely related with a set of requirements and if the potential impact that can be caused by solution onto its environment is unknown (Fig. 1) and *vice and versa*. Thus, "*there is no interest to identify the problems if there are no adapted solutions just as there is no interest to give solutions if the problems are not clearly identified*".

First, for a given expectation, several solutions can be available. However, all relevant solutions are not necessarily known and, naturally, the stakeholders favor the solution they control without further investigation and at the risk that such solution covers partially the problem or, in the worst case, is not adapted to the problem in the end (in operational phase for instance). To face up this problem, all solutions have to be

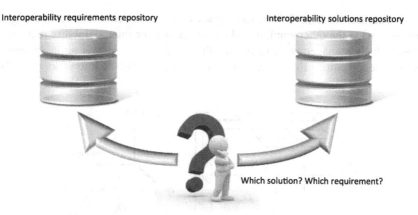

Fig. 1. The selection of solution dilemma

(1) fully and clearly identified in order to avoid to stakeholders to miss out on a relevant solution and (2), mirrored from the (or the set of) need(s) they allow to satisfy. That means to make available a relevant structure in which requirements and solutions are properly related and in agreements with the considered problem namely the ability to interoperate whether conceptually, technically or else, organizationally and during all the life cycle of the partnership.

Second, a given solution, and this independently of the covered field, is developed to satisfy a need. However, it is often forgotten that a solution can fully match an (or a set of) expectation but at the same time, this one can have an impact on other expectation and further on the system to be developed. In that case, the problem is not reduced to the choice of "the" solution but to choice of "the best" solution that means the solution which will satisfy the need for which it is developed but also the solution for which its impacts on the context will be fully identified and defined to allow stakeholders to choose it in confidence. Thus, beyond to have a set of solutions related to a set of requirements as mentioned before, it is also required to guide the stakeholders in their process of selection according to identified criteria that characterize the solution precisely (for instance in term of impact on other requirements).

3 Interoperability Requirements and Solutions: A Quick Scan

Numerous works deal with interoperability requirements for collaborative enterprises on the one hand and with the development of interoperability solutions - either conceptual technical or organizational - on the other hand. However, few works are concerned with the definition of the relation that can exist between the world of interoperability requirements and the world of interoperability solutions.

First, the world of interoperability requirements engineering focuses on two aspects. On the one hand, it is about to identify, to define precisely [15, 16] and writing requirements [17] in order to allow their verification - by stakeholders - either by the way of automatized and formal techniques (*e.g.* model checker) or not (*e.g.* test, expertise…). On the other hand, it is about to classify the interoperability requirements to ensure their management and traceability [18]. This aspect is strongly based on existing categorizations that are proposed by interoperability frameworks (Fig. 2).

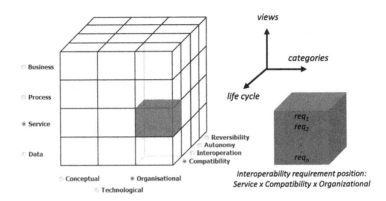

Fig. 2. The Framework for enterprise interoperability requirements

These two aspects are fundamentals since the principle of requirements engineering is that, the more the requirements are accurately identified the more a solution fully adapted can be found. However, if the consideration of the interoperability as requirement is accepted and widely studied, the connection with existing interoperability solutions is weak and their choice is often at the discretion of the stakeholders without any guidelines or support.

Second, some approaches make interoperability solutions available and rely strongly on the structuration of interoperability through interoperability frameworks. Let's mention the enterprise interoperability framework [13] that proposes no less than 66 interoperability solutions sorted onto its three axes such as interoperability concerns, interoperability approaches and interoperability categories [19]. However, the exploitation of this framework is difficult and does not allow stakeholders to know if a given solution is fully adapted to their interoperability needs since (1), they don't know the possible impact (and its evaluation) on the environment, (2), several solutions can be proposed for a given intersection between axes, (3), they don't know if a selected solution does not go beyond their effective needs (some solutions cover several categories and concerns that are not necessarily interesting for partners) and (4), these solutions are not formally related to requirements since those latter are not clearly and explicitly formulated *i.e.* following a structured and accepted format [23]. Thus, although a large number of solutions is proposed, this remains too general in terms of guide in the choice of solutions (not related to specific needs) and without precision this large sample can lead stakeholders to select "*a*" solution and not "*their*" solution (Fig. 3). In the same vein, let's mention also [20] that proposes a state of the art on enterprise interoperability services (business, semantic, data…).

Name of solution, author	
Interoperability concern	To choose in the interoperability framework
Interoperability barrier	To choose in the interoperability framework
Interoperability approach	To choose in the interoperability framework
Interoperability problem	Short and precise description of the knowledge
Interoperability knowledge	Description of the knowledge vs. problem Contribution of the knowledge to remove the barrier
Example (optional)	To illustrate the use of the knowledge through a concrete example
Remark	Open issues and limitations
References	List of references

Fig. 3. Template for interoperability solution proposal [19]

Other approaches propose a set of solutions - according interoperability aspects - but without necessarily be positioned precisely into a framework. In this case, let's mention [21] that proposes interoperability solutions (strategic interoperability, process interoperability, technical interoperability and semantic interoperability) for SMEs. This kind of approach grasps the necessity to consider a solution not only as a simple answer to a problem but to also to position it into a context allowing to consider other aspects that can be linked to this one. Thus, it examines and proposes solution according to interoperability such as technical, process-based and semantic but also taking into account characteristics - allowing to evaluate their relevance and usability for an SME (from high relevance to not applicable) – such as:

- *Startup-costs:* it represents the cost to implement technology or standard. This cost has to be as inexpensive as possible for SMEs.
- *Running costs:* SMEs are not able to afford high running costs for their interoperability solutions. This cost has to be, also, as inexpensive as possible for SMEs.
- *Implementation effort:* usually SMEs do not possess IT-system technically advanced as well as they do not employ IT-experts. Thus interoperability solution has to be easy to implement that means without strong efforts and advanced skills.
- *Direct use for an SME interoperability solution:* this aspect is concerned by the evaluation of the use of an interoperability solution that fulfills the needs of SMEs.
- *Conceptual input for an SME interoperability solution:* interoperability solutions are also analyzed in term of conceptual input for further researches on interoperability for SMEs.

Thus, this approach does not stop to the simple proposition of a set of interoperability solutions but, because of the specifics of SMEs, it has evaluated a set of interoperability solutions (BFC, BPMN, SAP…) according to defined criteria and it has provided an analysis allowing to guide SMES in their choice of interoperability solutions.

From these considerations, it appears that interoperability requirements on the one hand and solutions for interoperability on the other hand are clearly identified, but the link between them is not obvious or, at least, fully weaved. However the underlying difficulty remains the same for stakeholders: to select the better solution for their needs. In this way, it is required (1) to link solutions and requirements and (2), to highlight criteria that guide stakeholders in their choice of interoperability solution when one of them is identified as relevant to meet expectations.

4 Reference Model for Interoperability Solutions

The reference model for interoperability solutions is a structure that embeds parameters aiming to make a set of solutions available (this set is fully related to those proposed in the enterprise interoperability framework [13]) according to a (or a set of) requirement considered and positioned in agreements with the dimensions of the enterprise interoperability requirements framework (interoperability views – interoperability lifecycle – interoperability problems) [18]. However, as mentioned hereinbefore, the simple relation "requirements-solutions" is not sufficient to define accurately if a solution is really a well candidate solution regarding to interoperability project between partners and more broadly the partnership itself. Indeed, although a given solution allows to meet a requirement satisfaction, its implementation can have collateral effects on several parameters. As a consequence these parameters have to be integral part in the choice of an interoperability solution. To this purpose, the proposed model includes four parameters such as: *interoperability problems resolution, solution overview, other requirements impact*, and *granularity impact*.

Interoperability Problems Resolution. This parameter allows stakeholders to know precisely which problem(s) the proposed solution can solve in term of interoperability. These highlighted solutions depend not only on the resolved problem but also on fields covered in enterprises and the phase of the partnership. Thus the solution is positioned in agreements with the dimension of the framework for interoperability requirements that means according to (1) the *interoperability views* that represent the enterprises' domains that can be impacted by a problem of interoperability (business, process, service and data/resources/material), (2) the *interoperability lifecycle levels* that represent the moment of the partnership at which interoperability is requested by partners (*e.g.* the beginning of the partnership involves solutions that come under interfacing and thus, of compatibility) and (3), the *abstraction levels* that represent the categories of interoperability that can be developed in enterprise and thereby the problems of interoperability (conceptual, organizational ant technical). It is to note that a given solution can cover several interoperability views or else, interoperability life cycle levels. For instance solution such as semantic annotation can be used for each levels and can be implemented at the beginning of the partnership to solve existing - and avoid future - problems of misunderstanding (of models, data...). Solution such as Business Process Modeling and associated workflow engine are suitable for the process level to solve organizational and technical problems and can be implemented at the beginning of the partnership in order to align processes and useful for interoperation phase by the execution of the common process.

Solution Overview. This parameter takes into consideration the general information about the proposed solution. It makes available a quick overview of the solution and allows stakeholders to identify easily relevant solutions from those that are not adapted (*e.g.* solutions previously implemented without success). To this purpose, it gives information about the name of the solution (not limited to its acronym, source of misunderstanding), applications that are possibly existing and that support the solution (*e.g.* BPMN modeler software to support processes modeling and execution), average cost (or range) for implementation, average time (or range) to implement the solution and, material and human means requested to implement the solution.

Other Requirements Impact. A solution is implemented to satisfy one (or a set of, for a solution that covers several aspects of interoperability) interoperability requirement. However, if a given solution allows to improve interoperability it can also induce a degradation by impacting requirements that are related to its application domain. For instance, let's consider the requirement defined such as *"if task requires aptitude then resource has aptitude"* that has to be satisfy when resources (human, material, software) are shared by partners. This requirement affects the domain of task, resources and aptitude. The non-satisfaction of this requirement can lead, at best, to a bad achievement of the considered task and, at worst, to its non-achievement. A solution could be the replacement of the allocated resource by another one that has the requested aptitude or to train the current resource for the task. However, the choice of a solution (*e.g.* changing of resource) can impact the satisfaction of other requirement, in this case, those ones that take an interest in the realization of other tasks and the availability of the shared resources (*e.g.* *"It is possible that task is starting and resource is available"*). It is to note that the impact is not limited to other interoperability requirements but includes also other ones (functional as well as non-functional, *e.g.* performance requirements). For instance, the possible solution previously proposed can impact the duration of the realization of the task. As a consequence, when an interoperability solution is developed or proposed, it has to highlight which other requirements can be impacted.

Granularity Impact. It represents the level of detail of the object impacted by interoperability. The more precise the identification of the object impacted by interoperability is, the more the solutions selected and implemented by partners will be fully adapted and efficient. Indeed, interoperability can impact a partnership (mission, objectives...) as well as a given partner (mission, objectives but also component, resources...). For instance, the requirement *"partners have necessary authorization to access shared data"* has an impact on the good unwinding of the activities of the partnership (loss of time to access the information required to perform an activity). On the other side, the requirement *"function f, performed by resource r involved in partnership, is even though performed"* has a direct impact on a partner (precisely the execution of a function). From these knowledge, partners can select/adapt interoperability solutions or, possibly, relax requirements. As a consequence, the interoperability requirements (as other ones) are a part of a whole and their impacts must not be considered solely as a local matter but also as an overall matter (Fig. 4).

Finally, an important aspect of the model is the knowledge of the impact of a solution onto other requirements and stakeholders. Beyond the simple knowledge of the impacted elements, it is important for partners to know in which measure they are impacted. To this purpose, it would be interesting to quantify it or, at least, to define a

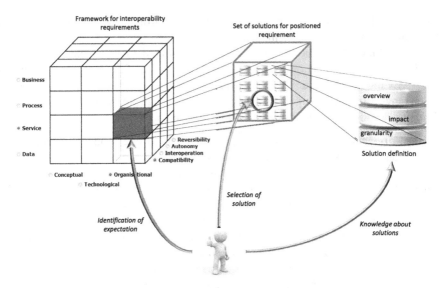

Fig. 4. Reference model for interoperability solution.

trend showing the importance of the impact in order to guide more precisely stake-holders in their choice. Moreover, regarding the choice, itself, it would be interesting to rely on existing tools used in Systems Engineering to select a candidate solution [22]. Indeed, a solution is characterized in the proposed model with different parameters (impact granularity, cost/time to implement…) and the use of these kind of tools allow to weight them and implement mechanisms that partially automatize the selection.

As a case study, the drug circuit process, available online at goo.gl/chclk7, shows a possible first implementation of the proposed model of interoperability solutions (partially since the proposed model has to be validated). This illustration focuses on the verification of interoperability requirements - written or selected by stakeholders but the paper does not consider this problematic – and the proposition of adapted solution according to the unsatisfied requirement, the potential interoperability problem as well as the proposed solution and its possible impact on other requirements if it is implemented.

5   Conclusion and Prospects

In a collaborative context, having mechanisms allowing to choose fully adapted interoperability solutions is a serious benefits, for enterprises, in term of costs for implementation and time to launch work. Furthermore, beyond the simple interoper-ability capabilities, benefits have an impact on the functioning of the whole partner-ship. The paper has presented a first proposition of a model that links interoperability requirements and interoperability solutions and, further, attempts to define a set of parameters allowing to guide stakeholders finely and accurately in their selection of a solution.

The advantage of such model is to guide precisely stakeholders in their choice rather than to have a sample list leading, too often, to select solutions unsuitable for their requirements. Obviously, parameters can be added depending on the special features of requirements (special needs in term of interoperability) or on the special features of partnership. However, having a link between requirements and solutions as well as general parameters characterizing them can be used as a base of selection.

Finally, it is to note this model - after its validation - will have to be integrated and technically implemented with existing tool and approach allowing to manage the lifecycle of an interoperability requirement from its elicitation and writing to the selection of a an adapted solution to satisfy it and via its verification [15].

References

1. ISO: Advanced automation technologies and their applications — Part 1: framework for enterprise interoperability, International Organization for Standardization, ISO 11354, ISO/TC 184/SC 5 (2011)
2. ISO: « ISO 15745 – 1, Industrial automation systems and integration – Open systems application integration framework – Part 1 : generic reference description », ISO TC184/SC5 (2003)
3. Chen, D., Doumeingts, G., Vernadat, F.: Architectures for enterprise integration and interoperability: past, present and future. Comput. Ind. **59**(7), 647–659 (2008)
4. Daclin, N., Chen, D., Vallespir, B.: Developing enterprise collaboration: a methodology to implement and improve interoperability. Enterp. Inf. Syst. (2014). doi:10.1080/17517575.2014.932013
5. Bourey, J.P., Grangel, R., Doumeingts, G., Berre, A.J.: Report on Model Driven Interoperability, INTEROP Network of Excellence IS 508011, deliverable DTG 2.3 (2007)
6. C4ISR Architecture Working Group (AWG): Levels of Information Systems Interoperability (LISI), USA Department of Defense (1998)
7. Ford, C.T.: Interoperability measurement, Ph.D. thesis, Department of the Air Force Air University, Air Force Institute of Technology (2008)
8. IEEE: IEEE Standard Computer Dictionary: A Compilation of IEEE Standard Computer Glossaries. Institute of Electrical and Electronics Engineers, New York (1990)
9. Wang, X., Xu, X.W.: DIMP: an interoperable solution for software integration and product data exchange. Enterp. Inf. Syst. **6**(3), 291–314 (2012)
10. Jardim-Goncalves, R., Grilo, A., Agostinho, C., Lampathaki, F., Charalabidis, Y.: Systematisation of interoperability body of knowledge: the foundation for enterprise interoperability as a science. Enterp. Inf. Syst. **7**(1), 7–32 (2013)
11. Panetto, H., Cecil, J.: Information systems for enterprise integration, interoperability and networking: theory and applications. Enterp. Inf. Syst. **7**(1), 1–6 (2013)
12. Vallespir, B., Chen, D., Ducq, Y.: Enterprise modelling for interoperability. In: 16th IFAC World Congress, Prague, Czech Republic, July 2005
13. Chen, D., Dassisti, M., Elveaeter, B.: Enterprise interoperability framework and knowledge corpus – final report. Interop deliverable DI.3, May 2007
14. Willis, J.: Systems engineering and the forgotten '-Illities. In: 14th Annual Systems Engineering Conference, San Diego, CA, USA (2011)

15. Mallek, S., Daclin, N., Chapurlat, V.: The application of interoperability requirement specification and verification to collaborative processes in industry. Comput. Ind. **63**(7), 643–658 (2012)
16. The Open Group Architecture Framework: TOGAF version 9, chap. 29 Interoperability requirements (2011)
17. Open Management Group (OMG): Semantics of Business Vocabulary and Business Rules (SBVR) – version 1.0 (2008). http://www.omg.org/spec/SBVR/1.0/PDF
18. Daclin, N., Mallek, S.: Capturing and structuring interoperability requirements: a framework for interoperability requirements. In: 7th International Conference on Interoperability for Enterprises Systems and Applications (I-ESA 2014), Albi, France, pp. 24–28, March 2014
19. Chen, D., Dassisti, M., Elveaeter, B.: Enterprise interoperability framework and knowledge corpus – final report – Annex: Knowledge Pieces. Interop deliverable DI.3 - Annex, May 2007
20. Elvesæter, B., Benguria, G., Capellini, A., Del Grosso, E., Taglino, F.: State-of-the-Art and Baseline EI Services Specifications. COIN Project, Deliverable D5.1.1 (2008)
21. Balzert, S., Burkhart, T., Werth, D., Laclavik, M., Seleng, M., Mehandjiev, N., Carpenter, M., Stalker, I.D.: State of the art solutions in enterprise interoperability. In: Cruz-Cunha, M. M. (ed.) Enterprise Information Systems for Business Integration in SMEs: Technological, Organizational and Social Dimensions, pp. 201–229. IGI Global, Hershey (2012)
22. Couturier, P., Lô, M., Imoussaten, A., Chapurlat, V., Montmain, J.: Tracking the consequences of design decisions in mechatronic systems engineering. Mechatronics **24** (7), 763–774 (2014)
23. INCOSE: Guide for writing requirements, v1.0, Requirements WG-INCOSE, INCOSE-TP-2010-006-01 (2012)

Introducing a Socio-Technical Perspective on Business Processes into Enterprise Interoperability Frameworks

Charles Crick[✉] and Eng K. Chew

Faculty of Engineering and Information Technology, University of Technology,
Sydney, Australia
charlescrick@computer.org, eng.chew@uts.edu.au

Abstract. This paper looks at enterprise interoperability (EI), specifically process-level interoperability, and suggests that the inherent non-determinacy of human-centred business processes introduces another ingredient into the EI puzzle that has thus far been understated in EIF ontologies. A conceptualisation of business process based on socio-technical concepts is presented. It is argued that this provides a better way to accommodate human agency factors, and under the influence of these factors, how business processes inevitably evolve over time, potentially affecting their interoperability. We suggest the extant body of knowledge on the theory of dynamic capabilities is relevant to understanding how organisations can control this potentially undirected process evolution and thereby sustain interoperability. Some initial observations are made concerning how this new ontological element could be accommodated into existing EIFs. The paper aims to stimulate discussion in this area and make a contribution to the EI body of knowledge.

Keywords: Socio-technical systems · Business process ontology · Technology affordance · Enterprise interoperability · Dynamic capabilities

1 Introduction

Generally, an Enterprise Interoperability Framework (EIF) is a way of structuring knowledge in the enterprise interoperability (EI) domain, such that we may reason about problems such as barriers to interoperability and understand possible solutions. As pointed out by Guédria et al. [1], in their review of the state of research in this area, there are several EIFs in existence, well known examples including the ATHENA (Advanced Technologies for interoperability Heterogeneous Enterprise Networks and Applications) Interoperability Framework [2]; the European Interoperability Framework [3]; and the FEI [4, 5], the latter is also a published ISO standard.

These frameworks have their foundations in the discipline of Enterprise Architecture [6], where the enterprise is modeled across a number of domains (such as business, data, technology), at a number of levels of abstraction (e.g. conceptual to physical) and generally in terms of deterministic artefacts such as business processes, data entities, applications and so forth. We use the term *deterministic* in the sense that the artefacts are well defined objects that can be designed, analysed and modeled etc.

© IFIP International Federation for Information Processing 2015
M. van Sinderen and V. Chapurlat (Eds.): IWEI 2015, LNBIP 213, pp. 83–91, 2015.
DOI: 10.1007/978-3-662-47157-9_8

In this paradigm, interoperability is characterised in terms of relationships between these objects, for example, communicating IT applications or business processes that need to interoperate in order to deliver an outcome. This representation also facilitates fairly straightforward quantification of interoperability, such as with the i-Score method [7], since the relationships and artefacts can be reduced to deterministic graph structures that can be analysed with mature algorithms.

In this paper we suggest the need for an additional ingredient in this EI picture, one that is bound up in the intrinsic non-determinacy of the human actors that take part in the activities of the enterprise, and which must therefore, we believe, be taken into account when we want to talk about behavioral aspects of EI. Naudet et al. [8] hint at this issue in their characterisation of organisational interoperability concerns, but in our view fall short of catering for the implicit dynamics involved.

Our response to this issue is to include a socio-technical dimension in the conceptualisation of business process, informing this view, in particular, with the theory of organisational routines [9] and technology affordances [10, 11], drawn from management sciences, both of which centre around the role of the human agency. We argue that these concepts introduce an adaptive element into the idea of interoperating processes such that a barrier in, for example, the technology layer may be simply "worked around" by improvisation. Our main point is that this occurs as part of business-as-usual, rather than through any intentional intervention. As argued by Schreyögg and Kliesch-Eberl [12], this type of organisational learning places a requirement on the part of management to exercise a second-order activity that monitors business-as-usual to detect and make corrections. Such second-order activities, or dynamic capabilities [13], are crucial mechanisms by which organisations maintain their alignment with the environment, or their evolutionary fitness [14], which includes their ability to maintain interoperability.

The remainder of this paper is structured as follows. First we set out our conceptual model of business process and provide its theoretical underpinnings. We then go on to discuss how this impacts the EI ontological model [4, 8].

2 Conceptualising Business Process as a Socio-Technical Object

2.1 Ontological Perspectives

The *business process* (BP) is a familiar Information Systems (IS) concept. Weske's definition is a typical definition used in the IS literature: "A business process consists of a set of activities that are performed in coordination in an organisational and technical environment. These activities jointly realize a business goal. Each business process is enacted by a single organisation, but it may interact with business processes performed by other organisations." [15 p. 6]. The idea of BP as deterministic, executable entities is central to this conceptualisation and has led to the rise of Business Process Management (BPM) and associated technologies as a popular IS discipline [16]. The conventional modeling and analysis of the interoperability of business processes also relies on this view. In some cases, of course, business processes are fully automated and operate without any human participation, and are in that sense deterministic. However, we argue, when there is human agency involved in the processes, this is an overly simplistic perspective, and any ontology that underpins a model of interoperability needs a way of teasing apart the deterministic and the non-deterministic elements.

Attempts have been made to admit other ontological perspectives into the business process concept, such as BP based on complex systems theory [e.g. 17, 18], for example. The importance of context when considering the instantiation of a BP has been recognised, both in terms of how it contributes to flexibility [19] and how it can be modeled [20]. There are several dimensions that provide context, such as, for example, the circumstances of the organisational environment providing the backdrop for the particular BP instance, or substitution of different participant roles when the process is actually executed. The BP literature is mostly silent, however, on the contextualisation attributable to the human participants, or other words, how the human participants construct the business process instance, in the act of practicing it, within a given situation.

The *organisational routine* concept [9], which has been developed in the management sciences largely outside of IS, provides a relevant insight into the role of human agency. This theory distinguishes a duality of "ostensive" and "performative" facets – the former representing the idealised, codified representation of the routine and the latter the routine-in-use, or what actually happens in practice. The implication here is that the routine may be performed differently each time it is repeated even if the ostensive aspect remains the same. We argue the distinction between the ostensive and performative aspects also has relevance to how business process should be conceptualised. It suggests that there has been a missing ingredient in the traditional IS orthodoxy when it comes to business processes [e.g. 15, 16, 21]. That is, we cannot treat a business process merely as an artefact that can be deterministically executed. Instead we argue that the non-determinacy of human agency must be factored in: the process-as-designed is different from the process-as-performed. Human factors such as motivation, skills, tacit knowledge and experience, intrinsically mean the process may not deliver what was "intended".

2.2 The Role of Technology

The idea of the performative routine is taken a step further into the socio-technical realm by the concept of the technology affordance [10, 11, 22, 23]. An affordance represents the perception of what can be done with an item of technology by a user with a particular goal – i.e. the affordance is the potentiality for action of a technology feature, not necessarily how the feature was designed. Thus the way technology is used (by a human user) in the business process is a function of the potentiality of the technology (for action) as perceived by the users, rather than just a set of pre-designed technology features.

2.3   Conceptual Model

In this section we explain our conceptualisation of *business process* that has been informed by the theoretical foundations discussed above. The purpose here is to understand how the human-centred factors give rise to intrinsically adaptive behavior whereby the business processes can evolve away from any a priori design, with ramifications for process-based enterprise interoperability.

We start with the intra-organisational view depicted in Fig. 1. This model situates the business process concept within the enterprise using the idea of organisational capability [24, 25] to model the outcome achieved by the business process. The numbered labels on the diagram refer to key component relationships in the model that are explained below.

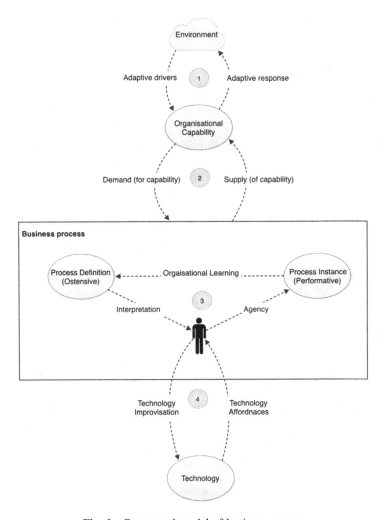

Fig. 1. Conceptual model of business process

1. Adaptive response. This relationship represents the requirement for "evolutionary fitness" [14] on the part of the organisation's capabilities. The environment exerts pressure for the organisation to adapt its portfolio of organisational capabilities. The organisation responds to meet this selective pressure by detecting the need to change and then redesigning or redeploying its resources, including business processes, to achieve the necessary outcome. In a commercial environment, a capability such as "manufacture cars" has an evolutionary fitness that is a function of the market demand and the competitors' products. For a non-commercial business, the adaptive imperative may come from a regulatory change, for example.
2. Demand/Supply Alignment. This is the central organisational alignment relationship whereby the external demand pressure for a given capability is met (or not) by the supply side: or in other words the ability of the organisation's business processes to deliver such a capability.
3. Process Evolution. The ostensive business process is interpreted every time it is practiced by the human actor. The loop back from the performative to the ostensive means that the ostensive is not a static representation of some a priori design: instead it is a definition that moves in line with what is learned from practice. "Learned" is used in a wide sense here: it not only refers to an intentional activity but also it is the necessary by-product of performative-ostensive relationship. So in this latter sense, it is inevitable that the practice will induce a drift away from the process-as-designed. This is consistent with the Feldman and Pentland's original characterisation of routines [26] and their more recent work on modeling this experiential learning [27]. This form of organisational learning confers a bottom-up adaptive capacity whereby the business processes can evolve to meet a new organisational capability need and thus enable or maintain evolutionary fitness.
4. Technology Imbrication. This represents the socio-technical relationship whereby the features available in the technology are interpreted by the user into a set of affordances [10]. These affordances are the product of the user's particular goals, experience and skills providing a unique context for how the technology features (as designed) are perceived as part of the business process. In line with Leonardi [11], the value of the technology only emerges when there is *imbrication* with human agency, or in other words, there is an interdependent relationship between the two. The other side of the imbrications relationship is that technology is improvised, or worked-around, when the affordance presented by the technology is inadequate for the task at hand. These improvisations, in turn, give rise to more affordances for other actors.

2.4   Inter-organisational View

If we look at a process-level interoperability, as is described in the FEI [4, 5], a consequence of this is illustrated in Fig. 2. In the top part of the diagram (A) we have interoperating processes between the two enterprises. After some elapsed time we get a situation where the interoperability may be threatened, for example, by a constraint that is operating in the technology layer. The process, due to the human agency, adapts

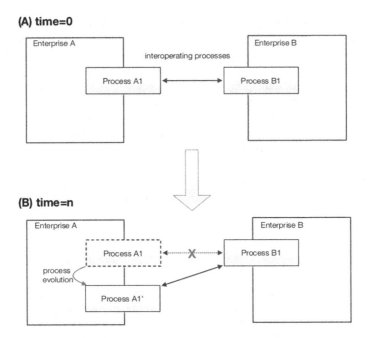

Fig. 2. Interoperability and process evolution

so as to maintain the interoperability, as shown in Fig. 2(B). People learn to work-around constraints and their improvised solutions become "business as usual" over time. Common instances of this phenomenon are where spreadsheets are used to augment data not (or perceived not to be) catered for in corporate IT systems. These evolve to become de facto systems of record rather than temporary fixes. In an order to cash process between a customer and supplier, the process is often sustained by the inter-relationships of human intermediaries, such as when the procurement officer in one company knows who to call in the supplier company to get prompt attention.

A corollary of the unilateral "evolutionary drift" of the business processes depicted in Fig. 2, is that interoperation may stop working rather than continue to be maintained.

The important point is that in both cases adaptation has occurred through the normal interpret-agency-learn cycle, labeled (3) in Fig. 1, rather than through any intentional process redesign.

3   Insights for Enterprise Interoperability Frameworks

The conceptual model we have presented above contains two aspects that we argue need to be addressed in the discussion relating to enterprise interoperability, and thence in the formulation of EIFs that seek to describe and structure knowledge about this domain. The first is that there is an inherently non-deterministic component in the concept of business process that is a function of the agency of human actors.

The second is that in the course of a (human-centered) business process being practiced, what the enterprise *understands* the process to be, or its ostensive component, will inevitably drift away from any a priori version that may have been designed. We suggest that if our objective in formulating EIFs is to provide a way to structure and thence gain insight into the interoperability problem domain, we need to understand these effects and incorporate them into the EIF ontology.

So, how might we proceed with this objective of accommodating the human agency effects into an EIF ontology? If we take the Chen and Daclin (then nascent) ontology for FEI [4], we can see that (business) process is represented as a type of *concern*, which forms one of the dimensions in their EI model of the Problem Space, the other being *barrier*. The FEI then addresses interoperability as the solution to a problem in terms of how a concern/barrier is mapped to an *approach* in the Solution Space. Thus, in FEI parlance, processes across two enterprises will interoperate if all the barriers are solved. The focus is not so much conditions *for* EI, then, but conditions for where EI will fail. Clearly this model, as does Naudet et al. [8], relates to a situation at a point in time, be that a priori, when a potential EI problem can be designed for; or a posteriori, when an interoperability problem actually surfaces. What is needed to accommodate the evolutionary process we describe, is a more dynamic approach. The relationship between problem and solution is more complex than these existing models allow for. The process whereby an interoperability problem is "headed off" before it actually happens by an adaptation of the business processes involved, is an example of this type of dynamics. The concept of dynamic capability [13, 28], from the management sciences literature, provides a theoretical basis for further understanding this phenomenon. It suggests [12, 29] the existence of a second-order cybernetic capacity that performs a monitor and alignment function that operates on the first-order business process system described. This function would act to maintain the alignment of the interoperating business processes to the required outcome, characterised in terms of the required organisational capability (e.g. a successful order to cash process between customer and supplier). Without this higher order function, there is no guarantee where the evolutionary process drift will lead.

4   Conclusion and Perspectives

In this paper, we have introduced a new theoretical element into the EI discourse, namely duality of ostensive and performative business processes that emerges from human agency. In this we have sought to stimulate discussion on how well studied organisational phenomena, drawn from management sciences and organisational science, factor into the traditionally technical realm of EI and EIFs. Some questions that arise have been touched on: how does the intrinsic adaptive nature of human-centered business processes play into EI and EIFs? When is EI "broken" at the business process level, given there is some capacity within the organisation to "fix" problems without any special intervention? Are these process-level workarounds compensating for inadequate technology? What are the implications for enterprise managers whose business model relies on process-level EI - e.g. with partner organisations – to deliver capability to their end-customers? In particular how can we apply the extant body of knowledge from the management sciences, including the theory of dynamic capabilities, to this area? We hope to investigate these issues further and to add to the burgeoning body of knowledge in this important field.

References

1. Guédria, W., Naudet, Y., Chen, D.: Maturity Model for Enterprise Interoperability. Enterprise Information Systems, pp. 1–28. Taylor & Francis, Boca Raton (2013)
2. Ruggaber, R.: ATHENA – advanced technologies for interoperability of heterogeneous enterprise networks and their applications. In: Konstantas, D., Bourrières, J.-P., Léonard, M., Boudjlida, N. (eds.) Interoperability of Enterprise Software and Applications, pp. 459–462. Springer, London (2006)
3. EIF: European Interoperability Framework, White Paper. European Commission, Brussels (2004)
4. Chen, D., Daclin, N.: Framework for enterprise interoperability. In: Proceedings of IFAC Work, EI2N, pp. 77–88 (2006)
5. Chen, D.: Enterprise interoperability. In: EMOI-INTEROP (2006)
6. Chen, D., Doumeingts, G., Vernadat, F.: Architectures for enterprise integration and interoperability: past, present and future. Comput. Ind. **59**, 647–659 (2008)
7. Ford, T., Colombi, J., Graham, S., Jacques, D.: The interoperability score. In: Proceeding of the 5th Annual Conference on Systems Engineering Research, Hoboken, NJ (2007)
8. Naudet, Y., Latour, T., Guedria, W., Chen, D.: Towards a systemic formalisation of interoperability. Comput. Ind. **61**, 176–185 (2010)
9. Pentland, B., Feldman, M.: Organizational routines as a unit of analysis. Ind. Corp. Chang. **14**, 793–815 (2005)
10. Zammuto, R.F., Griffith, T.L., Majchrzak, A., Dougherty, D.J., Faraj, S.: Information technology and the changing fabric of organization. Organ. Sci. **18**, 749–762 (2007)
11. Leonardi, P.: When flexible routines meet flexible technologies: affordance, constraint, and the imbrication of human and material agencies. MIS Q. **35**, 147–167 (2011)
12. Schreyogg, G., Kliesch-Eberl, M.: How dynamic can organizational capabilities be? Towards a dual-process model of capability dynamization. Strateg. Manag. J. **28**, 913–933 (2007)
13. Teece, D., Pisano, G., Shuen, A.: Dynamic capabilities and strategic management. Strateg. Manag. J. **18**, 509–533 (1997)
14. Helfat, C., Finkelstein, S., Mitchell, W., Peteraf, M., Singh, H., Teece, D., Winter, S.: Dynamic Capabilities: Understanding Strategic Change in Organizations. Blackwell, Oxford (2007)
15. Weske, M.: Business Process Management - Concepts Languages Architectures. Springer, New York (2012)
16. van der Aalst, Wil M.P., ter Hofstede, Arthur H.M., Weske, Mathias: Business process management: a survey. In: van der Aalst, Wil M.P., ter Hofstede, Arthur H.M., Weske, Mathias (eds.) BPM 2003. LNCS, vol. 2678, pp. 1–12. Springer, Heidelberg (2003)
17. Melão, N., Pidd, M.: A conceptual framework for understanding business processes and business process modelling. Inf. Syst. J. **10**, 105–129 (2000)
18. Vidgen, R., Wang, X.: From business process management to business process ecosystem. J. Inf. Technol. **21**, 262–271 (2006)

19. Rosemann, M., Recker, J., Flender, C.: Contextualisation of business processes. Int. J. Bus. Process Integr. Manag. **3**, 47–60 (2008)
20. Saidani, O., Nurcan, S.: Towards context aware business process modelling. In: Proceedings of the 8th Workshop on Business Process Modeling, Development, and Support, BPMDS 2007 (2007)
21. Hammer, M., Champy, J.: Reengineering the Corporation: Manifesto for Business Revolution. Harper Business, New York (1993)
22. Majchrzak, A., Markus, M.: Technology affordances and constraints. In: Kessler, E. (ed.) Encyclopedia of Management Theory. Sage, Thousand Oaks (2012)
23. Yoo, Y., Boland, R.: Organizing for innovation in the digitized world. Organ. Sci. **23**, 1398–1408 (2012)
24. Helfat, C.: The evolution of firm capabilities. Strateg. Manag. J. **21**, 955–959 (2000)
25. Helfat, C., Winter, S.: Untangling dynamic and operational capabilities: strategy for the (n) ever-changing world. Strateg. Manag. J. **32**, 1243–1250 (2011)
26. Feldman, M., Pentland, B.: Reconceptualizing organizational routines as a source of flexibility and change. Adm. Sci. Q. **48**, 94–118 (2003)
27. Pentland, B., Feldman, M., Becker, M., Liu, P.: Dynamics of organizational routines: a generative model. J. Manag. Stud. **49**, 1484–1508 (2012)
28. Teece, D., Pisano, G.: The dynamic capabilities of firms: an introduction. Ind. Corp. Chang. **3**, 537–556 (1994)
29. van der Weerdt, N.P., Volberda, H.W., Verwaal, E., Stienstra, M.: Organizing for flexibility: addressing dynamic capabilities and organization design. In: Bøllingtoft, A., Donaldson, L., Huber, G.P., Håkonsson, D.D., Snow, C.C. (eds.) Collaborative Communities of Firms: Purpose, Process, and Design. Information and Organization Design Series, vol. 9, pp. 283–296. Springer, New York (2012)

Humans in the Enterprise Interoperability Ecosystem

Fernando Luis-Ferreira[1,2(✉)], Hervé Panetto[3,4],
and Ricardo Jardim-Goncalves[1,2]

[1] Departamento de Engenharia Electrotécnica, Faculdade de Ciências
e Tecnologia, FCT, Universidade Nova de Lisboa,
2829-516 Caparica, Portugal
[2] Centre of Technology and Systems, CTS, UNINOVA,
2829-516 Caparica, Portugal
{flf, rg}@uninova.pt
[3] CNRS, CRAN UMR 7039, Vandœuvre-lès-Nancy, France
[4] Université de Lorraine, CRAN UMR 7039, B.P. 70239
F-54506 Vandœuvre-lès-Nancy, France
herve.panetto@univ-lorraine.fr

Abstract. Enterprises are complex live organisms of humans and networked machines including diverse types of computational devices. Enterprise interoperability promotes the interaction between companies based in the interoperability between such companies and between devices and services inside the company. Knowledge management is another important aspect that is extensively observed in the dynamic enterprise ecosystem. It is understandable that studies make different types of assessment for machines and people. In this sense we can ask on the interest of studying humans along machines in the chain of collaboration inside the Enterprise Interoperability Ecosystem. What we propose is to establish measures that promote interoperability between computational devices and humans, at the same time that we can promote interoperability between humans using computational devices to interact between each other.

Keywords: Enterprise interoperability · Emotions · Human computer interaction

1 Introduction

Today enterprise's competitiveness is, to a large extent, determined by its ability to seamlessly interoperate with other companies. The advantage of one enterprise over another stems from the way it manages its process of innovation. Enterprise Interoperability (EI) has therefore become an important area of research to ensure the competitiveness and growth of European enterprises [1]. The activities within an enterprise are complex as companies manufacture a variety of products using different production methods to satisfy different customer demands. An enterprise model is defined as "the art of externalising enterprise knowledge, which adds value to the enterprise or needs to be shared" [2]. The word interoperability has many different uses.

© IFIP International Federation for Information Processing 2015
M. van Sinderen and V. Chapurlat (Eds.): IWEI 2015, LNBIP 213, pp. 92–98, 2015.
DOI: 10.1007/978-3-662-47157-9_9

The term interoperability is increasingly used in enterprise engineering and its related standardization activities [3]. While interoperable systems can function independently, an integrated system loses significant functionality if the flow of services is interrupted. An integrated family of systems must, by necessity, be interoperable, but interoperable systems need not be integrated. Integration also deals with organisational issues, in possibly a less formalised manner due to dealing with people, but integration is much more difficult to solve, while interoperability is more of a technical issue. Compatibility is something less than interoperability. It means that systems/units do not interfere with each other's functioning. But it does not imply the ability to exchange services. Inter-operable systems are by necessity compatible, but the converse is not necessarily true. To realize the power of networking through robust information exchange, one must go beyond compatibility. [4]. In what regards to the human aspect we should not expect that difficulties with one person could interfere to the whole network and the knowledge exchange process within the enterprise. By knowledge we can consider the Individual Knowledge that can be found in the hands of an individual worker who serves as a fundamental unit in the process of knowledge creation, storage, and use within the enterprise. Many times this knowledge is tacit and therefore not well documented. Group knowledge is more powerful than the sum of the knowledge acquired by an individual. This knowledge can be both formal and informal and is frequently intangible but is one of the most important knowledge assets within a company. The organization, in turn, serves as a storehouse of knowledge with its own peculiar structure and divisions of functions, with multiple processes and activities to aid in the search for knowledge [5]. The present research paper departs from the analysis made in this section on the enterprise environment with a focus on the goal of pursuing Interoperability. Then in Sect. 2 an overview is made on the emotions as distinguishing characteristic of the humans to be attained for the improvement of interactions both Human to Human (H2H) and Human Computer Interaction HCI. In Sect. 3 an experiment is proposed with the objectives of allowing the emotional assessment and the preparation of a strategy for performing emotional assessment within enterprise environment. In Sect. 4 results are analysed and discussed leading to conclusions in Sect. 5. The main goal of this research work is to develop tools that, in a less-obstructive manner, allow the improvement and valuation on the role of humans in the Enterprise Interoperability Ecosystem.

2   Mediated Human to Human Interaction and Human Computer Interaction

The most distinguishing characteristic of humans, apart from the body, is the fact that humans feel emotions. Alan Turing back in 1950, questioned if a machine can think and for that he elaborated a test that is still in use and that could evaluate if machines can think [6]. At the same time, Jefferson was saying that "Not until a machine can write a sonnet or compose a concerto because of thoughts and emotions felt, and not by the chance fall of symbols, could we agree that machine equals brain that is, not only write it but know that it had written it. No mechanism could feel (and not merely artificially signal, an easy contrivance) pleasure at its successes, grief when its valves fuse, be warmed by flattery, be made miserable by its mistakes, be charmed by sex, be angry or depressed when it cannot get what it wants" what has become known as Jefferson's Oration [7]. Machines can fake the appearance of an emotion quite well, without having any feelings similar to those we would have: They can separate expression from feeling. With a machine it is easy to see how emotion expression does not imply "having" the underlying feeling [8]. As emotions play an important role in our life it is important to consider their role in human computer interaction (HCI). Affective computing is a research area developed by Rosalind Picard since the decade of ninety that addresses affective aspects in HCI. In her definition, affective computing is computing that relates to, arises from, or influences emotions [9]. In a broad sense it means, for one side, how emotions influence our behaviour in interacting with computational devices and, on the other side, how that interaction influences our emotions. In affective computing, we can separately examine functions that are not so easily separated in humans which enables a computational handle of affect related measurements [10]. Several measurements can be performed, integrating data acquired from physical environment which will increases the factor for unreliability to the overall system because of the unpredictable behaviours of the physical world [11]. Thus if we want to assess a person's emotional cues, it is necessary to develop a methodology that enables the evaluation of physiological information and correlate that information with known emotional states so that, later, becomes possible to infer emotional states from such measurements. Such measurements type of assessments is missing in what regards enterprise oriented studies as they have been made mostly for psychological studies [12,13]. In order to be used in the enterprise ecosystem, such measurements should be the less invasive and less disturbing of daily activity as possible. The objective would be, to monitor how interaction with computational environment affects humans' emotional states and how the interaction of humans by means of using computational channels can be evaluated and mediated if needed. Envisaging this non-disturbing approach, measurement of heartbeat seems to be an interesting option, from the ergonomic point of view, as today there are many devices on the market that can be used for fitness and are used like a normal watch (e.g. Nike+ Fuelband,[1] Fitbit,[2] Jawbone[3]).

It is also relevant to notice that emotional states can bias judgement and can alter perceptions. Emotions often seem to overpower us and to influence our judgements in profound ways. Our decisions and our actions when we feel angry or frightened or enthusiastic appear not to agree with the dictates of reason and prudence [14]. According to Saks and Johns, there are 3 factors that can influence the perceptions: experience, motivational state and, finally, emotional state [15]. Emotional states can diminish workers judgment and diminish conscientious decision capacity; in some cases it can also put them at risk. Finally, assessing emotional states can be a most

---

[1] http://www.nike.com/us/en_us/c/nikeplus-fuelband.

[2] http://www.fitbit.com/.

[3] https://jawbone.com/up.

relevant step for business as Nobel prize Daniel Kahneman stated, the study of peoples well-being can have a profound impact on economy [16]. In the next sections we pursue the goal of knowing more about a person's emotional state.

3   Design Experiment on Emotional Assessment

The observations presented in previous sections led to the need of obtaining physiological information about a person, which could lead us to establish possible inferences about that person's emotional states. A setup to perform physiological measurements was prepared with selected laboratory equipment. A group of 24 individuals where randomly chosen to perform an experience that was meant to provide clues on assessment of human emotional states from physiological readings. The result would introduce Human Emotions as a new variable in the enterprise interoperability ecosystem. The process of inclusion is based on considering humans beyond a simplified view of knowledge managers, by valuating their nature of emotional beings. The physiological responses were based on heart rate indicators collected during visual stimulus presentation. The pictures were classified in three different categories (animals, humans and food pictures) that were organized for each of the stimulus in positive, neutral and negative, according to the scores provided by Lang et al. in their Manual for the IAPS (International Affective Picture System) [17] (partially in Fig. 1 left).

Fig. 1. Selection of images from the IAPS database (left), experimental setup (right)

The results were collected in samples for each intervenient and we have performed an ANOVA with repeated measures with two with-subjects factors: the stimulus category with 3 levels (animals vs. humans vs. food) and the valence of these stimuli also with 3 levels (positive vs. neutral vs. negative). The main effects of each factor were analysed further using multiple comparisons with Bonferroni comparisons and the interaction effects between factors with simple main effects also with Bonferroni correction given the small sample size. The ANOVA is a F-test based on the F probability distribution. The F is estimated according to the Sum of Squares (SS) between groups dividing by the SS within groups.

4 Results and Discussion

The collected results were analysed taking in account data from self-assessment and physiological readings.

The results showed significant associations between the physiological and the SAM (Self Assessment Manikin) assessments for valence, activation and dominance. The correlations between these variables were significant for an alpha level of 0.05 and the Pearson r coefficient ranged between 0.41 and 0.63 for the significant correlations. The most reliable indicator of the subjective assessments through the SAM scales, for several measurements performed, for the heart rate that was moderately correlated with the subjective arousal (r = .41; p < 0.05), as seen in Fig. 2.

The correlation obtained denotes an interesting adhesion from the expressed self-assessment and the physiological measurements for heartbeat.

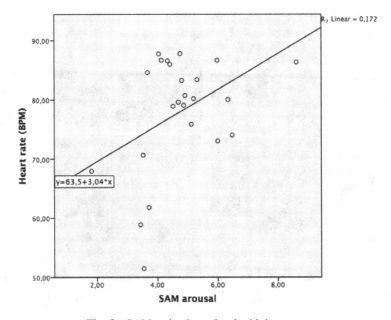

Fig. 2. SAM activation related with heart rate

The dispersed values in the graph are most probably due to persons that, even without notice, they were most affected by the images. On the other side there should be individuals that think that pictures are impressing, their body didn't react in the same way. Those persons are probably calmer then they think. The measurements were made with a set of images within those three categories; it is possible that other images, like those related to sexual content, could produce other effects. Those images use to be relevant in such tests, however in about two decades the patterns of beauty or disgust change as the society change in time with new trends and new contexts, and that is the age of the IAPS picture set.

In the work performed the objective was not to determine if a person is happy, sad, with fear or in euphoria. By the contrary the objective was to analyse if with such an approach it is possible to predict, or verify, the degree of interoperability between persons in the sense that they share the same physiological manifestation. Also the protection of workers, especially for those who require most concentration (e.g. air traffic controllers) or those who may put a person at risk (e.g. using dangerous cutting or drilling tools) can be monitored and scheduled in shifts according to the results from measurements presented in this paper. It is also convenient (or mandatory) to ensure privacy of the workers. That could be achieved by a policy of only issuing warnings to the worker about measurements outside established parameters and in that case recommending a pause or some exercise. Only dangerous or risky parameters would be issued to supervisors or to the human resources department or, in extreme cases, asking for medical assistance.

The continuous update of the working model deployed in this setup can ensure the validity and adequacy of each work for each individual, according to specific environmental conditions, and which workers will better cooperate within specific tasks in the enterprise environment.

5   Conclusions and Future Work

The results obtained show a promising path towards emotional assessment based on physiological readings. The results show that physiological measurements are not detached from the indications given by a person's expression. Interoperability within the company can benefit by the inferences obtained about people's emotions. Workers with high variations should be spared and should not be assigned to dangerous or sensitive tasks. Emotional indicators could also give notice about the proper moment to perform a certain task within the enterprise or about the best time for performing a negotiation. Would be interesting to evaluate the result of a negotiation after the assessment to be performed. In future work would be interesting to evaluate the interoperability between people while performing a negotiation. Another interesting feature would be to perform the measurements while people are interacting with computers. Would be interesting to verify if when a person has an emotional change, interaction with computers would be affected. Future work should advance in the direction of the measurements to be performed with available fitness devices as stated before. The unnoticed use of devices would allow it to be used seamlessly within the enterprise thus supporting new applications and new strategies to promote people's interoperability between themselves and towards interaction with machines. Also future work should include other types of measurements that did not fit in the scope of this paper but that can be coupled with the presented measurements in order to obtain more rigorous correspondences between physiology and emotional assessment.

Acknowledgements. The research leading to these results has received funding from the EC H2020 Program under grant agreement AQUASMART N° 644715 and EC 7th Framework Programme under grant agreement FITMAN N° 604674 (http://www.fitman-fi.eu).

References

1. Charalabidis, Y., Gionis, G., Hermann, K.M., Martinez, C.: Enterprise Interoperability Research Roadmap. European. Commission. (2008) ftp://ftp.cordis.europa.eu/pub/fp7/ict/docs/enet/ei-research-roadmap-v5-final_en.pdf
2. Vernadat, F.: UEML: Towards a unified enterprise modelling language. Int. J. Prod. Res. **40**, 4309–4321 (2002). UEML: Towards a unif (2002)
3. Chen, D., Vernadat, F.: Enterprise interoperability: a standards view. In: Kosanke, R., Jochem, J.G., Nell, B. (eds.) Enterprise Inter- and Intra-Organizational Integration. Kluwer, Boston (2003)
4. Panetto, H.: Towards a classification framework for interoperability of enterprise applications. Int. J. Comput. Integr. Manuf. **20**, 727–740 (2007)
5. Whitman, L.E., Panetto, H.: The missing link: culture and language barriers to interoperability. Annu. Rev. Control **30**, 233–241 (2006)
6. Turing, A.M.: Computing machinery and intelligence. Mind. **59**, 433–460 (1950)
7. Jefferson, G.: The mind of mechanical man. Br. Med. J. **1**, 1105–1110 (1949)
8. Picard, R.W.: Affective computing: challenges. Int. J. Hum Comput Stud. **59**, 55–64 (2003)
9. Picard, R.W.: Affective Computing. MIT Press, Cambridge (1997)
10. López, J.M., Gil, R., Garc\'ia, R., Cearreta, I., Garay, N.: Towards an ontology for describing emotions. In: Lytras, M.D., Damiani, E., Tennyson, R.D. (eds.) WSKS 2008. LNCS (LNAI), vol. 5288, pp. 96–104. Springer, Heidelberg (2008)
11. Ghimire, S., Luís-Ferreira, F., Jardim-Goncalves, R.: Towards self-evolutionary cyber physical systems. In: Advances in Transdisciplinary Engineering, pp. 547–554 (2014)
12. Mikels, J.A., Fredrickson, B.L., Larkin, G.R., Lindberg, C.M., Maglio, S.J., Reuter-Lorenz, P.A.: Emotional category data on images from the international affective picture system. Behav. Res. Methods. **37**, 626–630 (2005)
13. Machajdik, J., Hanbury, A.: Affective image classification using features inspired by psychology and art theory. Proceedings of the International Conference on Multimedia - MM 2010, p. 83. ACM Press, New York (2010)
14. Easterby-Smith, M., Lyles, M.A.: Handbook of Organizational Learning and Knowledge Management. Wiley, New York (2011)
15. Alan, S., Gary, J.: Perception, Attribution, and Judgment of Others. In: Organizational Behaviour: Understanding and Managing Life at Work, vol. 7 (2011)
16. Kahneman, D., Krueger, A.B.: Developments in the measurement of subjective well-being. J. Econ. Perspect. **20**, 3–24 (2006)
17. Lang, P.J., Bradley, M.M., Cuthbert, B.N.: International affective picture system (IAPS): Technical manual and affective ratings (1999)

Short and Position Papers

Multi-agent Product Life Cycle Environment. Interoperability Issues

Yulia V. Yadgarova[1], Victor V. Taratukhin[2(✉)], and Ekaterina N. Skachko[1]

[1] Bauman Moscow State Technical University, Moscow 105045, Russia
y.yadgarova@bmstu.ru, ekaterina_skachko@inbox.ru
[2] European Research Center for Information Systems (ERCIS),
Leonardo-Campus 3, 48149 Muenster, Germany
victor.taratoukhine@ercis.uni-muenster.de

Abstract. The main goal of this paper is to describe the integrated approach to product lifecycle management in the context of enterprise information system landscape. Product lifecycle management is a part of the common information area in the enterprise. In this work the analysis of enterprise interoperability problems was presented. To classify such problems and solution approaches we use a framework for enterprise interoperability, described by D. Chen at [1].

The paper suggests reference architecture for product lifecycle management systems based on multi-agent concept. It promotes understanding of the interrelationships of different lifecycle stages for acquiring and manipulating concurrent engineering knowledge.

Keywords: Future product lifecycle management · Enterprise interoperability · Intelligent design and manufacturing · Multi-agent framework

1 Introduction

Nowadays the concept of the enterprise interoperability plays a major role in development of high-technology products. Complex industrial production in aerospace industry, rapid development of automotive and electronic industries require management and collaboration of thousands of different suppliers and manufacturers. Industry 4.0 concept [2] implies reduction of time, growth of complexity and values of production and rapid customisation of the production lines. Different enterprise architectures and wide range of business capabilities lead to increasing of complexity and volumes of data. This extensive development has limitations associated with computational complexity. For example, change management and configuration management are performed via workflow coordination and agreement of several responsible persons distributed over the workflow (due to their roles in the project). If quantity of versions of the parts exceeds ten, a lot of work and agreements between several roles arise, as well as a lot of down time which, therefore, slows down the main design process. In this research the authors present multi-agent enterprise architecture framework

© IFIP International Federation for Information Processing 2015
M. van Sinderen and V. Chapurlat (Eds.): IWEI 2015, LNBIP 213, pp. 101–112, 2015.
DOI: 10.1007/978-3-662-47157-9_10

and decision-support system in product lifecycle environment domain. The key problem is to simulate human-like decision-making process to provide an agile product lifecycle management process. Multi-agent technologies play a key role in this problem and form an integration platform between human and manufacturing.

The wide range of different enterprise architectures, high value products and infrastructure are typically technology intensive, expensive and reliability-critical. They also require engineering services, such as maintenance and support throughout the life-cycle. The future product lifecycle management should provide a strong new level of integration of product development stages based on socio-supportive level of communication between designers, manufacturers, intelligent software, M2M (Machine-to-Machine) shop floor communication, etc. [3–5].

The paper analyses different types of product lifecycle management approaches and common enterprise interoperability problems for such systems and suggests multi-agent reference architecture of such system. Different phases of product lifecycle require different architectures of the agent and semantic-based protocols for their negotiation. It provides understanding of the interrelationships of different lifecycle stages for acquiring and manipulating concurrent engineering knowledge and processes.

2   Product Lifecycle Management in the Context of Enterprise Interoperability

Automation of discrete stages of product lifecycle is being developed since 1970. This process includes developing programs for automated design (Computer-aided design, CAD) and manufacturing (Computer-aided manufacturing, CAM), also office and accountant's programs. With the help of information technologies, evolving since 1980, the new step, a concept of FMS (Flexible manufacturing system), was reached. In the end of 80-th – beginning of 90-th the concept of PDM (Product Data Management) and PLM (Product Lifecycle Management) was developed. PDM is the system that stores data about production process and has an interface with CAD/CAM systems. Development and integration of these systems leads to arising of PLM concept [6]. Years ago PLM concept was understood as an integration of marketing, design, maintenance and service phases of product development [6]. However at present time PLM systems control the overall process of developing and maintenance of production in the factory including control of innovations, configuration management and change management processes. In other works current PLM task is not only automation of production process, but business concept for effective approval of the whole lifecycle processes. This concept, based on building an information model of the product and production process as well as workflow processes, allows collective design, improving of production processes and simulation of innovations on each stage. PLM integrates several approaches: PDM concept, collective design, digital factories. This concept focuses on the industry solutions and uses several technologies and methods. The main functions of PLM system [7] are:

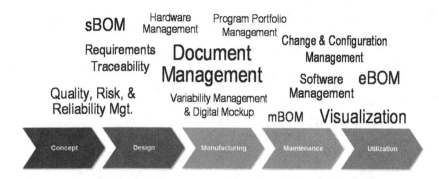

Fig. 1. Product lifecycle management concept [7]

- Manage CAD and process documents
- Provide an electronic file repository
- Include "attributes" – built-in and custom part and document metadata
- Construct and control bill of material (product structure) records
- Identify materials content for environmental compliance
- Change and workflow management
- Control multi-user secured access ("electronic signature")
- Export data for ERP (Enterprise Resource Planning) systems

The model of the product lifecycle management concept is presented at Fig. 1. Described functions are available on each stage of production process.

One of the main functions of a PLM system is data exchange and integration between other enterprise services like MES (Manufacturing Execution System), ERP, CRM (Customer Relationship System) [7]. The location and link between these systems is presented on Fig. 2. Providing interoperability between these products is a complex task, which can be solved by using similar data models, connectors and etc. We analyse the interoperability problems appearing in the PLM systems and classify these problems according to enterprise interoperability framework, described at [1].

2.1 Enterprise Interoperability Problem Space in PLM Domain

There are three main barriers with the interoperability of exchanging information:

Conceptual – syntactic and semantic incompatibility

Technological – incompatibility of IT architecture and platforms

Organisational – incompatibility of organisation structure and management techniques implemented in different enterprises

Several interoperability concepts was presented in the framework:

Interoperability of data – ability to operate together different data models which can locate on different machines with different operating systems

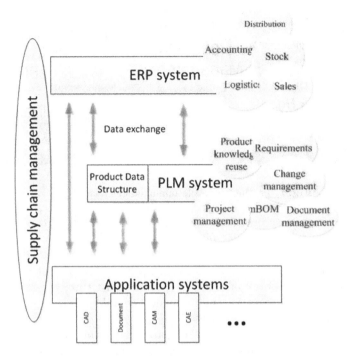

Fig. 2. Location of PLM system in the whole enterprise landscape

Interoperability of services – refers to operate together different applications with syntactic and semantic differences

Interoperability of processes – aims to make various processes work together

Interoperability of business – refers to work in a harmonised way at the levels of organization and company

The PLM system works mainly in intra-level of the enterprise and we define a specific problem space within product lifecycle managed domain in the context of interoperability:

1. *Interoperability of data* in the PLM domain: Within PLM system this problem is solved by using the integrated approach (a common format for all information models, single database (for example, Windchill PLM architecture, [8])). So, there are no problems with data interoperability within a single PLM system. But the problems appears when we aim for change a PLM vendor or integrate a PLM system in the whole information landscape (link with ERP, MES, CRM systems). Then there are syntax and semantic problems. Also there are several problems in technological and organisational interoperability between PLM-systems of several organisations: different information models and attributes of this models leads to mismatches in product definition (product structure).

2. *Interoperability of services* in the PLM domain: There is also a problem with integration between PLM and other systems. Also, interoperability of services

becomes a difficult task when we integrate organizations in single virtual enterprise with different systems and vendors of systems. As an example: integration with PLM services based on SOA with accounting system with strict architecture

3. *Interoperability of processes* in PLM domain: There are organisational barriers in the enterprise structure and conceptual interoperability with other systems and PLM solutions. Process description models in several PLM systems are different only if the product is same.

Our approach to problem of building reference architecture of the PLM system is based on the multi-agent concept of lifecycle stages. This reference architecture can be a good foundation both for building informational landscape of the single enterprise and for building virtual enterprise architecture. Loose coupling, unified interfaces and protocols in agent systems' architecture allows build a good reliability solution for linking enterprise system parts.

3   Multi-agent PLM Concept

One of the most appropriate technologies for developing large complex distributed systems is multi-agent concept. One of the benefits of multi-agent systems is their decentralization and simplicity of development of the agents. Also synergetic effect of such systems can be achieved. Agents, responsible for small simple parts of the system with negotiation with each other, can keep system status and achieve complex objectives together. Several common characteristics of the multi-agent systems (MAS) are:

- No explicit external control - system must be independent of external control unit
- Global order from local interactions - ability to achieve global order through local interactions
- Distributed control - in such systems control is distributed throughout the whole system. No central decision node is presented
- Robustness - self-organized systems are robust. System should thrive on randomness and fluctuations
- Adaptivity - self-organization is dynamic process. The system needs to be dynamic and reconfigurable
- Non-linearity - no direct relation between the fluctuations of the environment and system behavior [9].

Also one of the key trends in manufacturing is the ability of machines and devices to be self-organized, to communicate independently with each other and to provide agile and adaptive design and manufacturing environment.

Multi-agent systems allow to distance from the strict workflow process among the development and production processes. In proposed MAS, the first physical and second syntactic levels are well standardised by Foundation for Intelligent Physical Agents (FIPA [10]), but communication between agents in such systems builds based on semantic meaning of the message. To understand received block of information agent could parse this message at semantic level, the symbols must be understood in the same way. So, to communicate different agents with each other we use ontology describing approach. Building ontology depends on concrete specific of the enterprise and must be shared or explicitly expressed and accessible to be able to decode the information. FIPA standards includes Ontology Service Specification which describes usage of ontologies.

According to ISO 14258 [11] there are 3 basic ways to relate entities together:

1. *Common format* – used in presented PLM architectures.
2. *Unified format* – at present time used in integration processes between other information systems
3. *Federated format* – no predefined common format – used in proposed approach within MAS.

The key tasks for building robust distributed multi-agent PLM environment are:

– Build general reference architecture of multi-agent system. Each stage of PLM-concept environment has different functions and attributes. Each stage of PLM-concept environment has its own agent architecture
– Develop communication protocols between agents in similar layers and MAS with different types of agents (Horizontal and vertical integration).
– Define a data model for each stage for further integration and exchange
– Define problems of negotiation on similar lifecycle layers and develop semantic negotiation technics based on domain ontologies for agents for conflict resolution

A general several-layer architecture of multi-agent system with Design (DA), Manufacturing(MA), Support (SA) and Control/Change agents is presented at Fig. 3.

3.1   MAS of Design Phase

Concept of product as a MAS was presented by [5,12]. System of Design agents (DA) models the Design phase of product lifecycle management and represents the overall design view of the assembly (Fig. 4). Each DA represents simple part of the product. Each DA has a set of states presented by technological conversions. Present complex assembly of parts (parts of the large high-technology systems) consists of thousands simplest decomposed parts that have their own set of versions, alternates and other attributes. Every part interact with others to provide the whole assembly functionality. The utility function of the agent through negotiation process is complexity of the part. The cooperative utility function of the agent is complexity of the product $STC_{product}$.

Every design agent is responsible for a simple finite part of assembly. This means that we can describe assembly as a MAS. In this system negotiation of DA represents mismatch detection in the assembly part and minimization of utility function. Every change request to this system changes the whole multi-agent equipment and leads to negotiation procedure.

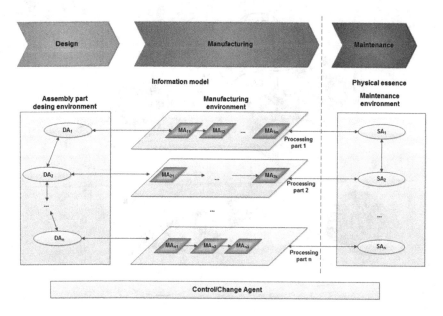

Fig. 3. Multi-agent product lifecycle system

In design process the part characterised by the set of elements:

$$Part = \{E_i | i = 1, 2, .., p\} \tag{1}$$

Each element E_i can be one of the several class of elements of $ez \in E_z$ and has the set of parameters

$$P = \{P_i | i = 1, 2, .., p\} \tag{2}$$

At this set parameters can be one of the part's class parameters (for example, length of the surface) and concrete object parameters.

We define Complexity characteristics of the part (Structural technological complexity):

$$STC_p = f(E, R_p, K_m) \tag{3}$$

where E – set of elements, R_p – set of relations between elements, K_m – coefficient of manufacturing complexity.

So, Complexity characteristic of assembly is:

$$STC_a = f(S, STC_p, R, P, TC) \tag{4}$$

where S – set of assemblies, STC_p – set of parts, R – set of relations between structural parts, P – set of parameters, TC – set of technological conversions.

STC of final product define as function of STC products' parts and technological conversions:

$$STC_{product} = \sum_{i=1}^{n} STC_a + \sum_{j=1}^{m} STC_p \tag{5}$$

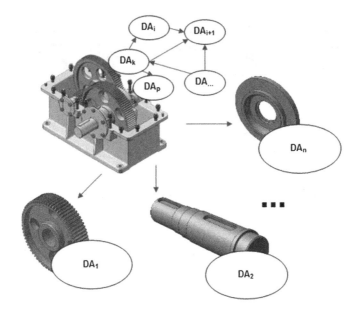

Fig. 4. Design agent's overview

MAS of Design agents has a strong link to MAS of manufacturing. It represents vertical integration of the product lifecycle stages and performs feedback between manufacturing and design layers.

3.2   MAS of Manufacturing Phase

One of the main task in the manufacturing phase of production process is control and scheduling tasks in shop floor. The production Manufacturing Execution Systems (MES) provide mechanisms to control the manufacturing shop floor in real time. These functions in modern PLM systems are performed by the MES-module (preparing and control processing). Integration between MES and PLM means that data values from PDM are transferred into MES [13] and, based on this data, MES builds a schedule of the processing. The meaning of processing part is decomposition of the whole manufacturing process on several simple subprocesses [14]. The single agent in this phase models the simplest process from the decomposition. The sequence of the processes makes the technological process of the part.

At the task's entry on the shop flor the task agent finds in the systems' database the relevant manufacturing process. The process interoperability is provided by independence of process model language stored in the database. Agent can works with ARIS diagrams, BPMN models and other concepts with multi-level decomposition (Fig. 5). Ontology-based approach provides semantic of the messages. While this manufacturing process is specified with entry parameters of the part (information from design agent) and manufacturing capabilities. Each manufacturing operation is presented by the relevant manufacturing agent (Fig. 5).

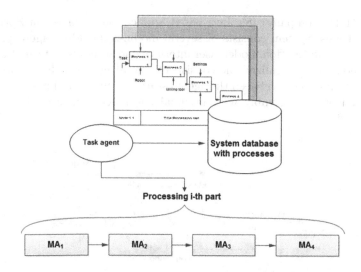

Fig. 5. Manufacturing agent's function overview

After finding the corresponding set of the manufacturing agents, each of them performs it's own function. Each agent is responsible for finding the resources, sequence of processing and operations. The negotiation process in this system is specified in [14].

Each manufacturing process (set of MA) has a link to the design agent (Each DA is responsible for the simple part). So, several MA linked with one DA form the vertical integration of this system. And from another side, single manufacturing process can be described as MAS subsystem. This subsystem is the part of the whole Manufacturing MAS.

3.3 MAS of the Mainenance Phase

In the maintenance phase we have physical instance of the product. The main task of product lifecycle management in this phase is making a closest link between physical state of the product and it's informational model [15]. Part of the multi-agent system responsible for the maintenance phase consists of the set of agents that represent information model of the product. Each maintenance agent has a one-to-one link to the DA and can store statistic and history data about product's functionality, maintenance, repair and other.

Every type of agents described below is under control of the Control/Change agent. Control/Change agent controlled the whole assembly part (one-to-one link) and is responsible for the changes and overall production process.

4   Evaluation and Implementation of the System

Based on the below model the part of integrated MAS system was presented. MAS desing agents subsystem is implemented as a module to PLM system

Windchill (PTC company) [8]. Java-based application is based on Spring and JSP-technologies. System consists of several modules including agent platform, link to product information model, user interface and standard information module. MAS module is centralized and consists of several agents such as shaft model. The negotiation process between the agents starts manually and finds the overall configuration of the assembly with minimal constructional-technological complexity (Fig. 6).

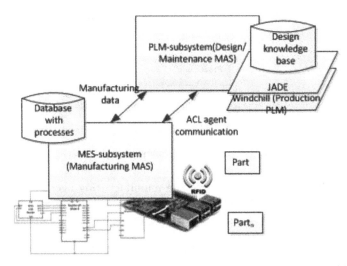

Fig. 6. Hardware-software architecture of the system

Among the variety of MAS designs we choose FIPA standards, which describe the overall architecture of the MAS and agent's ways of interactions. The reference architecture of the design agent includes several layers. The first layer is communication module. The second layer is run-time module which performs the transformation of product module part. The third level is control that performs the transformation of overall product module.

The manufacturing agent's layer is presented by hardware-software subsystem. In our subsystem the universal circuit board can be embedded in any device, controlled by a UNIX class operating system which contains an agent platform. This multi-agent architecture will support FIPA standards.

Agent communication is simulated at higher abstraction level than traditional data communication. Messages between processing devices, based on speech act theory (ACL-FIPA language) are transmitted across the network. Each module is capable of responding to a message from other agents by means of LEDs, connecting to other modules via IP network.

4.1 Position of MAS in the Framework

Proposed architecture contributes to remote several barriers according to [1]. The main benefits are eliminating conceptual barriers concerning data (due to single database usage), processes (due to usage the unified ACL language for agent communication and negotiation agents protocol) and services. The position of the proposed multi-agent architecture is described on Fig. 7.

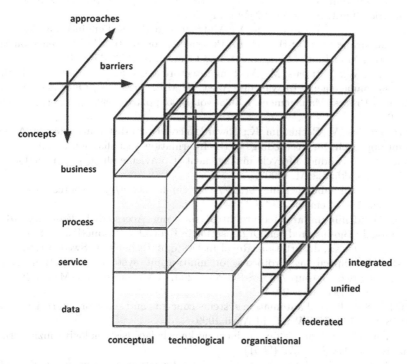

Fig. 7. Position of the MAS in the framework [1]

5   Conclusion

In this research we describe the integrated methodology for building an enterprise architecture in the product lifecycle management domain. Applying this architecture allows eliminating conceptual and technological barriers [16], due to use of standard semantic and architecture technologies. Also this approach bases on the multi-agent concept and provides the class of intelligent systems that helps to perform the full management of engineering production lifecycle and exchange data between several enterprises. Semantic approach to communication between agents allows increase interoperability and communication both between enterprises as between information parts within enterprise. In the further work we are going to present negotiation protocol between several multi-agent systems to extend this framework on virtual enterprise.

References

1. Chen, D.: Enterprise interoperability framework.http://ceur-ws.org/Vol-200/19. pdf. Accessed: 15 February 2015
2. BMBF: Zukunftsbild industrie 4.0. http://www.bmbf.de/pubRD/Zukunftsbild_ Industrie_40.pdf. Accessed: 16 February 2015
3. Tarchinskaya, E., Taratoukhine, V.: Matzner: Cloud-based engineering design and manufacturing: State-of-the-art. In: Proceedings of the IFAC Conference on Manufacturing Modelling, Management, and Control, pp. 353–358 (2013)
4. Scheer, A.-W., Nüttgens, M.: ARIS architecture and reference models for business process management. In: van der Aalst, W.M.P., Desel, J., Oberweis, A. (eds.) Business Process Management. LNCS, vol. 1806, pp. 376–389. Springer, Heidelberg (2000)
5. Taratoukhine, V., Bechkoum, K.: Towards a consistent distributed design: A multiagent approach. In: Proceedings of the Information Visualisation (1999)
6. Kolchin, A.: Product lifecycle management [Upravlenie zhiznennym tsiklom produktsii]. Anakharsis M. (2003)
7. Cimdata: All about plm. http://www.cimdata.com/en/resources/about-plm. Accessed: 15 December 2014
8. PTC: Windchill plm architecture. http://ptc.com. Accessed: 15 February 2014
9. Ferreira, J.: Bio-inspired Self-Organisation in Evolvable Production Systems. Tekn. Lic. Ph.D. thesis, dissertation, Royal Institute of Technology, Sweden (2013)
10. Poslad, S.: Specifying protocols for multi-agent systems interaction. http:// www.fipa.org/subgroups/ROFS-SG-docs/2007-TAAS-specifying-MAS.pdf. Accessed: 15 December 2014
11. ISO14258: Industrial automation systems-concepts and rules for enterprise models. In: ISO TC184/SC5/WG1, 14 April 1999
12. Evgenev, G.: Systemology of engineering knowledges [sistemologiya inzhenernykh znaniy]. M.: BMSTU 376 (2001)
13. Ben Khedher, A., Henry, S., Bouras, A.: Integration between mes and product lifecycle management. In: 2011 IEEE 16th Conference on Emerging Technologies & Factory Automation (ETFA), pp. 1–8. IEEE (2011)
14. Skobelev, P.: Multi-agent systems for real time resource allocation, scheduling, optimization and controlling: industrial applications. In: Mařík, V., Vrba, P., Leitão, P. (eds.) HoloMAS 2011. LNCS, vol. 6867, pp. 1–14. Springer, Heidelberg (2011)
15. Fedotova, A., Taratoukhine, V., Kupriyanov, Y.: Enterprise asset management systems: Methods and techniques for life-cycle management of high-value complex products. In: Very Large Business Applications (VLBA), pp. 69–78. Shaker Verlag, Aachen (2014)
16. Chen, D., Vallespir, B., Daclin, N.: An approach for enterprise interoperability measurement (2008)

Linked Data for Transaction Based Enterprise Interoperability

Erwin Folmer[1(✉)] and Dennis Krukkert[2]

[1] Univertity of Twente, Enschede, The Netherlands
e.j.a.folmer@utwente.nl
[2] TNO, Soesterberg, The Netherlands
dennis.krukkert@tno.nl

Abstract. Interoperability is of major importance in B2B environments. Starting with EDI in the '80s, currently interoperability relies heavily on XML-based standards. Although having great impact, still issues remain to be solved for improving B2B interoperability. These issues include lack of dynamics, cost of implementations, adoption and cross-industry exchange. Linked Data (part of the Semantic Web) technology, although originally not intended for the B2B domain, holds the promise of overcoming some of these issues.

This paper explores the potential of linked data technology within a B2B context by introducing and studying six scenarios for combining from light to heavy weight 'traditional' standards with Linked Data technology.

This research shows that using Linked Data technology has most potential for specifying semantics formally. This provides the 'best of both worlds' solution, in which legacy systems remain unaltered, and developers are supported in (semi) automated generation of transformation schema's to overcome different standards.

Keywords: Semantic Web · Linked data · Standards · Standardization · Interoperability

1 Introduction

Achieving interoperability in many industries is challenging but has great impact. Studies of the US automobile sector, for example, estimate that insufficient interoperability in the supply chain adds at least one billion dollars to operating costs, of which 86% is attributable to data exchange problems [1]. Later studies mention 5 billion dollars for the US automotive industry and 3.9 billion dollars for the electro technical industry, both representing an impressive 1.2% of the value of shipments in each industry [2]. The adoption of standards to improve interoperability in the automotive, aerospace, shipbuilding and other sectors could save billions [3].

The already huge importance of standards and interoperability will continue to grow. Networked business models are becoming indisputable reality in today's economy [4]. A recent Capgemini study concludes that to be ready for 2020 companies need to "significantly increase their degree of collaboration as well as their networking capability" [5].

© IFIP International Federation for Information Processing 2015
M. van Sinderen and V. Chapurlat (Eds.): IWEI 2015, LNBIP 213, pp. 113–125, 2015.
DOI: 10.1007/978-3-662-47157-9_11

Standards are important for ensuring interoperability [6]. "Standards are necessary both for integration and for interoperability" [7]. "Adopting standards-based integration solutions is the most promising way to reduce the long-term costs of integration and facilitate a flexible infrastructure" [8]. Some go even further: "Inter-organizational collaboration requires systems interoperability which is not possible in the absence of common standards" [9].

In an almost completely separated world, new developments take place under the umbrella of Semantic Web, Linked Data and even Big Data. Applications in the business transactions domain however are scarce. The question arises whether these two words can be combined.

2 Research Approach

In this paper is explored if, and how concepts from the Linked Data world, can be used in a different area: the world of inter-organizational interoperability where standardized message exchange for transactions is current practice but has some limitations.

In this explorative research a multi method approach is used. First of all requirements to the solution space are gathered The requirements are related to the current problems in the area of inter-organizational interoperability: the solution needs to solve identified problems otherwise it seems pointless. The authors are experienced in developing standards message based solutions for many industries and therefore have knowledge about the current limitations. Second, key assets from the Linked Data world are identified through literature search in the key journals (such as Semantic Web journal). Both these experts' based problems, and the outcome of the literature search are presented in the Background section.

Subsequently. scenarios are identified on how linked data can be used. These scenarios are structures using a very common structure for decomposition of transactions. The scenarios are tested, and validated in a workshop with linked data experts, and iteratively the scenarios are sharpened and pros and cons are gathered. Finally conclusion are presented in the final section.

3 Background

This section presents a background on the inter-organizational interoperability issues and continues with an exploration of Linked Data as background for defining potential solutions.

3.1 Interorganizational Interoperability

Business transaction standards reside at the presentation and application layer of the OSI model [10]. They include semantic standards, inter-organizational information system (IOS) standards, data standards, ontologies, vocabularies, messaging standards, document-based, e-business, horizontal (cross-industry) and vertical industry standards.

Examples are RosettaNet (electro technical industry), HealthLevel7 (health care) HR-XML (human resources industry) UBL (procurement). Semantic standards are designed to promote communication and coordination among organizations; these standards may address product identification, data definitions, business document layout, and/or business process sequences (adapted from [10]).

EDI and XML transaction based message exchange for enterprise interoperability have led to tremendous impact in the B2B world [11, 12]. However, still not all domains use the potential. Also, not all interoperability issues are solved, and new issues are introduced [13, 14]. Below we summarize the current issues:

Adoption issues: Many, both XML and EDI based, standards are not being used, or at least less than expected, leading to lower network effects and benefits.

Dynamic issues: The business world is changing, requiring flexibility from standards, This flexibility exits within standard for covering unforeseen business needs and variations of data or business processes, but is not harmonized. Also, many new versions for a standard arise, lowering interoperability.

Implementation cost issues: complexity of standards often lead to costly implementation projects. A part of these costs re-occur for every new version.

Quality issues: standards often offer different implementation choices for the same issue (relates to Dynamic Issue), and loads of optional elements. Different choices lead to interoperability issues. Also, semantics of the elements of the standard, data dictionary and associated rules are not always interpreted in the same way.

Limited interoperability in practice issue: Recent work shows that even a highly successful standard with acclaimed positive benefits does not necessary lead to interoperability on technical/syntax level. This might be caused by a conceptual mismatch: Business people do not want plug and play e-business, 80% interoperability might be enough [15].

Conceptual issues: standards often prescribe, or at least but restrictions on business processes. Although not proven, but still often heard that standards then limit innovation. For example: an innovation in business process will lead to a new version of the standard. However, the restrictions are needed since our conceptual goal has been set on automated business processes: plug and play e-business. Also, our economy and legislation traditionally is based on the notion of (paper) transactions. However, transaction often include information that has been exchanged before, and information that is not always needed. This transaction based thinking therefor has major impact in the message exchange.

Cross sector issue: Many of the current standards are developed for a single sector. Also standards exist that cover functional domain (such as procurement or invoicing). In the networked economy sectors become intertwined, introducing the issue of multiple, not interoperable standards.

Technology issue: There is currently still a lot of old technology in place, caused by the success of EDI/XML based standards. Migrating to newer technology has no positive business case simply because the "old situation" is working more than sufficient for many industries.

3.2   Linked Data (Semantic Web)

"The Semantic Web is here to stay" [16]. The Semantic Web is a vision by Tim Berners-Lee expressed in 2001, about the Internet evolving from a web of documents into a web of data (Web 3.0). Web 3.0 extends current Web 2.0 applications using Semantic Web technologies and graph-based (open) data [17]. In practice and literature terms like Semantic Web, Linked Data or Web 3.0 are used reversibly [18], and although its existence is way before the introduction of the rage around big data, linked data has become uncontroversial part of the Big Data Landscape [19].

The Semantic Web introduces fundamental paradigm shifts such as 'Anybody can say Anything about Any': The AAA principle, that can be extended to AAAAA if space and time are being added [19]. Which in practice means than multiple views (truths) can exist regarding a certain dataset. Another paradigm shift is that data should be kept at the source, without exchanging or duplicating the data, but referring (linking) to the source. So, information exchange contains references (URIs) to the source.

Hitzler and Van Harmelen [20] introduce the viewpoint that "semantics is a (possibly unobtainable) gold standard for shared inference" and based on that raises the questions: Why would a shared set of inferences have to consist of conclusions that are held to be either completely true or completely false? This questions the everlasting idea that all information being exchanged has to be complete and valid. In practice it means that not all necessary information for the task at hand will be make mandatory for sender to exchange, but only the information at hand will be exchanged regardless if that is enough for the task at hand for the receiving party. Although an interesting thought, but will it hold for a high value transaction data related to invoicing, or ordering products in the enterprise transaction context?

The goal of defining data semantics as well as the ideal of having a clear formal representation of semantics has not changed, but changing is the way of capturing and using data semantics as well as the formalisms for representation [21]. Data semantics can be used for semantic search, but also for data integration purposes: it is widely acclaimed that ontologies can play a valuable role for semantic data integration by providing a unified structure for linking information from different sources by providing a common interpretation of terminology used in different sources. On the same level it has been shown that semantic models are important for linking ontologies and schemas to each other. Typical use of semantic models is dis-ambiguation of terms, to derive implicit semantic relationships between data items and for detecting inconsistencies that arise due to wrong matches [21]. However many researchers seem to forget that ontologies are not made for their own sake, but that the purpose of an ontology is to help foster semantic interoperability between parties that want to exchange data [20].

Linked data uses RDF (triples) as basic data representation language to vanish syntactic issues, and uses vocabularies that are created in formally well-defined language such as OWL [19]. Triplification is often done without deep contemplation of semantic issues, or of usefulness of the resulting data [20]. A major source of interoperability problems is, however, the different vocabularies and ontologies that are used. And ontology matching in practice is often problematic, partly because semantic heterogeneities tend to be more subtle and owl: sameAs is not sufficient and misleading in practice, [22] and often rather abuse [20].

Again linked data brings in a paradigm shift: from resolving heterogeneity to accounting for it and acknowledging the importance of local conceptualizations by focussing on negotiation and semantic translation [22]. In this regard context becomes an important concept which is largely determined by space and time [22]. Others think that solving ontology interoperability problems is not the right direction, but the aim should be on preventing ontology interoperability problems by developing ontologies on a central (national) level and designing a system of mutually aligned domain ontologies [23].

Several researchers emphasize the distinction between modelling and encoding., with an emphasize on encoding (over modelling) within the Semantic Web community [24, 25]. Modeling semantics is a design task, encoding it is an implementation [24].

Although Semantic Web intended for web data, the technology is much broader useful. For instance Verma & Kass [26] describe usage in requirements engineering, functional and technical design for software engineering. Semantic Web is about semantic interoperability, which is also seen as important layer within inter-organizational inter-operability. Semantic Web is about offering support for complex information services by combining information sources that have been designed in a concurrent and distributed manner [25], a situation similar to the domain of inter-organizational information exchange.

4 The Scenarios for Linked Data Applications

There are different options to use Linked Data for enterprise interoperability. In this chapter, first the different scenarios are identified. Then, in Sect. 4.2, the different scenarios are compared and the most potential scenario is identified.

4.1 Identification of the Different Scenarios

In identifying the different scenarios, variation was applied in two aspects in which linked data and tradition (enterprise interoperability) standards differ.

First aspect is the exchange paradigm. Traditional standards rely on exchanging messaged at times that a relevant event has occurred. For example: a product has been send. In linked data however, the paradigm is not exchanging information, but keeping data at its source, link them to one another, and query for information once its needed.

The secons aspect is the way information is expressed and specified. In traditional standards XML messages are exchanged that are (more or less) digital representatives of paper messages that were used before (e.g. an invoice). The structure (syntax) of message instances is expressed in a separate schema. The semantics of information exchanged is typically expressed in a document written in natural language, and thus not interpretable for machines. In linked data, everything is expressed as triples, and there is no strict separation between instances and specification of these instances. Also, semantics can be expressed more formally.

Combining variation in both aspects led to seven possible scenarios which are described below.

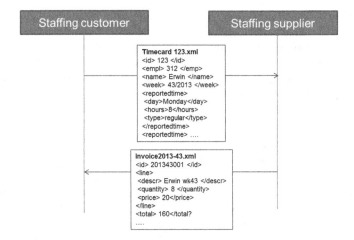

Fig. 1. Traditional exchange of XML messages

State of Practice. XML messages are exchanged which are based on XML schema. The schema specifies the structure (syntax) of the message. Typically a (PDF) document is written that provides, in natural language and sometimes UML models, the definition of each of the elements in the schema. Very often this document still gives to much space for interpretation, and therefore a (national or sectoral) localization is written in addition, or as replacement, of the natural language document. Figure 1 illustrates information exchange as we know it today.

"All in" Semantic Web. In this case no documents are exchanged. Instances, definitions and semantics are expressed using semantic web technology. Each organization has its own triple store to store information, and companies link to one another. For example: a timecard is stored as triples in the triplestore of the customer, while the invoice is stored as triples in the triplestore of the supplier. The invoice only references the timecard. Figure 2 illustrates this.

At first sight this option might seem like the ultimate B2B solution. Semantics are made explicit and interpretable by machines. Also, one doesn't get any closer to the best practice of 'keeping data at its source". But, there are some serious hurdles that have to be taken.

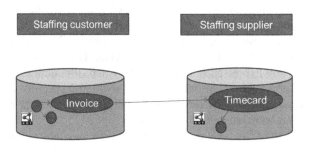

Fig. 2. All in semantic web

The first big issue is, maybe in contrast to what one might have expected, not a technical but a legislative issue. Current legislation is based on the notion that, in order to do business, organizations exchange 'business document'. For example Dutch tax authority states that "An invoice is a document that contains ….". In other words: exchanging documents is 'part of our system'. The implications are huge.

The promise of making semantics explicit and machine interpretable also needs a side note. Although it is possible to make explicit that one concept is the 'sameAs' another concept with another name (and a computer can reason with this), there are limitations to the expressiveness of semantic web technology. In practice it will still be necessary to have a document that, in natural language –and therefore not interpretable– specifies the different concepts.

A more 'technology driven' issue, or at least an issue that might be solved by technology, is the loss of notification. Traditionally, receiving a 'document' triggers an event. When using semantic web technology, there is no 'receiving'. So how to trigger an event? There are some initiative working providing a solution to this problem, but not is commonly used.

A more fundamental problem is driven by the 'open world' assumption behind the semantic web in combination with the lack of specifying structure. This means that there is no 'semantic web' counterpart of a 'mandatory field'. To take the Dutch authority example again: an invoice must contain a unique number. In XML schema this can be enforced so invoice instances without a unique number will not validate. In the semantic web this will not happen. A reasoner will just assume that such a number exists 'somewhere', even if this is not the case.

Security is also a major concern: you don't want your competitors to have insight in your data. SparQL endpoint do not contain any security or access policies. In practice this is mostly solved by putting a webservices in between that acts like an api.

A final issue is that the installed base of enterprise software will not support semantic web technology, making the introduction very difficult.

Semantic Web Based on Messaging Paradigm. Some of the issues mentioned in the previous scenario can be solved by actually exchanging the information besides storing it in a (local) triple store. RDF offers the possibility of serializing different triples in a

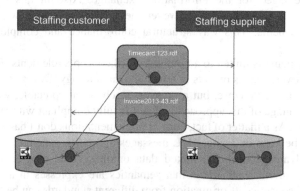

Fig. 3. RDF with an exchange paradigm

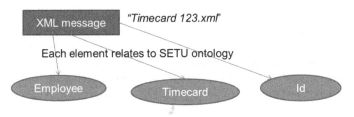

Fig. 4. XML message based on ontology

XML file that in its turn can be exchanged with other organizations. From within the XML serialization, references can be made to the original triples stored in the triple store. Figure 3 gives an example.

By exchanging the information in a RDF/XML serialization, one could argue that the issue of not exchanging messages is dealt with. Also, the issue of notifications is being dealt with. In return, some of the main advantages (like keeping data only at the source) are scarified. Also, the remaining issues mentioned in the "all in" semantic web scenario are not solved.

XML Messages Based on Semantic Web Ontology. In the "state of practice" scenario several issues are mention when adopting semantic web technology for B2B transactions. Even if this is solved, the installed base of enterprise software nowadays is accommodated to exchanging XML messages, not using to RDF based ontologies.

So, in order to accommodate current enterprise software solutions, it would be better to stick with exchanging XML messages. This scenario investigates the possibilities to actually do this, using a Linked Data ontology for the message definition, instead of XML schema (Fig. 4).

The drawback of this approach is that the possibility to check whether a XML instance complies to a standard (typically done using XML schema) is lost. Also, these ontologies, typically expressed in RDF, lack the expressiveness of XML schema when it comes to specifying structure.

Current Messages and Schema, Based on Ontologies for Semantics. The previous section already mentions that for legal and legacy reasons, it is preferred to keep on using XML messaged for the information exchange. Also in this scenario, XML messages will still be exchanged, however these XML messages will be based on tradition XML schema. This way structural conformance and completeness can be checked.

The XML schema is linked to an ontology. All concepts (elements) from the XML schema will be expressed as objects in a linked data ontology. Doing so, semantics can be described in a more precise, but moreover: machine interpretable, way (Fig. 5).

The big advantage of this approach is that it is fully compliant with current (legacy) implementations. As a matter of fact, current implementations don't have to be changed since they will be keep on using XML messages and XML schema.

So what advantage does the linked data ontology then provide us? The main difference with current standards is that semantics are expresses in a machine interpretable way. Also, concepts origination from different standards can be 'linked' to one

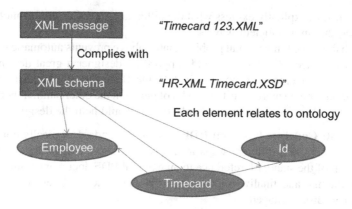

Fig. 5. XML schema linked to ontology

another. Although a couple of practical and more fundamental problems will be encountered, as will describe below, this approach does offers a starting point for automated transformations between different standards.

As shown in Fig. 6, a mapping can be defined (at the ontology level) between elements in different XML schema's. This mapping might be useable for automatic generation of XML transformation schema's (XSLT). Even though this systematics has already been implemented in a prototype (prestoprime.joanneum.at) to transform between different media metadata formats, we still see some hurdles to be taken for B2B applications.

One issue is that some elements in a schema are used for 'structuring purposes', and are not actual 'real world' concepts. Typically this is done for 'containers'. An example from the SETU standard is 'reference information' which contains various elements that can be used for referring to other objects or documents.

If two elements in different XML schema's have a different syntax, but semantically the same, then transformation is rather straightforward. However, a more fundamental problem is that in most cases elements from different standards are (semantically) not exactly the same. In order to make transformation possible in such a

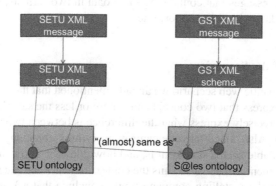

Fig. 6. Mapping between SETU and S@les

case, it is needed to explicitly express what the differences are. Current technology isn't capable to do this in a sufficient way.

Although the more fundamental problem stated above prevents automatic generation of transformationsheets (XSLT), is could support the designer a great deal by giving suggestions on what elements are potentially the same. If there are two standards that need a transformation scheme this doesn't offer a lot of gain. On the other hand, if there are tens of standard (e.g. electronic invoice standard), then it would help the designers a lot.

Mixed Content: Codelists Based on RDF. Semantic standards typically contain a lot of codelists. There are a different ways to use codelists in a standards: a table in the PDF document of the standard, reference to an external PDF document, enumeration as part of the schema, and finally: importing an external schema. Every option has it's advantages and disadvantaged.

When a codelist is in a PDF document (either as part of the standard or externally referenced), it is not possible to do automatic validation. When a codelist is part of the standard (either in the PDF document, or as enumeration in the schema), the dynamics are very low since the codelist can only change with the standard. Also, when a external codelist is used as source, manual synchronization is needed.

Linked data on the other hand is by nature very well suited to be 'maintained elsewhere'. So, one can imagine a situation where schema's 'link' to a codelist that is maintained elsewere. This does however require changes to legacy software to cope with this kind of codelists.

Combined Content: RDF as Additional Info in a Standard Message. All previous scenario's choices were made at different levels of the interoperability stack, for either 'the traditional' way or the 'linked data way'. There is however also another option: combine both.

The most obvious way to do this is by using RDFa to add concept from a Linked data ontology into a traditional XML message. Every element can be accompanied by a RDF counterpart. This does however require a change to the schema's. But, once realized, one can choose to add (optional) RDF data to a message.

The combination of traditional XML messaged and RDFa seems a nice approach for a 'transition period', but it would require additional effort from IT systems sending the messages. This also raises questions: which parties would be interested in putting effort in creating messages that contain the same data in two formats, while the parties that receives the data will only support one.

4.2   Analysis of the Scenarios

In the "All in" semantic web scenario we already mentioned that there is a fundamental issue on how to express that two concepts are 'more or less the same'. Moreover: how to explicitly and precisely express what the difference is between two 'more or less the same' concepts is. Also, since 'anyone can say everything about anything': how does one know how reliable such a statement is, and how does one know that the context in which such a statement is made also suits the context in which the statement is going to be used. For example: a staffing company might conclude that a Human Resource is more or less the same as a Person. An university might state that a Student is more or less the same as a Person. Giving this info the question arises what conclusions can be drawn. For most people a student and a Human Resource have a lot in common (both natural persons). However, for a procurement officer a Human Resource is more or less the same as a box of nails (both can be 'purchased').

We think the "Current messages and schema, based on ontologies for semantics" scenario is the most potential: linking a XML schema to an ontology, and use that ontology to help with creating transformation schema's.

Using an ontology for (semi) automated definition of transformation schemes can be implemented in two ways. The first option is to have an intermediate solution (during 'runtime' exchanging of messages) that receives XML messages in one format, does the transformation, and forwards the message in another format. For doing the transformation, the intermediate solution directly accesses and uses the knowledge in the ontology.

The second option is to first (in 'design time') distill an XML transformation schema (XSLT) based on the two original XML schema's and the ontology, and use this XSLT when exchanging messages.

The advantage of the first approach is that one is not limited to the expressiveness of XSLT (although we're not sure if this poses a problem), while the second approach had the advantaged that a lot of the enterprise services busses that are used today support XSLT.

5 Conclusions

Linked Data (Semantic Web) is an important technology approach within the container concept of Big Data. It is being developed to transform the document-centric world of the Internet transforming into a web of data instead of documents. However, the technology looks promising for the business transaction (e-business) world as well, although it was never designed with this application in mind.

This business transaction world has a long history of interoperability challenges covered by many standards based solutions starting from EDI solutions in the '80s to XML based standards that are used a lot nowadays. These solutions made an enormous positive impact but still several issues remains unsolved. This includes issues in the area of adoption, dynamics/flexibility, high implementation cost, quality, cross sectoral exchange and legacy solutions.

This paper aims to answer the question if Linked Data can contribute to solving these issues. Linked Data contains both conceptual and technical aspects. E.g. The principle that data is kept on the source and not being copied, just as the adagio: Anybody can say anything about anything, are examples on the conceptual level. Owl, RDF (the object-subject-predicate) and Sparql are examples of technical concepts of Linked Data.

Linked Data holds the promise to solve cross sector interoperability, its ability to handle (slightly) different semantics in communication, reduce redundant information exchange by linking, handles different versioning, make better reuse of existing data.

Six scenario's for inclusion of Linked Data concepts in the Enterprise transaction world are identified. These scenario's range from a full-blown Linked Data scenario down to using a small set of Linked Data concepts. The scenarios can by the way be implemented in incremental steps, making introduction easier.

Although all of the scenario's show a lot of potential advantaged, there are also some serious hurdles to take. One example is that Linked Data isn't meant for expressing structure which means that, combined with the open world assumption of Linked Data, it's very hard to enforce that specific information is actually exchanged. Also, from a legal perspective, the idea that 'exchange of messages' will be lost is a complex one. Other examples are mention in the paper as well.

The most realistic scenario is using Linked data at a 'design time' so support engineers, but at 'runtime' stick to current technology. This means that current XML messages, based on XML schema, will remain to be exchanged. For supporting the engineer, the schema will be related to an 'upper' ontology. For cross-sectoral exchange, the ontology and reasoners will give suggestions on what elements from different standards are potentially the same. Also, Linked Data could be used for specifying and reusing (elements within) codelists.

To sum up, although Linked Data is rapidly gaining importance and practical implementations are more and more common, it doesn't seem realistic that Linked Data within the world of business transactions becomes common in the near future (1-5 years). This paper shows that, although there is much potential in Linked Data, and at glance it seems that Linked Data is easy to implement in the business transactions world, the devil is in the details. And these details are quite essential, especially for the conceptual ones. However, since there is a lot of potential in Linked Data for business transaction, we urge to do more research on this topic and then aim for some large scale implementations to show the huge economic impact.

References

1. Brunnermeier, S.B., Martin, S.A.: Interoperability costs in the US automotive supply chain. Supply Chain Manag. **7**(2), 71–82 (2002)
2. Steinfield, C.W., Markus, M.L., Wigand, R.T.: Cooperative advantage and vertical information system standards: an automotive supply chain case study. In: 44th Hawaii International Conference on System Sciences (HICSS). Hawaii (2011)
3. Gallaher, M.P., O'Conner, A.C., Phelps, T.: Economic Impact Assessment of the International Standard for the Exchange of Product Model Data (STEP) in Transportation Equipment Industries (2002)
4. Legner, C., Lebreton, B.: Preface to the focus theme section: 'business interoperability' business interoperability research: present achievements and upcoming challenges. Electron. Mark. **17**(3), 176–186 (2007)
5. Falge, C., Otto, B., Österle, H.: Data quality requirements of collaborative business processes. In: 45th Hawaii International Conference on System Sciences (HICSS). Hawaii (2012)
6. Rada, R.: Standards: the language for success. Commun. ACM **36**(12), 17–23 (1993)

7. Dogac, A., et al.: Collaborative business process support in eHealth: Integrating IHE profiles through ebXML business process specification language. IEEE Trans. Inf Technol. Biomed. **12**(6), 754–762 (2008)
8. Chari, K., Seshadri, S.: Demystifying integration. Commun. ACM **47**(7), 58–63 (2004)
9. Gerst, M., Bunduchi, R., Williams, R.: Social shaping & standardization: a case study from auto industry. In 38th Hawaii International Conference on System Sciences (HICSS). Hawaii (2005)
10. Steinfield, C.W., et al.: Promoting e-business through vertical IS standards: lessons from the US home mortgage industry. In: Greenstein, S., Stango, V. (eds.) Standards and Public Policy, pp. 160–207. Cambridge University Press, Cambridge (2007)
11. Wang, E.T.G., Seidmann, A.: Electronic data interchange: competitive externalities and strategic implementation policies. Manag. Sci. **41**(3), 401–418 (1995)
12. Wigand, R.T., Steinfield, C.W., Markus, M.L.: Information technology standards choices and industry structure outcomes: the case of the U.S. home mortgage industry. J. Manag. Inf. Syst. **22**(2), 165–191 (2005)
13. Damsgaard, J., Truex, D.: Binary trading relations and the limits of EDI standards: The Procrustean bed of standards. Eur. J. Inf. Syst. **9**(3), 173–188 (2000)
14. Rukanova, B.D., van Slooten, K., Stegwee, R.A.: Business process requirements, modeling technique and standard: how to identify interoperability gaps on a process level. In: Konstantas, D., et al. (eds.) Interoperability of Enterprise Software and Applications, pp. 13–23. Springer-Verlag, London (2006)
15. Folmer, E., Wu, H.: Semantic standards quality measured for achieving enterprise interoperability: the case of the setu standard for flexible staffing. In: IWEI 2013. ISTE Wiley, Enschede, The Netherlands (2013)
16. Hitzler, P., Janowicz, K.: Semantic Web - interoperability, usability Applicability. Semant. Web **1**(1), 1–2 (2010)
17. Hendler, J.: Web 3.0 emerging. Computer **42**(1), 111–113 (2009)
18. Heath, T., Bizer, C.: Linked data - evolving the web into a global data space. In: Hendler, J., van Harmelen, F. (eds.) Synthesis Lectures on The Semantic Web: Theory and Technology, vol. 1, pp. 13–23. Morgan & Claypool, San Rafael (2011)
19. Hitzler, P., Janowicz, K.: Linked data, big data, and the 4th paradigm. Semant. Web **4**(1), 233–235 (2013)
20. Hitzler, P., van Harmelen, F.: A reasonable Semantic Web. Semant. Web **1**(1), 39–44 (2010)
21. Stuckenschmidt, H.: Data semantics on the web. J. Data Semant. **1**, 1–9 (2012)
22. Janowicz, K.: The role of space and time for knowledge organization on the Semantic Web. Semant. Web **1**(1), 25–32 (2010)
23. Hyvönen, E.: Preventing ontology interoperability problems instead of solving them. Semant. Web. **1**(1), 33–37 (2010)
24. Janowicz, K.: Modeling vs encoding for the Semantic Web. Semant. Web **1**(1), 11–15 (2010)
25. Guizzardi, G.: Theoretical foundations and engineering tools for building ontologies as reference conceptual models. Semant. Web **1**(1), 3–10 (2010)
26. Verma, K., Kass, A.: Model-Assisted Software Development: Using a 'semantic bus' to automate steps in the software development process. Semant. Web **1**(1), 17–24 (2010)

Interoperability Architecture for Electric Mobility

Allard Brand[1], Maria-Eugenia Iacob[2], and Marten J. van Sinderen[2(✉)]

[1] Energie Data Services Nederland, Baarnsche Dijk 4D, 3741 LR Baarn,
The Netherlands
allard.brand@edsn.nl
[2] University of Twente, P.O. Box 217, 7500 AE Enschede, The Netherlands
{m.e.iacob,m.j.vansinderen}@utwente.nl

Abstract. The current architecture for electric mobility provides insufficient integration with the electricity system, since at this moment there is no possibility for influencing the charge process based on information from market parties such as the distribution system operator. Charging can neither be influenced by grid constraints nor by the amount of (renewable) energy supply available. Because of the potential threats and opportunities and the impact these could have on the business model, there is a need for further integration of the energy and electric mobility markets. The aim of the current research is to define a reference architecture based on the current developments and concepts from literature to help market players in making the right steps forward. As main objectives, the reference architecture should (1) optimally integrate with the electricity system, (2) accommodate the adoption of renewable energy sources, (3) be aligned with European standardization developments and (4) have a positive impact on the current business model. The main concept behind the reference architecture is the concept of 'smart charging'. Based on a literature study, a reference architecture is defined for electric mobility. To provide a path for implementation and migration, a migration architecture is proposed.

Keywords: Interoperability · Electric mobility · Electricity system · Electric vehicles · Smart charging

1 Introduction[1]

The energy provisioning will change dramatically in the coming decades. The European Union has committed to reduce Europe's greenhouse gas emissions by 20% in 2020, and by 80–95% in 2050, compared to the level in 1990 [9]. In order to make this happen, non-renewable energy sources such as coal are expected to be replaced by renewable and sustainable energy sources. At the same time, the transition to (more)

---

[1] The current research has been conducted at Alliander, one of the main distribution system operators in the Netherlands.

© IFIP International Federation for Information Processing 2015
M. van Sinderen and V. Chapurlat (Eds.): IWEI 2015, LNBIP 213, pp. 126–140, 2015.
DOI: 10.1007/978-3-662-47157-9_12

electric mobility is considered as a contributing factor. Car manufacturers, consumers and grid operators show a growing interest in electric mobility.

Up to now, attention has mainly focused on the development of electric vehicles and the realization of an accessible charging infrastructure. However, massive use of electric mobility also introduces threats and opportunities in relation to the electricity system, which requires an increased degree of integration between the markets of electric mobility and the electricity system. The current architecture for electric mobility is inadequate, since there is a lack of integration between electric mobility and the electricity system. The main reason is that currently, there is no possibility for influencing the charging process based on information from market parties such as the operator of the distribution system or the energy supplier. Charging can neither be influenced by grid constraints nor by the amount of (renewable) energy sources available. In the current situation, charge points can only be controlled by the charge spot operator, which indicates a low amount of interoperability in the current architecture. Thus, the main goal of this research is to define *a reference architecture for electric mobility with the purpose of facilitating interoperability between involved parties from the markets of electric mobility and the electricity system.*

A *reference architecture* captures the essence of existing architectures for a class of problems (in our case that of designing an integration solution for the energy and electric mobility markets), and a vision of future needs and evolution to provide guidance to assist in developing new system architectures [5]. For the concept of *interoperability* we adopt the definition proposed by Chen et al. [4] stating that interoperability can be defined as the ability of two systems to understand one another and/or use one another's functionality.

We adhere to the 'Design Science Research Methodology' as defined by Peffers et al. [19]. The approach we take to develop our reference architecture is as follows. After we investigate the concept of electric mobility (Sect. 2), the objectives for the reference architecture will be defined on basis of the main problems and limitations in the current situation (Sect. 3). Given these objectives, we provide an elaboration of the smart charging concept (Sect. 4), and are able to derive a reference architecture for electric mobility (Sect. 5). For the design of the reference architecture, we apply the enterprise architecture approach as proposed by Iacob et al. [11]. This approach is based on open standards; using the 'Architecture Development Method' from TOGAF, and ArchiMate as the modeling language and framework. In line with this method we also formulate an implementation plan expressed as migration architecture (Sect. 5). The reference architecture is then evaluated by means of interviews with experts (Sect. 6).

We follow the approach depicted in Fig. 1. Based on the concepts defined in the ArchiMate core, architectures can be created that fill in the views related to phase B, C and D of the TOGAF ADM cycle; the phases concerned with creating the business, information systems and technology architectures. For describing the implementation and migration paths, a migration architecture will be established, providing an interim solution as a first step towards the reference architecture (phases E and F).

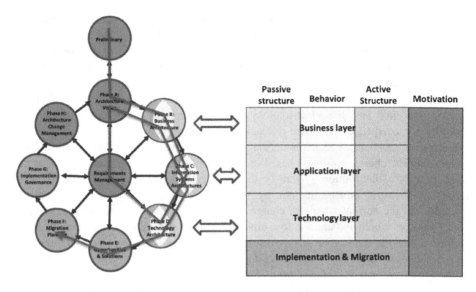

Fig. 1. Approach of the current research [10]

2   Energy Market Overview

In order to create a clear and comprehensive understanding of the concepts, services and structure in the current situation, we will review the markets of electric mobility and the electricity system.

2.1   Electric Mobility

Based on the definition by Gartner, we define *electric mobility* as the concept of using electric technologies, in-vehicle information, and communication technologies and connected infrastructures to enable the electric propulsion of vehicles and fleets [9].

In the current market for electric mobility, five main roles are evident. These roles are depicted in Fig. 2. The charge spot operator (CSO) is responsible for managing and operating several charge points. The e-mobility or charge service provider (CSP) is the central point of contact for the customer, providing them with the ability to charge at public charge points, irrespective of the responsible CSO. In order to realize this, the role of a clearing house exists, which unburdens both CSO and CSP, making it possible

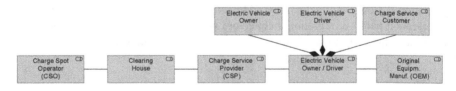

Fig. 2. Overview of the market roles within the market of electric mobility

to provide roaming functionality to their customers. The original equipment manu-
facturer (OEM) is the producer of electric vehicles and/or charge points, and provides
EV related services. The remaining role is the role of electric vehicle owner and/or
driver. This role aggregates several sub roles: the owner of the electric vehicle, the
driver of the electric vehicle that influences its charging needs, and the charge service
customer, who owns the contract with the CSP.

For the charging of electric vehicles, charging infrastructure is needed. The current
research is focused on the charging infrastructure in the public and semi-public space,
concerning charge points for customers that cannot charge at home or need to charge
during their travel. The main reason behind this decision is that most citizens do not
have a private driveway and depend on public charging infrastructure.

2.2   The Electricity System

De Vries [6] defines the electricity system as the combination of systems that produce,
transport and deliver power and provide related services, including the actors and
institutions that control the physical components of the system. The electricity system
consists of a technical and an economic subsystem. The technical subsystem is defined
as the physical part of the electricity system, consisting of the hardware that physically
produces and transports electric energy to customers, as well as the devices that use the
electricity. The economic subsystem is defined as the actors that are involved in the
production, trade or consumption of electricity, in supporting activities or their regulation, and their mutual relations [6] (see Fig. 3).

Energy producers feed their electricity directly into the transmission grid, based on
contractual agreements with the transmission system operator (TSO). The electricity is
then transported to the distribution system operator (DSO), from where it is distributed
to (small) consumers. The metering responsible party is responsible for the metering
processes. In the Netherlands, the DSO used to perform this role; however, since the
introduction of the 'supplier model', the energy supplier has been given this responsibility [7]. For the sake of understandability, we identify the metering responsible as a
separate role. On the market, organized by the market operator, electricity gets traded.
Energy producers offer their electricity on this market. Balance responsible parties
(BRP) buy commodity on the wholesale market in order to serve the customers of the

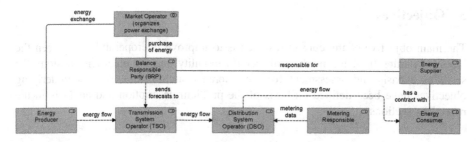

Fig. 3. Overview of the market roles within the electricity system

energy supplier they represent. The energy supplier sells electricity to its customers. Very large electricity consumers can buy electricity directly on the wholesale market [6].

The liberalization of the energy market has led to the establishment of a separate balancing market in the Netherlands. This market is controlled by the TSO, who is the single buyer on this market. When there is imbalance in the network, the TSO corrects this by buying the lowest priced offer in the balancing market. Most of the offers come from large power producers. However, sometimes smaller energy producers or energy suppliers offer electricity as well. The TSO charges the balance responsible parties that caused the imbalance on basis of the price that it has paid on the balancing market. The mechanism works the other way as well: in case of a surplus of produced electricity, the TSO accepts and receives the highest bid in the balancing market for adjusting generating units downwards [6].

2.3 Changing Nature of the Electricity System

According to [14] two inter-related movements can be seen in electricity generation, impacting the way the electricity system will be managed in the future. The first movement is the increase of electricity generated from sustainable energy sources in order to reduce greenhouse gas emissions. The second movement entails the decentralization of electricity generation; instead of centralized power plants with high capacity, the number of smaller electricity generating units is growing and moving closer to the load centers.

Fossil fuel usage is one of the greatest contributors to greenhouse gas emissions, leading to a significant increase in the concentration of carbon dioxide in the atmosphere [14]. This introduces one of the greatest global challenges of our time: climate change [21]. Issues concerning climate change are high on the political agenda; as illustrated by the commitment of the European Union to reduce Europe's greenhouse gas emissions to 80–95% in 2050 [9]. Worldwide, energy provision is radically changing; under the influence of climate change a strong drive exists to reduce fossil fuels usage and make the transition to renewable sources instead [22].

The second movement described by [14] concerns the decentralization of electricity generation. Thus, electricity generation capacity is increasingly realized in the distribution part of the electricity system as small-scale generation units are directly connected into the distribution grid.

3 Objectives

The main objective of the current research is to improve interoperability between the involved parties from the markets of electric mobility and the electricity system. To serve as a basis and assessment for the reference architecture, various underlying objectives have been defined on basis of the problem description and analysis in the preceding sections.

3.1   Optimal Integration of Electric Mobility and the Electricity System

Verzijlbergh et al. [23] investigated the impact of electric vehicle charging on residential low-voltage networks. Their results, based on data from Enexis, show that the charging of electric vehicle has a significant potential impact on residential low-voltage networks. This impact can be reduced by influencing the charge process, shifting demand away from (household) peaks. This way, the number of overloaded transformers and cables can be reduced drastically. In an impact scenario, this reduction is approximately 25% and 8% for overloaded transformers and cables. Therefore, the reference architecture should reflect and accommodate the ability to let distribution network operators influence the charge process, with the goal of using current assets as efficient as possible and avoiding unnecessary investments in assets.

3.2   Accommodation of the Adoption of Renewable Energy Sources

As mentioned in Sect. 2.3, a movement is expected from centralized electricity generation based on fossil fuels towards electricity generated from sustainable energy sources. The main driver for this movement is the reduction of greenhouse gas emissions [14]. However, renewable energy sources and distributed generation are generally unpredictable and introduce fluctuation in supply [17]. Electric vehicles can improve the economics of distributed energy generation when integrated in an optimal manner [20], and offer an enormous ability to temporarily adjust demand. Therefore, the reference architecture should reflect and accommodate the advantage offered by electric vehicles to optimally integrate renewable energy sources.

3.3   Optimization of the Business Model for Electric Mobility

The business case for charge points has been a negative business case up to now [24]. The market model as originally proposed by [17] has been implemented, but does not seem to succeed very well. In addition, the current architecture implies a situation where customers have no choice of energy supplier, since the energy contract is established between the supplier and charge spot operator. For the reference architecture, various alternative solutions have to be compared to see whether other implementations could result in a better business model [14].

4   The Concept of 'Smart Charging'

In the current situation, no external control is involved in the charging process. This basic form of charging electric vehicles is called 'uncontrolled' or 'dumb' charging [2]. As stated in the problem analysis and objectives, integration is needed between the process of charging electric vehicles and external influences based on fluctuations in demand and supply. In an ideal situation, charging should be influenced based on grid constraints and the amount of (renewable) energy supply available. This concept is not

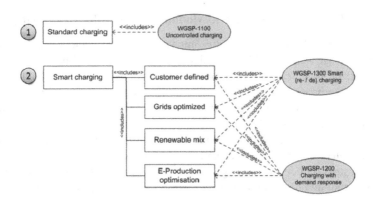

Fig. 4. Drivers for 'smart charging' [2]

new, and is widely regarded as 'smart charging'. The concept of smart charging is one of the central concepts that has been applied in the reference architecture.

The main idea of smart charging is that by taking control of the charging process, the use of the grid and available energy can be optimized to minimize additional investments and facilitate the integration and storage of renewable energy [2].

The concept of smart charging is positioned as an alternative to 'standard' or uncontrolled charging. Movares defines smart charging as a method for charging electric vehicles optimized according to the available grid capacity and/or fluctuations in the supply of (sustainable) energy [16].

Based on a use-case analysis by CEN, CENELEC & ETSI [2] four drivers can be identified, that are depicted in Fig. 4. The four drivers can be summarized as follows: (1) Charging has to be performed within boundaries as specified by the customer. (2) The process of charging should be optimized to meet grid constraints. (3) Charging should be based on supply and availability of renewable energy sources. (4) Charging should be optimized to 'avoid' peaks and efficiently use production capacity.

As hinted in Fig. 4, there are essentially two ways to 'implement' the concept of smart charging. In the following sections we will present these two options.

4.1 Controlled Charging

Controlled charging is a realization of smart charging based on flexible contracts and technical signals for load control [2]. Control signals can be sent to either the charging station or the electric vehicle. These control signals can range from simply switching between on and off, charging with a specific rate or can involve communication about sophisticated charge schedules. Controlled charging should be seen as a 'top-down' approach in demand-side management, where measures are taken by market actors in order to control the electricity demand [2]. In other words, market roles (such as utilities) decide to implement measures on the demand side to increase the efficiency of the energy system. This is the approach that has been used by the vast majority of the power industry over the last thirty years [8].

In the scenario of controlled charging, the role of the 'aggregator' (also referred to as 'flexibility operator') arises. This is a generic role that links the role customer and its possibility to provide flexibilities to the roles market and grid [2]. The aggregator is responsible for summing up flexibilities from several customers, and actively partici-pates in energy market commercial transactions to market these flexibilities [1]. The aggregator coordinates the charging process on basis of based on control signals.

4.2 Demand-Response Charging

Demand-response charging involves extra communication that makes it possible to receive price signals or other incentives, providing the possibility for a customer to respond [2]. In contrary to the controlled charging approach, the concept of demand-response implies a 'bottom-up' approach, where customers become active in adapting their consumption patterns [8]. According to the International Energy Agency, demand response refers to a set of strategies which can be used in competitive electricity markets to increase the participation of the demand-side, or customers, in setting prices and clearing the market [13]. Demand response can be seen as a concept describing an incentivizing of customers in order to initiate a change in their consumption or feed-in pattern [2].

In a demand-response approach, customers are exposed to (near) real-time prices or other incentives, to which they may respond in two ways [13]: shifting their demand in time to an off-peak period, or reducing their total or peak demand (either by energy efficiency measures, or self-generation). Of course, customers are free to choose to not respond and pay the market price instead.

Demand-response can be implemented in two ways, based on the method in which customers can respond to the price signals. The first option is a manual implementation: customers get price information, for example on a display, and based on this infor-mation they decide whether or not to shift their consumption. The second option considers an automated implementation: customers shift their consumption automati-cally, based on technical signals and some kind of an energy management system. For instance, the system could set-up the system in such a way that (part of) their con-sumption is shifted when prices are at a certain level [8]. In contrast to the scenario of controlled charging, the external control of the charging process could be fully auto-mated based on a demand-response energy management system (EMS). This EMS acts as a software agent that represents the customer. The EMS communicates about demand-response price signals over some sort of communications network, such as the internet [18]. Based on the price signals, the EMS can adjust the charging process automatically. The PowerMatcher technology [15] is an example of agent-based system for demand-response energy management.

4.3 Consequences for Design Choices

Adopting the concept of smart charging affects several other design decisions, ranging from consequences on the structure of the energy market to changes in the metering functionality. The main question to be answered is how to relate the relevant stakeholders to the charging process; how can the role specific objectives be translated into either price or control signals (such as start charging, stop charging, and charge at a specific level).

In the demand-response approach, price signals or other incentives are used to influence the charging process. In order to realize this approach, new kinds of energy markets need to emerge. In the 'European conceptual model of Smart Grids' [2], three markets are identified that are expected to emerge in the smart grid of the future: the energy market, the grid capacity market and the flexibility market. The grid capacity market gives distribution system operators the possibility to attach variable prices to grid capacity, in contrast to the fixed grip capacity prices as reflected in the current situation. In this way, the DSO can use a demand-response approach for congestion management. As identified in the previous section, automated demand-response requires some kind of energy management system (EMS). A logical location to implement this EMS would be inside the electric vehicle.

In the controlled charging scenario, control is performed by a secondary actor, outside the scope of the electric vehicle. The aggregator needs to be able to send control signals to the charge point management system of the charge spot operator, which translates these control signals into commands towards the charge point. The charge point reacts to these control signals by adjusting its charging process.

5 Reference and Migration Architecture

Based on [15], the automated demand-response approach using two-way communication is considered as the most favorable scenario. According to Kok, this scenario forms the hot spot in his 'smart energy management matrix' [15]. The main advantages of this approach when compared to controlled charging is that it mitigates privacy issues and enables distributed control with full power and responsibility at the customer. At the same time however, demand-response involves radical changes when compared to the current situation. Flexible energy and grid prices are needed and energy management systems need to be implemented within electric vehicles. Because of this radical change, we choose to establish two architectures: a reference architecture, based on the demand-response approach towards smart charging, and a migration architecture, providing an interim solution as a first step towards the reference architecture. The migration architecture focuses on the realization of the objectives as identified for the current research that are feasible on a shorter timescale, and implements the scenario of controlled charging.

For both the reference and migration architecture, a new 'type' connection is introduced for charging stations, on which various energy suppliers are allowed to deliver energy. This introduces the ability to 'switch' between energy suppliers, and allows the customer to have their 'own' contract for the provision of energy. To distinguish between separate charging sessions, it is desirable to replace the currently separated meters of the DSO and CSO with a single certified meter per outlet, managed and controlled by a trusted third party. Based on a shared registry for the metering data of charge points, metering values can be exchanged between energy supplier, DSO and

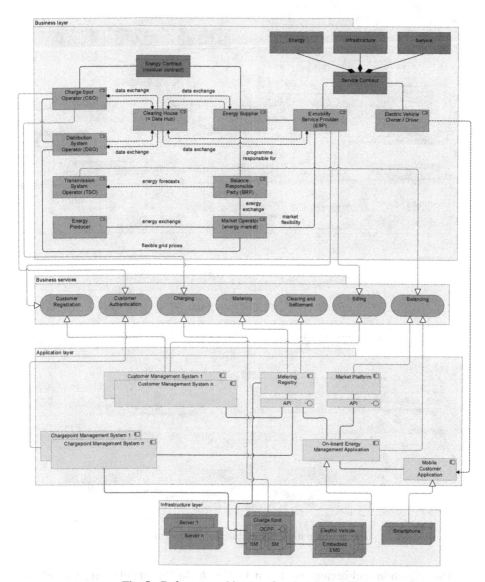

Fig. 5. Reference architecture for electric mobility

CSO. This situation would be in line with the current 'meter values registry' for regular connections, as mentioned in [7].

The reference architecture is shown in Fig. 5, Please note that for comprehensibility, some relationships have not been drawn [2]. The servers in the infrastructure layer realize the applications in the application layer, except for the on-board management system which runs on a local server inside the electric vehicle. However, these realization relationships have not been drawn. Although, both smart meters are related to the metering database; for simplicity, only one of the relationships has been drawn.

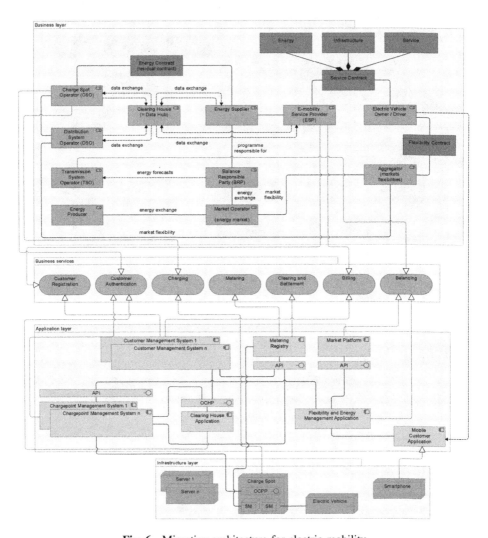

Fig. 6. Migration architecture for electric mobility

The migration architecture is shown in Fig. 6. In this architecture, the role of 'aggregator' is depicted, reflecting the controlled charging approach as described in Sect. 4.1. The aggregator is the key mediator between the consumers on one side and the markets and the other power system participants on the other side [1]. By externally controlling the charge process, the aggregator combines flexibilities from several customers. In the migration architecture, the radical changes that are required to support an automated demand-response approach (that forms the basis of the reference architecture) are absent.

6   Validation

For the validation of the architectures, we used a qualitative approach. A series of structured interviews (of about 90 min) have been carried out with six experts in the fields of energy, electric mobility, and of (enterprise) architecture (in Table 1 the experts that have been interviewed are listed, including their experience in years). The interview consisted of an initial presentation on the background, motivation and design choices as made for the reference architecture. Following on this presentation, the reference architecture has been presented to each of the interviewees.

Overall, the interviewees showed confidence in the model and outlined that in principle, it can greatly improve the identified problems. The results of the validation are graphically displayed in Fig. 7. All of the interviewees with experience in the energy sector agreed that the situation as modeled in the reference architecture would enhance the integration between electric mobility and the electricity system, and reduce the potential impact of electric mobility. One of the main reasons given was that smart charging results in a better utilization of the electricity net. By applying control and scheduling in charging, less of the electricity cables need to be replaced.

The interviewees confirmed that the reference architecture depicts a situation that drives the adoption of renewable energy sources (RES) in the electricity system. When compared to household devices such as washing machines, electric vehicles have an enormous potential capacity. The idea of dynamic demand and supply can helps significantly in solving the intermittency problem of renewable energy, which concerns its stochastic behavior. Being able to 'follow' the availability of energy supply offers a

Table 1. Validation interviewees (including their years of experience)

Company	Profession	Energy	Architecture
E-laad	Manager R&D and innovation	12	n/a
Enexis	Manager smart grids	28	n/a
EDSN	Manager architecture and services	25	15
Eneco	Senior project manager	12,5	n/a
University of Twente	Professor, information systems	n/a	10
Delf University, UCPartners	Senior researcher and CTO	15	15–20

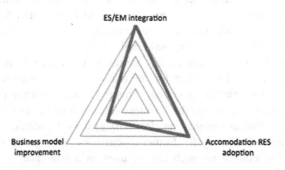

Fig. 7. Validation results (outermost contours represent highest scores)

more effective solution than the globally examined opportunity of storage, since the latter involves an energy loss. Some interviewees mentioned the importance of regulation for the success of RES adoption. The interviewees agreed that the current business model does not yield a profitable situation. Several of them pointed out that this is only the case for the realization of public charging infrastructure (the focus of the current research); for private and semi-public charging infrastructure positive business cases can be made. It was also pointed out that the main reason for the negative business case of the current business model is its narrow scope. The realization and commercialization of public charging infrastructure is not profitable when considering just the provisioning of uncontrolled charging. However, there is financial potential in the reduction of grid investments, the balancing of the electricity system and the storage of energy. In the discussion about the implementation of smart charging, various viewpoints have been mentioned. Overall, the interviewees agree that smart charging has to be based on incentives. However, the opinions concerning the implementation of these incentives vary. Real-time price signals (as in the demand-response approach) are desirable for the future, but are not feasible in a short timescale since they are radically different from the current organization of the energy market. The current energy market is based on forecasts and reconciliation, and involves financial risks. One of the interviewees mentions that for the distribution system operator (DSO), price signals are not an adequate instrument at all; he mentions that the component of the energy prices that a DSO can influence is insignificant (since it concerns only a few cents); prices need to be increased at least a tenfold before having a little effect. Even though it was confirmed that price signals offer the simplest mechanism and are preferred on long term, most interviewees mentioned that controlled charging is more feasible on a short term. This confirms the migration path as proposed in the current research.

7 Conclusions

To address the drawbacks of the current architecture for electric mobility, we proposed a reference architecture that facilitates interoperability between the involved parties from the markets of electric mobility and the electricity system. The main architectural choices that have been made involve the implementation of 'smart charging'; the integration of flexibility and intelligence in the charging process, the location of control and the metering of the usage of electricity for individual charging sessions. The reference and migration architectures are depicted in Figs. 5 and 6, and have been validated qualitatively, through a series of interviews with experts in the fields of energy, electric mobility, and (enterprise) architecture.

Reflecting on the main result of this research, we conclude that the proposed architecture forms a useful blueprint for the realization of an integrated solution for electric mobility and the electricity system. This is expected to drive the integration of RES, to have a positive impact on the business case for the charging infrastructure and to prevent potential threats towards the electricity system. In addition, the architecture provides a common vocabulary for further discussions, aggregating various concepts from literature. The current research can be used as a reference for helping market players make the right steps forward.

As any other research, the current research involves certain limitations. Even though the reference architecture seems to provide a promising solution, the level of abstraction is relatively high. The field of electric mobility is still immature, and therefore the main focus of our research has been on analyzing market roles, processes and high-level design choices to provide an integrated architecture for electric mobility and the electricity system. Especially the application layer needs further refinement in order to provide concrete guidelines for involved stakeholders.

Another limitation regards the validation of the reference architecture. Although the reference architecture has been discussed extensively with leading experts, the number of interviews that could be performed is relatively low. We believe that further validation research might result in improved feedback and uncover further issues in the reference architecture. Also, the development of one or more concrete business cases can help to open the discussion with the stakeholders.

Finally, we have not examined the concept of inductive charging. Further research is needed in this area and may have implications for the reference architecture.

References

1. ADDRESS. Technical and commercial conceptual architectures (2009)
2. van Buuren, R., Jonkers, H., Iacob, M.-E., Strating, P.: Composition of relations in enterprise architecture models. In: Ehrig, H., Engels, G., Parisi-Presicce, F., Rozenberg, G. (eds.) ICGT 2004. LNCS, vol. 3256, pp. 39–53. Springer, Heidelberg (2004)
3. CEN, CENELEC & ETSI. Smart Grid Coordination Group – Sustainable Processes (2012)
4. Chen, D., Doumeingts, G., Vernadat, F.: Architectures for enterprise integration and interoperability: past, present and future. Comput. Ind. **59**, 647–659 (2008)
5. Cloutier, R., Muller, G., Verma, D., Nilchiani, R., Hole, E., Bone, M.: The concept of reference architectures. Syst. Eng. **13**(1), 14–27 (2010)
6. De Vries, L.J.: Securing the public interest in electricity generation markets: the myths of the invisible hand and the copper plate. Technical report (2004)
7. EDSN. Stroomopwaarts: Gezamenlijk stapsgewijs naar een beter functionerend marktmodel voor kleinverbruik (2013)
8. Eurelectric.Power Choices: Pathways to Carbon-Neutral Electricity in Eur. by 2050 (2011)
9. European Commission. What is the EU doing about climate change? July 2013. Obtained online from: http://ec.europa.eu/clima/policies/brief/eu/index_en.htm
10. Gartner. IT Glossary: Electro Mobility, April 2012. Obtained online from: http://www.gartner.com/it-glossary/electro-mobility-e-mobility/
11. Iacob, M.E., Jonkers, H., Quartel, D., Franken, H., Van den Berg, H.: Delivering Enterprise Architecture with TOGAF and ArchiMate. Van Haren, The Netherlands (2012)
12. Iacob, M.E., Meertens, L.O., Jonkers, H., Quartel, D.A.C., Nieuwenhuis, L.J.M., Van Sinderen, M.J.: From enterprise architecture to business models and back. Softw. Syst. Model. **13**(3), 1059–1083 (2013)
13. International Energy Agency. The Power to Choose: Demand Response in Liberalised Electricity Markets (2003)
14. Kok, J., Scheepers, M., Kamphuis, I.: Intelligence in electricity networks for embedding renewables and distributed generation. In: Negenborn, R.R., Lukszo, Z., Hellendoorn, H. (eds.) Intelligent Infrastructures, pp. 179–209. Springer, The Netherlands (2009)

15. Kok, J.K.: The powermatcher: smart coordination for the smart electricity grid (2013)
16. Movares. Laadstrategie Elektrisch Wegvervoer (2013)
17. Netbeheer Nederland. Net voor de toekomst: een verkenning (2011)
18. OpenADR. Openadr overview, June 2013. http://www.openadr.org
19. Peffers, K., Tuunamen, T., Rothenberger, M., Chatterjee, S.: A design science research methodology for information systems research. J. Manage. Inf. Syst. **24**, 45–77 (2007)
20. Richardson, D.B.: Electric vehicles and the electric grid: A review of modeling approaches, impacts, and renewable energy integration. Renew. Sustain. Energy Rev. **19**, 247–254 (2013)
21. Rijksoverheid. Nieuwe energie voor het klimaat: Werkprogramma schoon en zuinig (2010)
22. TNO, UUtrecht, ECN. Naar een toekomstbestendig energiesysteem voor Nederland (2013)
23. Verzijlbergh, R., Lukszo, Z., Slootweg, J., Ilic, M.: The impact of controlled electric vehicle charging on residential low voltage networks, pp. 14–19 (2011)
24. VNO-NCW. Onoph Caron: 'Hoe financieren we de aanleg van laadpalen?'

Model Based Enterprise Modeling for Testing PLM Interoperability in Dynamic Manufacturing Network

Nicolas Figay[1(✉)], Parisa Ghodous[2], Bezhad Shariat[2],
Ernesto Exposito[3], David Tchoffa[4], Lyes Kermad[4],
El Mouloudi Dafaoui[4], and Thomas Vosgien[5]

[1] Airbus Group Innovations, Suresnes, France
nicolas.figay@airbus.com
[2] University Lyon 1, Lyon, France
{parisa.ghodous,bezhad.shariat}@univ-lyon1.fr
[3] LAAS, Toulouse, France
ernesto.exposito@laas.fr
[4] University Paris 8, Paris, France
{d.tchoffa,l.kermad,e.dafaou}@iut.univ-paris8.fr
[5] IRT, Saclay, France
Thomas.vosgien@irt-systemx.fr

Abstract. When willing to prepare and to build operational Product Life cycle Management interoperability within a Dynamic Manufacturing Network (DMN) in a mature digital business ecosystem such as Aeronautic, Space and Defense, the approaches proposed by the Enterprise Application Interoperability are insufficient when willing to address the existing interoperability brakes Some of these brakes have been addressed in project such as IMAGINE and SIP@ SystemX, allowing to experiment innovative way of using standards based enterprise modeling and also to identify some additional gaps for applying model base enterprise modeling to PLM interoperability within a DMN. After defining the business and the scientific contexts, the paper describes this new approach which consists in federating the usage of several PLM, Business, Information and ICT standard through the usage of an enterprise modeling standardized language, ArchiMate, and associated modeling tool Archi created using ArchiMate as an EMF DSL. The defined methodology is based on producing a set of DMN blueprints and associated templates. Then, through model to model transformation, other more detailed models using more specialized languages are created and used for software component generation and deployment enterprise hub platform based on standards. Using the methodology, the associated framework and the developed resulting from our research activity, we are now able to prepare and build interoperability within a DMN. Ability of preserving investment performed with the legacy and reducing risks associated to future evolution was demonstrated through IMAGINE Aeronautic Lab experimentation within SIP. Such experimentation also highlighted some issues related to model based engineering in such a context, and allowed identifying needs for new extensions of the federative PLM interoperability framework for Collaborative Networked Product Development initiated during the ATHENA project. It will be addressed in future work.

© IFIP International Federation for Information Processing 2015
M. van Sinderen and V. Chapurlat (Eds.): IWEI 2015, LNBIP 213, pp. 141–153, 2015.
DOI: 10.1007/978-3-662-47157-9_13

Keywords: Model based enterprise modeling · PLM · Interoperability · Standards · Cloud · Simulation · MDA

1 Introduction

The approach described in this paper results from several successive research projects, each of them followed by operational projects allowing to assess the results and to provide new identified gaps and challenges for the next research projects. The approach, aiming at building continuous interoperability, has been developed supporting successively different industrial drivers in the PLM area: concurrent engineering, sharing of digital mock-up units distributed between heterogeneous tools, networked collaborative product development, enterprise technical applications interoperability, DMN and factory of the future. It is consequently important reminding in the introduction business and research context in order clearly understanding the challenges addressed.

1.1 Business Contexts

Nowadays in order to remain competitive and within a global economic context where the complexity of the products is still increasing, enterprises have been developing new approaches the last years, in particular the Product Lifecycle Management (PLM) approach. Reference [1] defines PLM as a strategic approach aiming to put in place appropriate processes related to production and consumption of data describing the product, through the different phases of the lifecycle of manufactured products and within the supply chain.

Along the lifecycle of the product and during the different PLM phases, the processes (e.g. Product Design Process) of the different enterprise functions (e.g. Design Function attributed to the Design Office) are supported by different PLM solutions constituting the Information System (IS): Product Data Management (PDM) system for the design office, Enterprise Resource Planning (ERP) systems and Manufacturing Execution System (MES) for production, Customer Service and Support (CSS) systems for support, etc. Such systems encompass processes, methods and tools which are today systematically computer aided, using software products deployed on Information and Communication technological infrastructure. A PLM application is realized by one or several instances of software products deployed in operational and technical environments PLM. PLM solutions include PLM Hubs (e.g. Boost Aerospace) which aim at interconnecting PLM applications and processes of partners collaborating around products. The need for governed standards in digital business ecosystem was identified by mature communities (e.g. eHealth in Australia working around NETHA or Automotive around VDA) for preparing and building operational interoperability. But PLM standardization governance organizations, such as ASD SSG for European Aeronautic, Space and Defense domain, are facing difficulties when elected eBusiness PLM standards and associated PLM standardization enterprise policies have to be applied in the enterprises. Different brakes exist for implementing and applying standards, which are politic, organizational or technical. Scientific gaps also exist for being able to properly establish continuous PLM interoperability, due to the complexity of complex systems of systems which are to be considered for supporting DMN in a continuously evolving environment.

1.2   Research Context

To deal with the complexity of PLM and required continuous interoperability, the authors of the paper have being collaborating around the establishment of a federated framework for interoperability of technical applications applied to networked collaborative product development [2]. It was done through participation to or assessment of several research projects in PLM area (RISESTEP – Enterprise Wide standard access to STEP distributed databases -Esprit Project 20459), SAVE (Step in a virtual enterprise-bright euram project 97-5073), OpenDevFactory (Paris cluster Usine Logicielle), CRESCENDO (FP7 Transport 234344 Collaborative and robust engineering using simulation capability enabling next design optimization), TOICA (Thermal Overall Integrated Conception of Aircraft), SIP@SystemX, Factory of the future area (IMAGINE FoF ICT 201173 Innovative end to end management of DMN), in enterprise application interoperability area (IDEAS IST 2001 37368, ATHENA FP6 IST 507849 Advanced technologies for interoperability of heterogeneous enterprise networks and their applications - COIN Collaboration and interoperability for networked enterprises IST FP7 IST IP project 216256, NEFFICS Networked enterprise transformation and resource management in future internet enabled innovation cloud FP7 ICT 258076) or in Digital Business Ecosystems (FP6 Integrated Project IST-2002-507953).

The assessment through operational projects of approaches coming from Enterprise Application Interoperability domain in one hand, PLM for manufacturing within a System Engineering context in the other hand, demonstrated some drawbacks, with identification of important brakes [2] for industrial usage of manufacturing PLM standards.

PLM interoperability in DMN involved in the development of complex systems requires an effective combination of standards coming from vertical, horizontal and ICT domains, as defined by Object Management Architecture. It also requires effective combination of enablers such as ontology, model driven/service oriented architecture and enterprise modeling, coupled with Model Based System Engineering, Computer Aided Design, Computer Aided Manufacturing and Computer Aided Support. Creating such effective combination of standards is a scientific challenge, due to the silos induced by each concerned community using heterogeneous technologies, languages and paradigms. Applying such effective combination of standards within a DMN is also a challenge because of the uncontrolled evolution of the technologies and solutions developed by each domain or used by each stakeholder.

In order addressing such issues, we have been developing a federative framework for eBusiness PLM interoperability within DMN. We integrated within this framework the Open Group's ArchiMate open and independent standardized enterprise modeling language, which supports the description, analysis and visualization of architecture within and across business domains in an unambiguous way. This choice was made after assessing other enterprise modeling standards, and was motivated by the simplicity of the language, its alignment with principles of governance of the evolution of the information system defined by enterprise modeling and control urbanism of enterprise information system, its intent of use for facilitating the communication between enterprise, process, information system and ICT architects, and the existence of the Archi modeling tool. Archi modeling tool (http://www.archimatetool.com) was created by Phil Beauvoir on top of the Eclipse Modeling Tools which implements OMG's specification related to Meta Object Facilities in order supporting Model Driven Architecture. It relies on a formalization of ArchiMate using eCore (http://eclipse.org/modeling/emf), on top of which visual modeling capabilities were develop with full alignment with underlying principles of ArchiMate, i.e. support of multiple views derived from predefined viewpoints associated to precise stakeholders, concerns and authorized subset of language modeling constructs. Archi also provides ability to the user for definition of properties as (name, value) couples, which can be used as a way for annotating an Archi model. In addition, Archi is open source and is an implementation of reference of the open ArchiMate standard, which is a mature standard, as several implementations are available, being on top of commercial or free open source solutions. It makes Archi an appropriate ground for including ArchiMate as a branch of an extended hypermodel for interoperability [3].

1.3   Problem Statement

Within the last research projects contributing to the establishment of the federated interoperability framework for PLM Interoperability, i.e. IMAGINE and SIP@ SystemX, different ways of using Archi have been explored:

- Modeling of the goals, objectives, capabilities, work package, outputs and infrastructure for supporting better communication and decision making between industrial program participants, clients and involved architects and realization teams (e.g. A380 program with about 50 first level sub-contractors and many Airline companies as clients). It is facilitated by the ability to visually represent and interconnect motivation, business, application, technologies, implementation and migration.
- Definition of Blueprint and blueprint templates for design and monitoring of a DMN (IMAGINE), with combination of contract model derived from the decomposition of a product (e.g. Airbus' A380) as a set of configuration items (e.g. SNECMA engine), each configuration item being developed by an enterprise which will be a node of the DMN, partner blueprints, cross organizational collaboration process (e.g. external change management, Technical Data Package secured interchange) blueprints, collaboration capabilities blueprints including collaborative manufacturing PLM hub on the cloud (realized by the cPlatform) and each partner capabilities which are to be involved and interconnected during collaborative product development (e.g. PDM systems of partners for their respective products)

- High level AS IS and TO BE high level representations of interconnected Platform models, Platform Independent Models, Business models and Motivation models
- Definition of blueprints of standards and underlying framework related to manufacturing PLM (e.g. ISO 10303, ISA 95) and System Engineering standards (e.g. ISO15288), Enterprise process standards (e.g. ArchiMate), Application family (e.g. PDM) standards or ICT standards (e.g. XML technologies), as inputs for being able to define how to jointly combine them all along their lifecycle in order supporting PLM interoperability with a DMN. A fist target is being able to use it for appropriate functional and non-functional specifications by the enterprises for implementation by software solutions, testing, deployment, integration and support. A second target is to support demonstration of appropriate and effective usage for supporting enterprise objectives, goals and processes.
- Definition of a model based approach for assessing PLM standards and their implementation through a test based approach, on top of a test bed which will allow in a first phase to simulate the expected collaboration in a DMN using the standards for targeted business collaboration scenarios, and in a second phase to validate implementations of the standards for supporting these scenarios reusing simulation process, scenarios and data for unitary and integration testing. Implementations of the standards concerns as well software products, applications, methods and business processes within the DMN, and between the partners, their applications and their specific business processes

Doing so, several issues arose concerning usage of model based enterprise modeling relying on Archi within PLM interoperability within System Engineering and manufacturing DMN context.

First ArchiMate scope and intent of use is not the same than other standardized languages such as UML used for Software development, BPMN used for Business Process modeling or XPDL used for design of workflow models and their execution on workflow engines. It's the reason why methods and tools build on top of Archi and enterprise modelling are to be interconnected with methods and tools relying on such standardized languages and associated modeling languages and platforms, implying to properly manage the produced models as consistent sets of artefacts, their relationships with used modeling platform and targeted enterprise execution platforms.

Second Archi is a modeling tool built on top of Eclipse that can be used only on a personal desktop. A single model is produced within a single XML file, but with multiple views. No capabilities exist allowing combining several model trunks, produced by different persons or tools (e.g. self-describing enterprise applications). Or the different blueprint models for support of a DMN have to be produced independently by several organizations and tools as separate artefacts, using ArchiMate with Archi, but also other languages and related modeling tools. As a consequence, as for a manufactured Product, Enterprise data management solution, similar to Product Data Management solutions, are required for collaborative production and consumption of Enterprise models.

Third the enterprise applications underlying conceptual models and the enterprise modeling language are not based on the same meta model and on the same semantic. They are also not implemented on the same technologies: implementation languages for the applications, including programming and serialization languages for applications, including modeling meta-language, notations but also programming and serialization languages of the underlying modeling platforms. As a consequence, the model transformation chain is complex when willing to support Model Based Enterprise Collaboration engineering with proper technical data package interchange within a DMN.

This paper describes a new approach for resolving the identify issues.

2 State of the Art and State of the Practice

2.1 State of the Art Combined with Technologies Assessment

Figay and Ghodous [4] presents the NEFFICS platform which combines an open innovation social media platform with a business modelling and operations platform, and provides a foundation for cloud based open business model innovation, process innovation and service innovation for networked enterprises. It combines usage of Value Delivery Modeling Language (VDML), of the Business Process Model and Notation (BPMN), of the Case Management Model and Notation (CMMN) and of Service Modelling Language (ServiceML) which extends the Service oriented architecture Modeling Language (SoaML).

Analyzing the NEFFICS architecture as described by Fig. 1, the platform appears as innovate platform embedding extended business process designers and dedicated engine. What is targeted as collaboration execution platform is integration of standardized enterprise application components, such as Enterprise Service Bus, respectively Enterprise Workflow System, Enterprise Portal, Enterprise Application Server, and Enterprise repository, based on a consistent set of mature open standards, respectively Java Business Integration, Wfmc'XPDL, Enterprise Java beans and LDAP, for which numerous interchangeable COTS are available on the market. The aim is ability of having interchangeable components, without being specific platform, component or product dependent. As a consequence, NEFFICS platform can't be the target. Due to the fact that both modeling and execution platforms are integrated in NEFFICS, needs for model transformation chain is not addressed in NEFFICS. Such a chain is important in particular for integration of manufacturing PLM standards.

Taentzer et al. [5] points out interest of model driven software engineering which emphasizes on model as primary artifacts in all phases of software development, from requirements analysis over system design to implementation, deployment, verification and validation. It should allow coping with intrinsic complexity of software intensive systems by raising the level of abstraction, and by hiding the complexity of the underlying technology as much as possible. However it requires installing a sophisticated mechanism of model transformation, which enables a wide range of different automated activities such as translation of models (expressed in different modeling languages), generating code from models, model refinement, model synthesis, model extraction and model refactoring. It proposes EMF refactoring usage in a transformation chain based on the AndroMDA tool for model driven software development. We assessed AndroMDA in ATHENA and OpenDevFactory projects. One issue

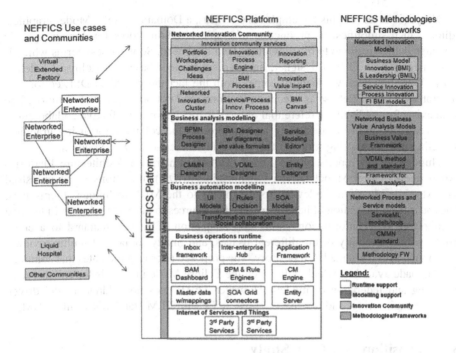

Fig. 1. The NEFFICS platform

identified comes from the fact that Platform Models are not provided and that transformation is based on velocity, which is not a model to text solution. Underlying technology is really hidden, making it difficult to establish communication between the functional and ICT infrastructure architects. Transformation and deployment logic is hidden and very difficult to correct or debug when something is going wrong. Finally, creating Platform Independent model from PLM standards is an important manual task. Transforming these standards formalization in Domain Specific Language, as UML profiles or as MOF/EMF based DSL, should allow generating the PIM from models of the PLM and System engineering standards, which include as well domain information models (e.g. ISO STEP application protocols, ISA 95), business processes (e.g. ISO15288, SCOR) or business services (e.g. OMG's PLM Services). An issue here is that formal language for specifying the standards are heterogeneous implementation languages which are not necessarily the one used in the execution platform. E.g. a STEP application protocol is formalized in EXPRESS, while languages considered by the targeted execution platform are based on AndroMDA profiles, which consider Manageable entities, value objects, services (local, remote, web), internal processes and user/machine interface interaction processes. Platform targeted for PLM hub are quite more complex than the one targeted by AndroMDA, and being able capturing infrastructure as visual model with appropriate DSL is an important need. Finally, hiding the infrastructure as aimed by model software driven engineering is not accurate when willing ensuring that infrastructure fits with enterprise motivation and when willing to deal appropriately with deployment and evolution.

Vivyovic et al. [6] puts the emphasis on Sirius, a Domain Specific Model graphical editor, which simplifies the production of graphical editing tools for domain specific language, which respond to the previously identified need. So we assess Sirius which is now integrated on OBEO designer, an open source tool based on Eclipse Modeling Tools. One drawback we identify comes from the fact the graphical DSL editors are generated on top of Eclipse as execution Platform, and not on top of Web solution. The need exists for publishing a referential of models for supporting effective collaboration, and eventually ability of designing and monitoring the collaboration using graphical modeling and monitoring tools on the web using the created DSL notation.

Hugo et al. [7] reports on the TEAP (TOGAF Enterprise Architecture Platform) experience to target Model Driven Organization (MDO) limitations in an industrial context while identifying relevant improvements to the MDE techniques themselves. The focus is on federation of heterogeneous data sources to integrate relevant Enterprise Architecture (EA) information, more easy adaptation of an EA standard to a client needs, with traceability of the different usages, and finally support of multiple views/ viewpoints over the same EA repository. The proposed approach indicates that solutions will be made available, which will enrich the Eclipse Modeling Tools for collaborative modeling and federation of models. However TEAP does not address model driven software engineering, and doesn't establish links with PLM standards within a DMN.

3 Proposition and Case Study

In this part, we will introduce the model based approach for establishing PLM interoperability within a DMN, following by a case study.

3.1 Model of Reference for the Collaborative PLM Hub

Unlike the other platforms proposed for enterprise interoperability, we propose a simplified reference model in Archi capturing the principle of collaboration supported by the collaborative platform and the applicative components which will be required for the collaborative platform acting as a PLM hub. It includes applicative components for delivering horizontal services usually provided by standardized enterprise solutions (enterprise portal, enterprise service bus, enterprise workflow, enterprise application servers), as well as vertical services related to PLM: PDM repositories and transformation services related to technological frameworks associated to PDM standards: STEP, XML or UML for model exchange, web service and BPEL for distributed Web services and their composition, in order being able to interconnect distributed systems implementing OMG's or OASIS's PLM services. Such generic platform should support PLM business collaborations around a configuration item of an integrated product, for which a component will be provided by a provider, implying exchange of different kind of work orders with associated technical data package. The technical data package will contain product and process data and associated metadata. Figure 2 is a view combining a blueprint template for collaboration, associated to a generic applicative model of the cPlatform.

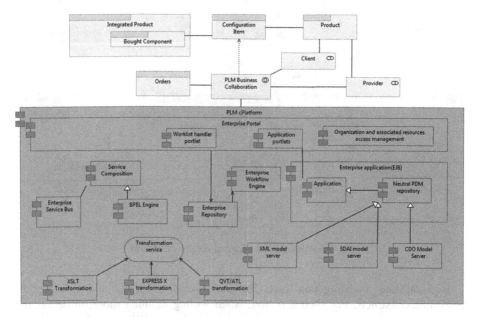

Fig. 2. ArchiMate model for cPlatform and supported collaboration

Each applicative component is associated to an open mature standard; all the selected standards have been chosen in order allowing their combination in order covering all the interoperability needs.

It is expected that each application (e.g. PDM system) of the partners involved in the collaboration will rely on standardized service contract elected by the considered digital business ecosystem, here Aeronautic, Space and Defense. Figure 3 is a view capturing the fact that PDM systems of the partners are interconnected through standardized contract, the OMG's PLM services.

The composition of the services is to be realized through cross organizational workflow process models enacted on the enterprise workflow model. Client's and Provider' PDM are (automate) participants of the workflow model, and the tasks they have to realize consist in invocation of operations defined in the PLM standard. Inputs and outputs for the operations are typed according PLM standard for data exchange and sharing, STEP within the aeronautic context.

The cross organization process workflow process is formalized by mean of an orchestration model. If BPMN 2.0 allows modeling orchestration models, it also supports modeling of conversation, collaboration and choreography that can't be executed. However, unlike Wfmc specifications, no architecture of reference is provided with BPMN. Wfmc provides XML process Definition language, which can be distributed between workflow designers and workflow engines provided by different software providers. In addition, since version 2, XPDL was extended with BPMN notation. In addition, only XPDL includes in the meta model task which are to be distributed to work list handlers or to applications.

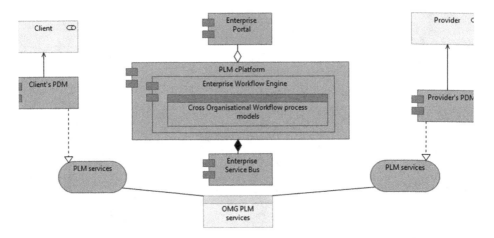

Fig. 3. Applications plugged on the cPlatform

If ArchiMate modeling constructs include processes, activity and task are not ArchiMate constructs. For such a reason, when willing defining more on details the collaboration processes, the link must be established with XPDL process models a consistent way. It can be done first by associating workflow process model data object and related artefact at ICT layer with the XPDL model defining a generic collaboration process: all the participants are roles defined in the ArchiMate model. Eventually, workflow process activity model can also be captured in ArchiMate, with a detailed view and by typing activities in the view as XPDL: activity. So some complementary constraints are to be put on the view in order ensuring alignment with the XPDL representation (hypermodel for interoperability approach).

The same approach is to be applied with services and data objects. Description of services with ArchiMate doesn't support capture of operations, which is a too low grain of detail. Description of data doesn't support capture of entities. So it will be needed associating services and data objects in Archi with representation based on other languages, supporting the appropriate level of detail. It can be UML for software design (deployment and component diagrams), EXPRESS, XML Schema, Json or EJB entities for data serialization, WSDL for web services, etc. Similarly, ICT layer can be mapped with underlying network and eventually virtualization servers (e.g. ProxMox) allowing automated generation of virtual network or creation of views querying the virtualization servers. At business layer, such mapping can be done with models using more rich languages such as BPMN, IDEF0 or SPEM. For motivation views, it can be mapped with more detailed decision models. Finally implementation and migration views can be related to project planning models. Archi model can be use as integration model dedicated to communication between the different architects and stakeholders, in order aligning CIM, PIM and PM models.

Two model transformation chains, one for software artefacts generation and deployment on the cPlatform, based on solution such as AndroMDA, one for model to model generation and DSL integration, based on solution such as Obeo Designer.

3.2 Blueprint Template for Manufacturing PLM Standards

Numerous types of manufacturing PLM standards have been produced, providing several frameworks for system engineering processes, product data exchange, sharing and long term archiving, PLM services, CAD services, etc.

Such processes don't aim at standardizing the business processes or the software tools. It is the reason why important work is still to be done when willing to implement them and to use them in operational context, as the link is to be made with the specific context, i.e. the actual processes and operational platforms.

In order facilitating assessment and implementation of the standards, our approach allows to produce blueprints describing the standards in order helping each stakeholders, and in particular the architects referenced in the ArchiMate specification (enterprise, process, information system, ICT technologies architects), to better understand how the proposed standards can be use. It also supports defining how the standards can be use together.

Such exercise has been performed on manufacturing standards for product and process data exchange, such as STEP and ISA95. Such standards adopted functional analysis in order capturing information flows between functions. Doing so, no process model is provided (orchestration). Activities of functional model can be mapped with activities of an orchestration model, and then associated to the task that will be distributed in order performing the activity. While relevant workflow data are exchanged between workflow engines and work list handler, application data flow is between workflow participants is not ensured by such system. As the definition of the actual participants is defined dynamically, the need for exchanging or sharing data is known at the very last time. The method for making data available between participants is then to be adapted to the context. In addition, data flow between functions is in fact to be mapped with data flow between participants realizing the tasks. The exception is for control flows, which will correspond to exchange between the participants and the workflow engine that control the distribution of task.

Here again, model transformation will be required for customizing the workflow systems and the data transportation services from data flow provided in such standards, e.g. from Application Activity Model in STEP application protocols, which is formalized using IDEF0. Similarly, ISA 95 provides the description of data flow between function without using a standardized language. This description was very easy to capture with Archi.

Similarly, process framework such as ISO15288 can be easily captured, as illustrated in Fig. 4. Such model can be used in order to produce cartography where usage of standards can be contextualized, as illustrated in Fig. 5.

Such models are inputs for model transformation which will allow to structure the workflow models of the cPlatform, and which will help the collaboration to rely on process of reference.

Other usage is to provide blueprint models for high level architecture of used technical solutions, of the ICT infrastructure or of the migration from an AS IS solution to a TO BE solution which will deal with ensuring continuous interoperability at an acceptable price.

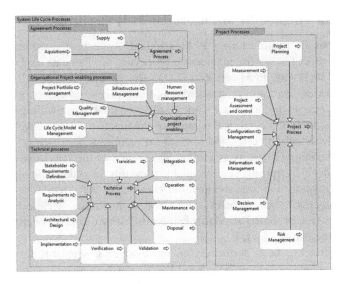

Fig. 4. ISO 15288 high level processes

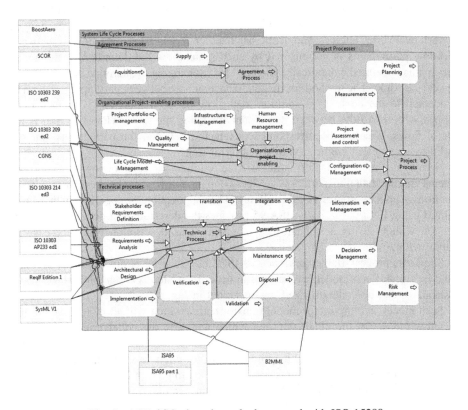

Fig. 5. ASD SSG elected standards mapped with ISO 15288

4   Conclusion and Future Work

In order preparing and building operational PLM interoperability within DMN, this paper proposes an innovative model driven approach which combines enterprise modeling, business modeling, information system modeling and ICT modeling. This approach has been developed through the IMAGINE project for DMN and the SIP@SystemX project, which aims at assessing PLM standards and their implementation on top of a test bed platform based on the cPlatform, and allowing to model use case, test scenarios and to managed them with test data in configuration. The future research in SIP will address simulation of DMN infrastructure and applications for industry being able to properly specify and prepare tests related to implementation of PLM standards to the software vendors, integrators and ICT departments, in alignment with enterprise strategy, processes and methods.

References

1. Product Lifecycle Management (PLM) Definition, CIMDATA (2009). https://www.cimdata. com/en/resources/about-plm
2. Figay, N., Ghodous, P.: Innovative interoperability framework for enterprise applications within virtual enterprises. In: MEDES 2009
3. Figay, N., Ghodous, P.: Extended hyper model for interoperability within the Virtual Enterprise. In: SITIS 2009
4. Berre, A.-J., de Man, H., Lew, Y., Elvesæter, B., Ursin-Holm, B.M.: Open business model, process and service innovation with VDML and ServiceML. In: Proceedings of the Standardisation for Interoperability in the Service-Oriented Enterprise Workshop, IWEI (2013)
5. Taentzer, G., Müller, D., Mens, T.: Specifying domain-specific refactorings for AndroMDA based on graph transformation. In: Schürr, A., Nagl, M., Zündorf, A. (eds.) AGTIVE 2007. LNCS, vol. 5088, pp. 104–119. Springer, Heidelberg (2008). http://dx.doi.org/10.1007/978-3-540-89020-1_9
6. Vivyovic, V., Maksimovic, M. , Perisic, B.: Sirius: a rapid developmet of DSM graphical editor. In: 2014 18th International Conference on Intelligent Engineering System (2014)
7. Hugo, B., Cabot, J., Frapeau, S., Somda, F., Piers, X., David, J., Calle, C., Lafaurie, J-C.: MDE support for enterprise architecture in an industrial context: the TEAP framework experience. In: AMINO 2013

Industrial Papers

PLM Standards Modelling for Enterprise Interoperability: A Manufacturing Case Study for ERP and MES Systems Integration Based on ISA-95

Emna Moones[1,2(✉)], Thomas Vosgien[1], Lyes Kermad[2],
El Mouloudi Dafaoui[2], Abderrahman El Mhamedi[2],
and Nicolas Figay[3]

[1] Technological Research Institute SystemX, Palaiseau, France
{emna.moones, thomas.vosgien}@irt-systemx.fr
[2] University Paris8, 140 Rue Nouvelle France, 93100 Montreuil, France
{l.kermad, e.dafaoui, a.elmhamedi}@iut.univ-paris8.fr
[3] Airbus Group Innovations, 12 Rue Pasteur, 92150 Suresnes, France
nicolas.figay@airbus.com

Abstract. Today Enterprise Interoperability is considered as a key factor of successful collaboration. It was identified as a critical need that has to be taken into account all along the lifecycle of a manufactured product. To deal with this problem and to reduce complexity of the different systems of interest used when different companies have to collaborate together, Enterprise Architecture (EA) and Enterprise Modelling (EM) are considered as solutions to facilitate Enterprise Interoperability. Dealing with interoperability issues in the context of Product Lifecycle Management (PLM), we have to mention the importance of product data and process standards implementation as interoperability enablers. In order to address the complexity of PLM standards, we propose to apply a model-driven methodology for modelling these standards and the related collaboration scenarios. This approach intends to make standards more comprehensive and to better manage standards evolutions, but also to instantiate and re-use these "generic" standards models to specify specific business collaboration scenarios. This proposal aims also to facilitate the exchange, testing and simulation of standards implementations. In this paper, the focus is on the ISA 95 standard for manufacturing-PLM integration, with an exchange scenario between Enterprise Resource Planning (ERP) and Manufacturing Execution System (MES) based on ISA 95 standard.

Keywords: Enterprise architecture · Enterprise interoperability · Manufacturing PLM standards · ERP/MES · ISA-95

1 Introduction

Nowadays in order to remain competitive within a global economic context where the complexity of products is still increasing, enterprises have been developing new strategic approaches such as the PLM approach. PLM is defined, by CIMDATA [1], as a

© IFIP International Federation for Information Processing 2015
M. van Sinderen and V. Chapurlat (Eds.): IWEI 2015, LNBIP 213, pp. 157–170, 2015.
DOI: 10.1007/978-3-662-47157-9_14

strategic approach aiming at setting-up appropriate processes related to production and consumption of product data, all along the different product lifecycle phases and across the whole supply chain. Along the product lifecycle phases, enterprise business functions and processes are supported by different PLM solutions including the Information System (IS) such as Product Data Management (PDM) systems for design engineering activities and configuration management, ERP and MES for manufacturing, business planning and logistic operations. PLM solutions include PLM Hubs, such as BoostAerospace.[1] In such a context, efficient, agile and interoperable IS and interfaces are required in order to ensure the continuity, consistency and integrity of the different/shared exchanged product and process data.

Governance of standards, as addressed by ASD SSG,[2] is facing difficulties when elected eBusinessPLM standards and associated PLM standardization enterprise policies have to be applied. New challenges related to factories and support taking advantage of emerging technologies are also to be considered in order to support competitiveness of enterprises. To deal with the context of PLM standards and their complexity, the Standard and Interoperability PLM (SIP[3]) project was launched within the frame of the IRT-SystemX.[4] The adopted approach in this project is based on a federating framework for interoperability of technical enterprise applications [2]. While different projects such as INTEROP [3] and ATHENA [4] has addressed the interoperability of enterprise applications relying on a common Application Interoperability Framework (AIF), our approach also relies on a federative interoperability framework defined by [2]. This framework defines a pragmatic methodology for preparing and building operational interoperability (as defined by System Of System Interoperability (SOSI) [5]) at an acceptable price for Dynamic Manufacturing Network (DMN) [6, 7].

SIP project aims at extending the federative network by addressing new identified brakes, in particular the importance to be able to assess standards and their implementations to support DMN collaboration. It introduces and analyses the ArchiMate standard as a way to properly rely on enterprise modelling as a key enabler for dealing with the specification and simulation of DMN business collaboration scenarios in order to better prepare enterprise interoperability. The SIP methodology relies on the use of a test bed allowing execution and simulation of DMN models. The testbed is built on top of a collaborative platform constituting a hub for interconnection of technical enterprise applications. It integrates enterprise collaboration technical solutions (enterprise portal, enterprise service bus, enterprise workflow system, etc.) using appropriate open standards. It also integrates PLM standard-based technical solutions for product data exchange and sharing, with appropriate applicative services. On such a platform, the test bed introduces testing specification, development and management of capabilities applying Model-Based System Engineering (MBSE).

The issue addressed in this paper concerns the reasons for modelling PLM standards and the way to model these standards so that we can re-use these models to

---

[1] http://www.boostaerospace.com/.

[2] http://www.asd-ssg.org/.

[3] http://www.irt-systemx.fr/project/sip/.

[4] http://www.irt-systemx.fr/.

specify and simulate standards-based collaboration scenarios. The idea is also to investigate the use of such approaches to specify testing procedures and related validation properties for assessing standards implementations.

In this context, we propose to apply and extend the SIP methodology on business manufacturing data exchange business cases and particularly for enabling efficient data integration between ERP and MES systems.

Section 2 hence provides a state of the art about enterprise modelling approaches languages and tools. Based on the literature, it also explains how the interoperability of business processes could be achieved by using models. A second sub-section of the state of the art present the used ISA-95 standard for ERP and MES systems integration. Section 3 introduce our proposal and illustrates how we managed to model different aspects of the ISA-95 standard. Finally we also introduce in this section the DEKENZ case study in which we specify a data exchange and integration scenario between an ERP system and different MES systems re-using and instantiating the ISA 95 standard model. Conclusions and future work are presented in Sect. 4.

2 State of the Art

Interoperability is the ability of several systems, whether identical or radically different, to communicate without ambiguity and operate together [8]. Considering a PLM strategy in a DMN context, standardized interfaces between processes and supporting resources (human and ICT resources) are required in order to ensure the continuity, consistency and integrity of the different shared/exchanged product and process data all along the product lifecycle and across business domains. As a result PLM Standards have largely been identified in the literature as interoperability enablers [2, 9]. A PLM standard is not only a technical solution for product data exchange but also a strategic answer that has to consider:

- The strategic business motivations of the organizations involved in the DMN;
- The business engineering needs of the addressed collaboration processes;
- The human and applicative resources supporting these business processes that intend to become interoperable;
- The ICT systems in which standards will be implemented;
- The technological solutions for using standardized data format;
- The infrastructures permitting to organizations to connect their applications and to share/exchange their standardized process and product data.

Therefore, PLM standards are very complex and hence difficult and costly to implement. One way to address this complexity is to model these standards and related business cases using Enterprise Architecture Modelling considering these different dimensions. One of the goal of this paper is to study these frameworks to use and/or to extend them in view to specify and model standards-based business collaboration scenarios. The finality is then to be able to simulate these scenarios to prepare and build the interoperability of future DMNs.

2.1   Enterprise Architecture Modelling for PLM Interoperability

An enterprise architecture (EA) description is usually very complex, because it comprises a large set of components and relationships between them. EA is a coherent whole of principles, methods and models that are used in the design and realisation of the enterprise's organisational structure, business processes, information systems, and infrastructure [10]. However, in practice, these domains are not approached in an integrated way. Every domain speaks its own language, draws its own models, and uses its own techniques and tools. According to [11], architecture allows managing complexity and risks due to various factors such as technology, size, interface, context and stakeholders. Therefore, it is important that EA can be represented with relevant information and at the appropriate level of detail for individual stakeholders. More generally, EA must show properties that can be verified with respect to user needs (e.g. open or closed architecture, interoperable or not, centralized or decentralized, etc.) [11]. It must be simple so that business people can easily understand, check, analyse, discuss in a 'language' shared at the corporate level. According to [11] enterprise architecture models describe the EA from various viewpoints to allow specifying and implementing the systems. For this purpose, numerous approaches, methods and frameworks (e.g. Zachman [12], CIMOSA [13], TOGAF [14]) have been developed to consider these different viewpoints related with different stakeholders.

In literature, it is possible to distinguish between simple methods of representation (SADT, IDEFx, GRAI, IEM, etc.) and reference architectures (CIMOSA, ARIS, PERA, GERAM, GIM, etc.). These latter offer a set of structured methods with a methodology to be followed to build the model. But, these methods are, in most cases, difficult to implement. In other cases, we note the existence, according to the viewpoints, of different languages that must be studied and mastered. Moreover, the models defined according to these different viewpoints are related and when a change occurs on one model, the consistency of the impacted related models must be insured. However, due to the heterogeneity of the methods and techniques used to document the architectures, it is very difficult to determine how the different domains are interrelated. Still, it is clear that there are strong dependencies between the domains [10]. Also, it should be possible to visualise models in a different way, tailored towards specific stakeholders with specific information requirements.

For all these reasons, we propose a modelling methodology based on the TOGAF framework and the ArchiMate[5] enterprise architecture language due to its ability to model an enterprise system interrelating domain specific architectures and cross-domain relationships. The ArchiMate language divides the enterprise architecture into a business, applicative and technological layer. In each layer, three aspects are considered: active elements that exhibit behaviour (e.g. Process and Function), an internal structure and elements that define use or communicate information. The use of ArchiMate language in our methodology allows us to model different system architectures. First it is used to model the standard architecture itself and related test procedures. Secondly it used to specify business collaboration processes and their related

---

[5] http://www.opengroup.org/subjectareas/enterprise/archimate.

applicative and technological chains. Finally it also used to specify the as-is and to-be applicative and technological integration platforms as well as the different SIP "test beds".

2.2 ISA-95 a Standard for ERP and MES Systems Integration

While addressing the role of PLM standards it is important to distinguish the different types of standards included in the scope of a PLM approach. Moreover, the interoperability across system information might be addressed distinguishing the product or system taken into account. The global and main role of information exchange standards is to reduce the number of inter-change protocols from the unmanageable multitude of one-to-one interchanges to a finite number of distinct and meaningful compositions of coherent information across time, space and multiple disciplines [9].

In our context, we are particularly interested by the ISA 95 standard developed to address interoperability issues between ERP systems and MES. ISA-95 is defined according to [15] as the international standard for the integration of enterprise and control systems. It consists of models and terminology that can be used to determine which information has to be exchanged between systems for sales, finance, logistics, production, maintenance and quality. Four functional levels are defined by ISA 95 standard. Levels 0, 1 and 2 are the levels of process control. Their objective is the control of equipment, in order to execute production processes that end in one or more products. Level 3 could be called the level of MES activities, it consists of several activities that must be executed to prepare, monitor and complete the production process that is executed at level 0, 1 and 2. The highest level (level 4) could be called the level of enterprise, including ERP systems and PDM Systems. At this level financial and logistic activities are executed in order to produce the product configuration ordered by the client. Next section, which introduces the proposed methodology, also provides extracts of the ISA-95 standard modelled with the use of the ArchiMate language.

3 Proposed Methodology and Case Study

In this section, the SIP methodology and the use of ISA-95 standard are introduced. The SIP methodological modelling framework is presented and its application is illustrated first by modelling the ISA-95 standard and secondly specifying/modelling an information exchange scenario between ERP and MES based on ISA-95.

3.1 SIP Methodology

SIP methodology aims at validating a set of coherent PLM standards and their implementations. The first objective is to develop an innovative interoperability framework (shown in Fig. 1) in order to provide a model-driven methodology for the development of a PLM standards assessment test bed which will be implemented as a service.

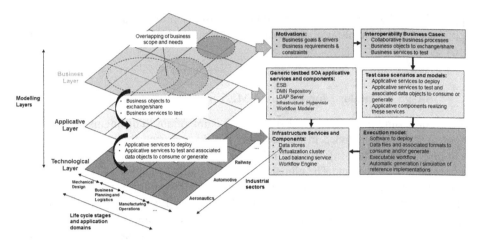

Fig. 1. SIP methodological modelling framework

First of all, we have to model the DMN and the strategic motivations of the different stakeholders. Still on the business layer, the second step consists in collecting and modelling interoperability business cases and related exchange and test scenarios. The supporting applicative chains that supports these scenarios are then specified at the applicative layer. Finally the execution model to simulate is modelled to prepare the appropriate test bed infrastructure configuration. In parallel the framework also provides architectural viewpoints to specify the generic and specific applicative and technological components of the test bed. This figure is not fully representative of the SIP framework since it does not include the step consisting in modelling PLM standards. However next section illustrates the way of performing this step using Archi-Mate language to model ISA-95.

Moreover, using models instead of text documents enables first to constitute a knowledge base of PLM standards models. These models should include a set of reusable standards-based collaboration templates of the different functional modules of the standard. A PLM standard can specify the supported business processes, as well as the product and process data models to implement in ICT systems., we will have a multi-layer view with the modelling of the processes (organizational layer), the data models (applicative layer) and specifying the software solutions (technological layer). Cross this way, modelling the standard allow us to show the link between the different layers, the information flow between each layer. Also with this method, we can put in place the exchange protocols described in the documentation of the standard, we can define a validation properties for the implementation of the standard and we will construct a templates of the standard that can be exploited in various specific implementation scenarios. The test and the validation will be based on the generation of recommended practices, test processes with the integration of real applications and single test, all this to generate solutions which implement standards and which can be easily integrated [6, 7].

3.2 The ISA-95 Standard

In this part we will introduce the structure of the ISA-95 standard and the application of the SIP methodology for modelling the standard with ArchiMate.

3.2.1 Content and Structure of the Standard

The ISA-95 standard is structured in five parts. The first part presents the models and terminologies for analysing and exchanging information between level 4 (ERP) and level3 (MES). The second part shows the data models in order to standardize the structure and the information flows defined by part 1. In part 3 ISA-95 defines the four operations group that it covers in manufacturing activities which are: Production, Maintenance, Quality and Inventory operations. Part 4 specifies the informational flow between the four types of operations defined in part 3. Finally part 5 standardizes the implementation format and transactions data messages which transit between ERP systems and MES systems.

3.2.2 Modelling ISA-95 with ArchiMate

Based on the ISA-95 specifications [16], we have modelled a set of reusable ISA-95-based collaboration templates of the different functional modules of the standard. This templates intend to be re-used in specific business collaboration scenarios requiring a strong ERP-MES integration. Figure 2 represents the functional model of ISA-95 gathering the several functions covered by the MES and the ERP and the information flow between these business functions. Indeed the functions supported by the ERP systems are: Order processing, Product cost accounting, Product shipping admin, Procurement, Research development and engineering. The MES supports the following functions: Production control, Quality assurance, Maintenance management. The rest of the functions which are Production scheduling, Product inventory control, Material and energy control are supported by both the ERP and the MES systems. Our ISA-95 model also includes several levels of abstraction providing more detailed views of these functions which are not shown in this paper. These standardized business functions will be re-used in the frame of case study described in Sect. 4.

In Fig. 3 the business functions of Fig. 2 have been categorized according to their belonging to the higher level business functions "Business Planning & Logistics" and "Manufacturing operations management" corresponding respectively to level 4 (supported by ERP and PDM system) and level 3 (supported by MES) of ISA-95 mentioned in Sect. 2.2. For instance, the functional level 3 is sub-divided in four sub-functions: Production, Maintenance, Quality and Inventory operations management. Different levels of abstraction appear in this diagram since all these sub-functions are also detailed with activities sequencing diagrams as defined in the ISA-95 standard.

Figure 3 also details the standardized data flows between these business functions. According to ISA-95 documentation, four categories of information are exchanged between the business and the manufacturing layers: schedule information, product definition information, performance information and product capability information. Each of these categories is also sub-divided into four sub-categories of data flows corresponding to the information consumed or generated by the level 3 sub-functions. For instance, the schedule information category includes production schedules,

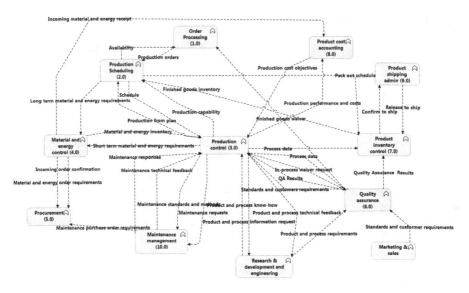

Fig. 2. Functional model of ISA-95in ArchiMate

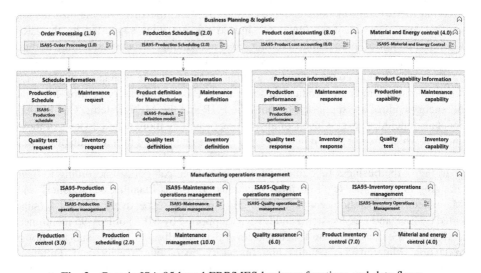

Fig. 3. Generic ISA-95-based ERP/MES business functions and data flows

maintenance requests, quality test requests and inventory requests. Each of these business objects are also detailed at the applicative layer to represent the various standardized data models defined by ISA-95. Figure 4 shows the product definition model as defined by ISA-95 in part 2 and permitting to define the shared information between product production rules, bill of materials and bill of resources. One limit of ArchiMate we had to deal with when capturing the information model of ISA95, which

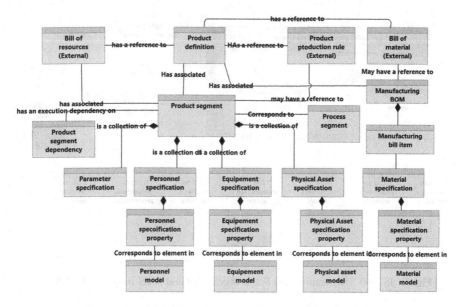

Fig. 4. ISA-95 Product definition object model in ArchiMate

is formalized in UML, is the missing ability of the language to capture reflexive relationship.

To exchange these data in standardized way, ISA-95 also defines the way to structure the transaction messages which transit between business and manufacturing layers. The different kind of ISA-95 transactions data set are represented in Fig. 5 where the content, structure and implementation ISA-95 format are defined. An ISA-95 transaction data set is first composed of an "application identification area" which includes information about the origin of the message and where it will be transmitted. It includes a "data area" which includes a "verb area" for sending a demand (get, change, cancel, etc.) or responding to a demand (show, confirm, respond, etc.) and the "noun area" specifying the kind of exchanged data objects (as defined in part 2 of ISA-95). The "noun area" contains the standardized information models as defined in part 2 and implemented in an ISA-95 compliant XML format: the Business To Manufacturing Mark-up Language (B2MML). The transaction message is based on three models, a pull model where a user of data requests the data from a provider of the data, a push model where a provider of data requests an action (processing, changing, or cancelling) on the data by another user and a publish model where the owner of data publishes it to users (subscribers) of the data.

This section introduced some extracts of the ISA-95 ArchiMate model. This model includes reusable ISA95-based collaboration templates, such as the ones shown in Fig. 3. In the next section these templates are re-used to model and specify an inter-operability business case study.

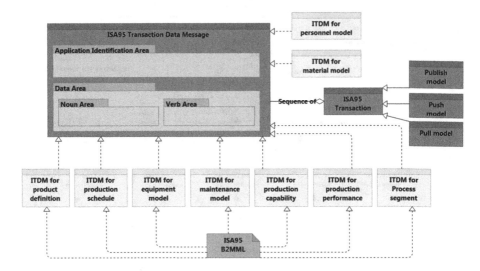

Fig. 5. ISA-95 Transaction Data Set between ERP and MES model in ArchiMate

3.3   Modelling and Specifying ISA-95-Based Data Exchange Scenarios with ArchiMate

DEKENZ[6] is a French company specialized in the development, the fabrication and the marketing of pens with the particularity that its labour is mainly ensured by students located in different universities in France. The objective of this concept was to provide to universities an operational training to the functioning of a company. The finished DEKENZ pen showed in Fig. 6 is a pen mainly composed of Aluminium. It is composed of a cap assembly (itself composed of cap, a cap stopper, a staple and an inner clip), a body assembly (itself composed of a body tube, a quill, a body stopper, a nose and a ring), a quill and a cartridge.

As shown on Fig. 7, the production of the cap and of the stopper as well as the integration of the cap and body assemblies is performed by students at "La Halle Technologique" of the IUT Montreuil.[7]

Figure 8 represents the business layer of the ERP-MES data integration scenario of the DEKENZ case study. The manufacturing process of this product is modelled on the bottom of the Fig. 8. On top of the Fig. 8 are represented the business planning and logistics operations of the scenario; i.e. the pen production order creation, the production planning creation according to the Manufacturing Bill of Materials (MBOM) and to the inventory level of the pen components. In the middle of the Fig. 8, the ISA-95 model shown in Fig. 3 is instantiated and re-used for this scenario permitting hence

---

[6] DEKENZ website: http://pm.flamant.free.fr/dekenz/?p=accueil.

[7] IUT Montreuil website: http://www.iut.univ-paris8.fr/.

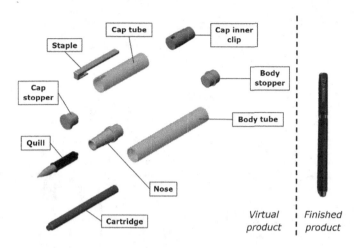

Fig. 6. DEKENZ product – Pen sub-components CAD models on the left and the finished product on the right

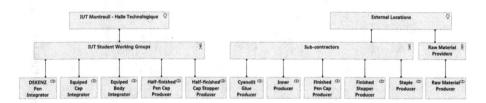

Fig. 7. DEKENZ case study - Map of actors and their roles

to specify the standardized data flows between the IUT ERP system and the IUT and the sub-contractors MES systems. For this paper we first focused on the exchange of MBOMs and production schedules/orders from the IUT ERP system and the MES systems but as well on the exchange of production performance and production capability information from the MES systems to the IUT ERP system.

Figure 9 below illustrates the To-Be applicative architecture supporting such a scenario as well as the data flows mentioned previously.

One limit of ArchiMate we had to deal with is the missing modelling construct "as-is" as we can find it in the Ontology Web Language, e.g. when willing to capture that a software system (ICT layer) is an instance of a software product (Business Layer) with an architecture (Applicative Layer) shared by all the instances of the product.

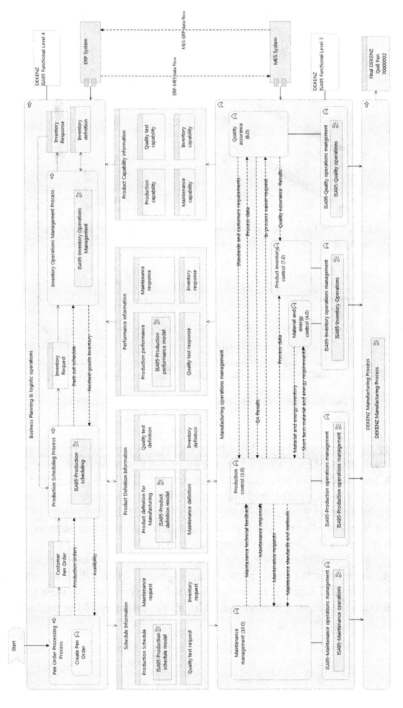

Fig. 8. DEKENZ Case study – ERP-MES data integration scenario

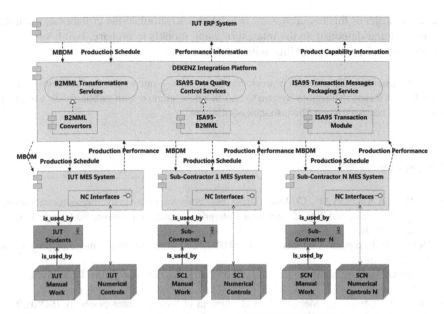

Fig. 9. To-Be applicative architecture for the DEKENZ ERP-MES integration scenario

4   Conclusion and Future Work

This paper intends to demonstrate how the use of enterprise architecture modelling languages could contribute to better specify and prepare interoperability business cases. Extending the SIP methodology, this paper introduces a manufacturing case study for ERP and MES systems integration based on the ISA-95 standard. Some extract of the ISA-95 ArchiMate model are shown to illustrate the approach and the interest of re-using templates of these models to be re-used in different collaboration scenarios. Last section shows how the templates have been re-used and instantiated in the context of the DEKENZ ERP-MES integration scenario. The next steps will be:

- To instantiate the ISA-95 object models with the concrete DEKENZ case study data (MBOM, Production schedules, etc.).
- To create the related B2MML files to understand and analyse this implementation solution in view to develop the future B2MML converters and quality checkers.
- To create the related ISA-95 compliant transaction data messages.
- Define the quality control procedures to assess the conformity to the standard and to verify the content of the exchanged B2MML files.
- Perform the mapping with the IUT ERP data model and the MES systems data models in order to further specify and/or develop the B2MML converters.
- Specify and/or develop the ISA-95 B2MML quality checkers.
- Address the limitations of the ArchiMate language by proposing some extensions to the community.

One of the target of this research work is to be able to simulate the collaboration on the SIP test bed and demonstrate the interest of using models to prepare, build, verify and validate enterprise interoperability with models.

Acknowledgments. This research work has been carried out under the leadership of the Technological Research Institute SystemX, and therefore granted with public funds within the scope of the French Program "Investissements d'avenir".

References

1. CIMDATA About PLM – CIMdata (2014). https://www.cimdata.com/en/resources/about-plm
2. Figay, N.: Interoperability of Technical Enterprise Application. Université Claude Bernard Lyon 1 (2009)
3. INTEROP European Commission: CORDIS (2007). http://cordis.europa.eu/project/rcn/71148_en.html
4. ATHENA Interoperability Framework v2.0 - NEHTA. "Interoperability Framework. v2.0" (2007)
5. Morris, E., Levine, L., Meyers, C, et al.: System of Systems Interoperability (SOSI): final report (No. CMU/SEI-2004-TR-004). Software Engineering Institute, Carnegie-Mellon University Pittsburgh, PA (2004)
6. Figay, N., Tchoffa, D., Ghodous, P., et al.: Dynamic manufacturing network, PLM hub and business standards testbed. In: Mertins, K., Bénabe, F., Poler, R., Bourrières, J.-P. (eds.) Enterprise Interoperability VI, pp. 453–463. Springer, Switzerland (2014)
7. Moones, E., Figay, N., Vosgien, T., et al.: Towards an extended interoperability systemic approach for dynamic manufacturing networks: role and assessment of PLM standards. In: Boulanger, F., Krob, D., Morel, G., Roussel, J.-C. (eds.) Complex Systems Design and Management, pp. 59–72. Springer, Switzerland (2014)
8. Bourey, J.P., Grangel, R., Ducq, Y, et al.: Report on Model Driven Interoperability (2007)
9. Rachuri, S., Subrahmanian, E., Bouras, A., et al.: Information sharing and exchange in the context of product lifecycle management: role of standards. CAD Comput. Aided. Des. **40**, 789–800 (2008). doi:10.1016/j.cad.2007.06.012
10. Lankhorst, M.M.: Enterprise architecture modelling - the issue of integration. Adv. Eng. Inform. **18**, 205–216 (2004). doi:10.1016/j.aei.2005.01.005
11. Chen, D., Doumeingts, G., Vernadat, F.: Architectures for enterprise integration and interoperability: Past, present and future. Comput. Ind. **59**, 647–659 (2008). doi:10.1016/j.compind.2007.12.016
12. Zachman, J.A.: The Zachman framework for enterprise architecture, primer for enterprise engineering and manufacturing. CA Mag. **128**, 15 (2003). doi:10.1109/CSIE.2009.478
13. Kosanke, K., Vernadat, F., Zelm, M.: CIMOSA: enterprise engineering and integration. Comput. Ind. **40**, 83–87 (1999). doi:10.1016/S0166-3615(99)00016-0
14. TOGAF® Version 9.1. http://www.opengroup.org/togaf/. Accessed 11 Feburary 2015
15. Harjunkoski, I., Bauer, R.: Sharing data for production scheduling using the ISA-95 standard. 2:1–15 (2014). doi:10.3389/fenrg.2014.00044
16. ISA95, Enterprise-Control System Integration - ISA. https://www.isa.org/isa95/. Accessed 11 Feburary 2015

An Interface Pattern Model for Supporting Design of Natively Interoperable Systems

Vincent Chapurlat[✉], Nicolas Daclin, and Stéphane Billaud

LGI2P, Parc Scientifique G. Besse – Ecole Des Mines D'Alès,
30035 Nîmes Cedex, France
{vincent.chapurlat,nicolas.daclin,stephane.billaud}
@mines-ales.fr

Abstract. This article focuses on the interoperability feature seen as a specific requirement. Indeed, any complex system (e.g. a train, an organisation or an IT system) need to interact with other systems, thereby forming a heterogeneous environment. All these systems are not necessarily designed to function properly and efficiently with one another, whether from a conceptual, technical, behavioural or organizational standpoint. This paper highlights what seems to be relevant in terms of conceptual definitions and modelling framework whenever a (group) of engineer(s) intends to design what we call here a "natively interoperable system" or, at least, a system maximizing its interoperability capabilities. To proceed, as a first prerequisite, a definition of the concept of interoperability is here proposed for complex system engineering. The second prerequisite consists of establishing the needs of a design team assigned to design such "natively interoperable system". An interface pattern model with sufficient generic, formal and pragmatic qualities is then proposed and illustrated briefly.

Keywords: System interoperability · Natively interoperable systems · Design for interoperability · Interface pattern model

1 Introduction

Many examples from industry have highlight that a lack of interoperability of systems leads to delays, failures, dysfunctions or shortcomings all along these systems' life cycle; problems that can be much more manageable if they are characterized and detected earlier in the system's design stage. So, various research and development were focused on interoperability management problematic particularly over the last decade considering interoperability as an essential feature of any kind of technical or socio technical complex system (e.g. a transportation system or a Collaborative Network of Organisations [1]). The goal is to design a system able to assume its mission and for this able to maximize and maintain its abilities to interact efficiently with other systems (technical or sociotechnical, more or less complex themselves) in various situations, even more or less unpredictable, throughout its life cycle and without unwanted effects that can affect the behaviour of each systems involved in the interaction. In this sense an interaction, requested or not, consists to exchange and share items from different nature (digital i.e. data/information/knowledge, physical i.e. any kind of energy field, or material e.g. raw material, product, part, or waste).

© IFIP International Federation for Information Processing 2015
M. van Sinderen and V. Chapurlat (Eds.): IWEI 2015, LNBIP 213, pp. 171–185, 2015.
DOI: 10.1007/978-3-662-47157-9_15

Further, an interoperable system must perform efficiently its mission independently from other systems with which it must interact for achieving this mission. However, lot of systems are currently more or less designed in order to be integrated into a given and fully identified upper-level system. These practices limit drastically the analysis of the real expected system interoperability, for instance, in avoiding unexpected or reverse effects that the interface is unable to prevent or, failing this, to protect the system itself. Last, even if important recommendations and standards are now available for instance concerning Health Care systems [2], IT systems [3], or Defence systems [4] design, the notions of interoperability requirements, interoperability analysis issues, interface or interaction still remain poorly formalised in engineering activities.

This article aims to propose conceptual elements for supporting complex system design stage taking into account requested system's interoperability. The goal is to help engineers' teams to design a so-called "*natively interoperable system*". First, definitions of system interoperability and interoperability requirements, obviously, of *natively interoperable complex system* are proposed. Second, an interface pattern model is needed to face design issues of such systems. This is done adopting a set of pre-requisites conceptual and then generic definitions (processor, interaction, effect…) that can be applied to various nature of systems. The goal is to provide engineers with modelling language and, by evidence, a verification tooled approach allowing them to confirm and to check whether the considered system can avoid defects due to its interaction with other systems under all specified conditions via its interfaces.

2 System Interoperability/Interoperability Requirements

Definition of interoperability depends of the application domain[1] and authors e.g. [5–9]. The goal here is to propose and adopt (in this paper at least) a definition of system interoperability for the purpose of system design stage. Classically, interoperability is "*connecting people, data and diverse systems. The term can be defined either technically or comprehensively, in taking into account social, political and organizational factors*". Then, "*two or more devices are said interoperable if, under a set of conditions, the devices are able to successfully establish, sustain and, if necessary, break a link while maintaining a certain level of performance*". In technical systems, interoperability is "*a property of a product or system, whose interfaces are completely understood, to work with other products or systems, present or future, without any restricted access or implementation*". In socio-technical systems, it is defined as "*a property referring to the ability of diverse systems and organizations to work together*", i.e., to inter-operate.

---

[1] The reader can find various interoperability definitions used in this section in glossaries available on [last visited and checked 2011-04-12]: http://dli.grainger.uiuc.edu/glossary.htm, http://www.eu-share. org/glossary.html, www.csa.com/discoveryguides/scholarship/gloss.php, www.naccho.org/topics/ infrastructure/informatics/glossary.cfm, ec.europa.eu/transport/inland/glossary_en.htm,www.nato. int/docu/logi-en/1997/defini.htm, www.cs.cornell.edu/wya/DigLib/MS1999/Glossary.html, www. ibtta.org/Information/content.cfm, dli.grainger.uiuc.edu/glossary.htm, cloud-standards.org/wiki/index. php, en.wikipedia.org/wiki/Interoperability, wordnetweb.princeton.edu/perl/webwn, www.anzlic.org. au/glossary_terms.html

For instance, enterprise interoperability is defined as "*a cooperative arrangement established between public and/or commercial entities (authorities, parking facility operators, etc.), wherein tags issued by one entity will be accepted at facilities belonging to all other entities without degradation in service performance*". In the same manner, interoperability is considered as "*the ability of a system or product to work with other systems or products without special effort from the customer*". In the military field, NATO defines also interoperability as "*the ability of systems, units or forces to provide services to - and accept services from - other systems, units or forces and to use these services so exchanged to enable them to operate efficiently together*". Last, in transportation systems, interoperability seems to be achieved when "*a transport network [is suitable] for movements without breaking bulk*".

Thus we propose defining system interoperability as:

"*The set of abilities and associated capabilities of a system (namely "S" from now) that allow S to be and to stay able to exchange and work harmoniously with other systems from its upper level all along its life cycle:*"

- *To fulfil a common mission (i.e. the main function for which the overall system is designed), possibly time-bounded, while remaining able to perform its own mission and to reach its own objectives through the use of exchanged items with other systems then when S is interacting with these systems whatever may be their nature;*
- *In all specified operational situations (e.g. nominal functioning mode, or functioning modes when facing a risky situation) met throughout its life cycle;*
- *Reflecting the stakeholders' requirements under every specified situation.*

This capability indicates and allows assessing before, during or after the interaction - and when placed in its environment – that S does not require or result in major changes to its operations, structure or behaviour; consequently, its functional and non-functional requirements (performance, security, safety, ergonomics, human factors, etc.) are not altered. Moreover, this does not induce undue adverse effects (dysfunctions, risks) when S is achieving its mission independently of every other system".

As a consequence a natively interoperable system S is "*a system designed to maximize its ability to interoperate all along its life-cycle*". During S design stage, engineer has to consider carefully this expectation and shall "*[...] ensure the compatibility, interoperability and integration of all functional and physical interfaces and then ensure that system definition and design reflect the requirements for all system elements: hardware, software, facilities, people, and data*" [10]. To this purpose, one or several interfaces are requested. An **interface** is defined in [11] as "*a boundary across which two independent systems meet and act on or communicate with each other*". That requires, at least by adhering to published interface standards or by making use of a 'broker' of services able to assume interface role between S and other systems, possibly, "*on the fly*". Communication, synchronization or even exchange protocols must be defined and applied.

3   Interface Elements: Prolegomena

Let's recall briefly a set of concepts from the literature on system sciences [12–14] and some theoretical foundations of Systems Engineering defined as *"an interdisciplinary approach and means to enable the realization of successful systems* [socio-technical or technical systems]. *It focuses on defining customer needs and required functionalities early in the development cycle, documenting requirements, and then proceeding with design synthesis and system validation while considering the complete problem"* [15–17].

A **processor** aims to transform **items** (*digital* i.e. data/information/knowledge, *physical* i.e. any kind of energy field, or *material* e.g. raw material, product, part, or waste) transported by input **flows**, into new items transported by output flows, under the control of other flows and by using **resources** that support or are involved in processor functioning. As an example, S is a processor, a function, an activity or a process when considering its functional view; moreover, a component or an organizational unit involved in S is a processor when considering physical view (organic, organizational).

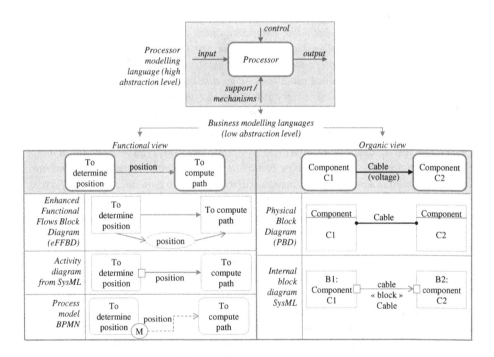

Fig. 1. From high abstraction level to low abstraction levels of modelling

Figure 1 shows the links between an abstract modelling language proposed in the SAGACE approach [13] and some equivalent notations used in various domains such as eFFBD (enhanced Functional Flows Block Diagram) [18], PBD (Physical Block Diagram), BPMN 2.0 (Business Processes Modelling Notation) [19], Activity or Internal Block Diagram from SysML [20]. So, all of the proposed concepts discussed below can be applied independently of the adopted modelling language. This step offers a freedom to the designer in choosing the most relevant modelling language when addressing system S interfaces design.

The processor behaviour is described by a **transformation** that details the inputs flows/outputs flows treatment provided by the processor. This transformation may be described by modelling the modification induced by the processor on one or more characteristics of each item transported by input flows, so as to obtain new or modified items transported by output flows. More generally, the characteristics of any concept are named formally Space, Shape, Time attributes i.e. **SST attributes** in the next: Space (e.g. type, definition domain, instantaneous value/default value…), Shape (e.g. optical, electromagnetic, signal, binary, or linked to the aspect of the pointed out item if it can be considered as dependent from one or several of five senses) and Time (update frequency, maximum life cycle before updating…) (Fig. 2).

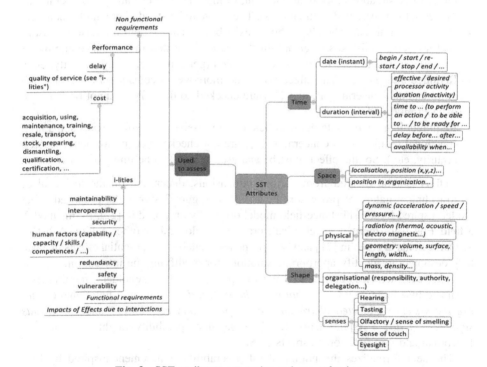

Fig. 2. SST attributes categories and examples in use

Analytical methods can be applied (1) to assess processor performance (e.g. in terms of costs, QoS or response time); and (2), to check some of the functional and/or non-functional **requirements** (e.g. by evaluating various "*-ilities*"[2]) the processor must respect in accordance with Stakeholders' expectations and constraints.

---

[2] « *developmental, operational and support requirements a program must address (e.g. availability, maintainability, vulnerability, reliability, or supportability)* » [15, 24] i.e. a kind of non-functional requirement (NFR).

An **interaction** is an oriented relation between an emitter processor P_1 and one or more receiver processors $\{P_2, ..., P_n\}$ denoted $\{P_i\}$. There is an interaction when (1) an exchange of one or more identified flows or service between P_1 and $\{P_i\}$ is identified and/or (2), one or more **fields** F generated by P_1 can impact $\{P_i\}$. An interaction is planned or desired, or alternatively unwanted or unintentional. In all cases, it can cause an **effect** if the interaction (1) affects one or more P_2 SST attributes, and/or (2), impacts the set of requirements (including interoperability requirements) to respect by $\{P_i\}$, in one of various characterized ways, that means [21]:

- Feared/Harmful. At least one characteristic of $\{P_i\}$ becomes inconsistent with the necessary conditions to survive. In this case, the identified relation causes the emergence of behaviours or physical phenomenon that are often inappropriate, such as resonances, electromagnetic interferences and thermal effects, thereby inducing rather risky situations (accident, incident, or malfunction) or damage to operational modes at the source and destination(s). They have to be avoided or simply modified.
- Required but absent. The effect should exist but remains absent for various reasons such as design mistakes or errors. In this case, some non-functional requirements concerning P_1 and $\{P_i\}$ have not been verified (performance, safety, security, etc.).
- Required and present. The effect exists and moreover is considered necessary. All requirements concerning P_1 and $\{P_i\}$ are checked so this effect cannot be removed or even modified.
- Required then appropriate but insufficient or excessive: The effect exists some non-functional requirements concerning $\{P_i\}$ are not checked yet (performance, safety, security, etc.). So, the effect must be analysed in order to be improved or reduced.

The **effect** can be derived from various dimensions, depending on the technical or socio-technical nature of processors P_1 and $\{P_i\}$. Figure 3 shows the proposed effect model inspired by the substance-field model originally proposed in [22]. In this model, a **field** F is from thermal, mechanical, pressure, biological or other nature. A list of available fields is given in [21] and [23] proposes a database of potential effects that can help designers to identify appropriate solutions for modifying the interaction.

After defining these concepts, S must respect [25, 26] stakeholders' requirements separated into functional (i.e. *"what must the system do?"*) and non-functional (*"what are the system's expected characteristics of performance, "-ilities" and constraints supposed to do?"*) requirements. In our case, interoperability might concern both functional and non-functional aspects of S.

The next formalizes the notion of interoperability requirement inspired by [27] (applied to collaborative processes).

These requirements are split up into 4 categories such as:

- **Compatibility.** S can send and receive flows from other systems in its environment whenever such interactions are needed. This ability is driven by respecting technical standards, communication protocols for technical compatibility or organizational rules and policies for organizational compatibility, described respectively as technical compatibility requirements e.g. required frequency of the exchange and organizational compatibility requirements. These must be recognized by all systems having to interact with S.

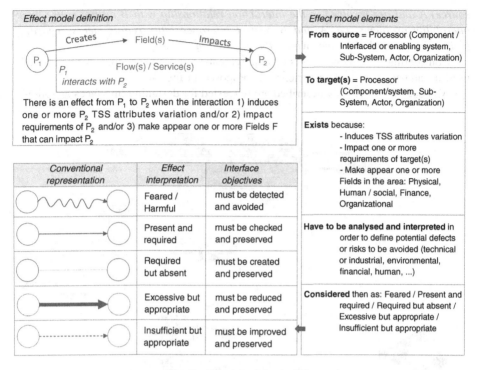

Fig. 3. Effect model principle

- **Inter-operation.** S operates seamlessly with the other systems in its environment by taking into account flows content being exchanged to fulfil its mission; moreover, it is able to control, adapt or anticipate problems promptly. S can also influence, not necessarily intentionally, other systems through both desirable and adverse effects. In this case, the term interoperation requirements could be referenced e.g. lifetime of any item transported before its obsolescence in taking into account states and modes of operation at the origin and relation target (ready, stop, etc.).

- **Autonomy.** S is independent of other system operations and behaviour. Autonomy may be decomposed into decisional autonomy (where S assumes its governance and remains capable of deciding actions) and operational autonomy (where S remains capable of preserving its performance in terms of cost, schedule and quality of service). At this point, it becomes necessary to consider decisional autonomy requirements and operational autonomy requirements.

- **Reversibility.** The relationships between S and the other systems are completely reversible, i.e. S can return to an identified configuration or state without causing any problems (dysfunctions, loss of performance, requirement violations, etc.) requiring difficult to manage changes once S no longer needs to exchange with the other systems in its environment. Relationship reversibility requirement is the term introduced here.

Last, a causality rule exists whereby: "*a processor A will be interoperable with processor B if all elements that compose (from different sources) or refine (from the same source) A and are involved in the interaction relationship with B do not cause inter-operability problems, i.e. A and B respect interoperability requirements regarding their own role and objectives within the interaction".*

Considering these new classes of requirements, requirements checklists classically used in industry can be then enriched as proposed in Fig. 4.

All concepts previously described are requested for designing interfaces as follows.

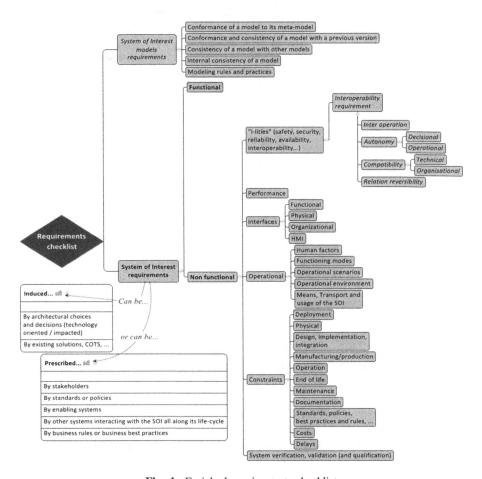

Fig. 4. Enriched requirements checklist

4   Interface Model Pattern

An interface is *"the common logical and/or physical border between two or more components* (here, processors) *or between the system* (a processor) *and its environment* (a upper-level processor), *at which the rules of exchange, compatibility, integrity and non-regression are to be respected throughout the system's life cycle".*

From a theoretical point of view, an interface allows P_1 and each P_i {P_i} to:

- Exchange the requested flow(s) or service(s). In due course, it must consider (in the receiver role) or make available (in the emitter role) the items carried out by the(se) flow(s) or requested by the service(s). Among other abilities, this set-up must:
  - Provide functional skills: emit, receive, transport, adapt (e.g. convert the input format of the exchanged flows), separate, protect, authorize the interaction, involve another processor, manage the items (e.g. store, retrieve), etc.
  - Respect all stakeholders' requirements, especially, interoperability requirements.
- Protect them from, or avoid, the potential effects induced by the interaction, or, at least, be able to contain the inappropriate effects within acceptable limits. To this purpose, its behaviour has to be adapted and/or a set of protection mechanisms or barriers must be designed to limit risky situations, for instance inspired by resilience engineering principles [28].

So we propose in the next an **interface pattern model** enabling engineers to model and analyse interactions between any type of systems and other systems composing the environment then to build and check interfaces.

An interface is conceptualized as a processor P intending to establish a connection between a processor P_1 (system, component, subsystem, business unit or actor) with its environment composed of a set of processors {P_i} in order to (*objective 1*) transport flows between P_1 and {P_i} (or vice versa) and/or (*objective 2*) protect from, in the sense of avoiding, unwanted effects between P_1 and (at least) one of the {P_i} processors resulting from relationship implementation. Considering interface design and following system design principles (e.g. as proposed in [16, 29]), three cases must be raised:

- Designing a native interoperable processor P induces the design of each needed or potential interface, by considering each interface as a sub-processor of P.
- Improving the interoperability of an existing processor P can induce global or partial re-engineering of each of its interfaces, considering that each processor P1 found to play the role of interface can either replace one of the parts of P or be added to P.
- Improving the interoperability of processor P, by considering P impossible to modify (e.g. P must be definitively integrated into a more complex processor P', perhaps assumed to be the upper-level system). It induces the design and addition of new interfaces between P and the other processors from the environment.

In accordance with the basic principles of Systems Engineering approach, and as illustrated in Fig. 5 an interface can be viewed as a processor characterized by:

- **Interface Purpose:** The interface (objective 1) *"allow to ensure the exchange of flows or services between two or more systems (components/functions/actors or business units having to be identified), as expected from an efficient (in terms of resources used) and effective (with positive results) way"*, or (objective 2) *"contributes to improve the protection of a system (to be identified) from an efficient and effective way, in taking into account other systems with which the interaction is not mandatory or even inevitable"*.

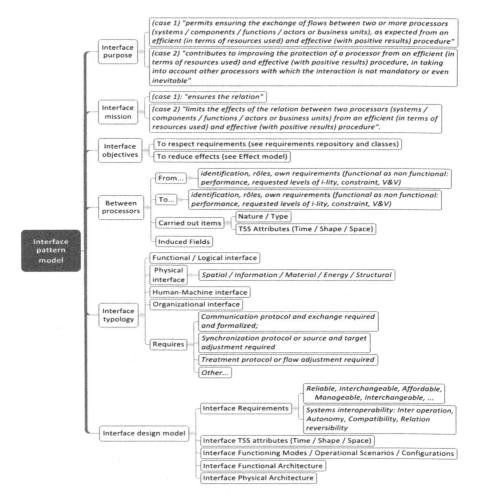

Fig. 5. Interface pattern model

- **Interface Mission:** An interface (objective 1): *"ensures the requested interaction i.e. exchange of flow(s), service(s) (themselves inducing exchange of flows)"* or (objective 2) *"limits the effects of the interaction between identified processors (systems/components/functions/actors or business units) from an efficient (in terms of resources used) and effective (with positive results) way"*.
- **Interface Objectives:** An interface must respect overall functional and non-functional requirements (including interoperability but also, for instance, performance, ergonomics, constraints, or verification requirements). They are induced or come from the identified processors in relation. At least, an interface must improve the identified processors interoperability (i.e. compatibility, interoperation, autonomy and reversibility), reduce effects (having to be detected, identified and then modelled

by an effect model) following the interface objectives, interchangeable, reliable, affordable, scalable, manageable and interchangeable (Fig. 5).

- **Interface Typology:** logical or functional at first during the design process, it will become physical, human-machine (HMI) or organizational interface. So, it is proposed to distinguish the functional or logical interface, from physical, human-machine and organizational interfaces as follows:

- *Functional interface*: between functional entities (e.g. functions from functional architecture). The designer creates functional interfaces between functions that model the flows to be exchanged (data, material, energy) in the role of input, output, control (trigger) or resource flows. This notion of function requires determining:

  - types of carried out items, contents, origin (external of the system of interest or internal), and respective roles in the system;
  - whether or not a communication protocol and exchange is requested and formalized;
  - whether a treatment protocol or flow adjustment is needed taking into account interoperability requirements;
  - whether a synchronization protocol or source and target(s) adjustment is requested.

After allocating functions to the processors, the functional interface evolves into the physical, human-machine and/or organizational interfaces, which are then required between the system under design, and its context, or else between subsystems and components.

- *Physical interface*: between the system to be designed and components or subsystems forming its context [11, 29, 30]. These interfaces are required to:
  - Enable operating functions on physical flows and hence meeting the functional requirements. For instance, [11] distinguished five types of physical interfaces:
    - Spatial: related to physical adjacency for alignment, orientation, serviceability, assembly or weight;
    - Structural: related to load transfer or content;
    - Material: related to the transfer of airflow, oil, fuel or water;
    - Energy: related to the transfer of heat, vibration, electric or noise energy;
    - Information: related to the transfer of signals or controls;
  - Respect non-functional requirements (performance, "*-ilities*" such as interoperability when considering non-functional aspect of interoperability, and abilities, e.g. emission, reception, or transport of a flow);

- *Human-Machine interface* (HMI): The activities required for user interface design are already detailed for instance in [30].
- *Organizational interface*: These interfaces are required between actors and organizational units involved in and required to play roles in the system of interest. Exchanges become necessary in conducting sharing, collaboration, communication

and cooperation when performing activities to: produce/manufacture, deliver, store, sell, buy, design, manage, control, verify, plan, teach and organize training periods for stakeholders, qualify actors' profiles, decide, etc. These interfaces can be modelled as a collaborative working process model or a virtual organization model for instance.

- **Interface SST Attributes.** The goal is to define what are the requested SST attributes of the requested interface, for instance, in terms of potential physical elements that can be used to implement the interface (communication components, connections, ports, links, etc.) as illustrated in Fig. 2 and such as:
  - Time e.g. duration for connection,/disconnection, maximum delay before updating value or life cycle duration before obsolescence of the carried out items;
  - Shape e.g. dimensions (L*H*D), geometry, weight, radiation from various nature (see the list of possible fields in the effect model);
  - Space e.g. position, speed, transfer speed...

- **Interface Functioning Modes/Operational Scenarios and Configurations:** As any component, an interface evolves all along its life cycle by passing from a functioning mode to another one, highlighting then various behavioural scenarios and configurations. An approach for discovering and analysing these characteristics are detailed in [31].

- **Interface Functional Architecture:** The interface must transform one or more flows stemming from an emitter system to a (set of) receiver system. This transformation allows avoiding physical effects that may impair the systems in interaction (e.g. disturbing or damaging structure/organization or behaviour) and moreover must verify the interoperability requirements. We propose to model the expected transformation by (1) a model of time, shape and space attribute transformation of the flow and of items transported by the flow, and (2) the effect model proposed above focusing on the potential effects to be avoided and anticipated. In design stage, the functional vision of an interface highlighting these two transformations can be for instance modelled by choosing and using one of the modelling languages introduced in Fig. 1 considering the nature of source and targets processors. This completes the interface pattern model with one or more functional architecture patterns models, more or less detailed aiming facilitating design by reusing partially or fully these models.

- **Interface Physical Architecture:** The interface is implemented by linking various sub-processors (physical subsystems or components, actors, sub-organizational units), on which the functions proposed in the functional architectures are to be allocated et then performed taking particularly into account all non-functional requirements. This description can be generated by using, for instance, any Physical Block modelling language and respecting SE principles.

5 Conclusion and Prospects

This paper has introduced conceptual aspects of an interface model pattern supporting engineers involved in natively interoperable system's design activities. This helps particularly and guides modelling activities but aims also to permit checking and testing conformity, coherence and adequacy [32] of proposed interfaces in order to design a system that will be able to maximise its interoperability in various situations even difficult to predict. The goal is now to develop modelling and analysis platform [33] integrating existing proof and simulation tools [34, 35] allowing then mixing formal properties proof and simulation as proposed in [36] when considering systems of systems [37] interoperability analysis.

References

1. Camarinha-Matos, L.M.: Collaborative networks: a mechanism for enterprise agility and resilience. In: Mertins, K., Bénaben, F., Poler, R., Bourrières, J.-P. (eds.) Enterprise Interoperability VI, pp. 1–8. Springer International Publishing, Switzerland (2014)
2. European Commission, Annex II - EIF (European Interoperability Framework) (2010). http://ec.europa.eu/isa/documents/isa_annex_ii_eif_en.pdf. Accessed 20 February 2015
3. ATHENA Interoperability Framework (AIF). http://athena.modelbased.net/model.html. Accessed 20 February 2015
4. Department of Defense (DoD) Architecture Framework (DoDAF), version 2007, 23 April, version 1.5 (Volumes I, II and III) (updated version 2.02 is available)
5. Daclin, N., Chen, D., Vallespir, B.: Methodology for enterprise interoperability. In: Proceedings of the 17th World Congress - The International Federation of Automatic Control - Seoul, Korea, 6–11 July 2008
6. Lavean, G.: Interoperability in defense communications. Commun. IEEE Trans. **28**, 1445–1455 (1980)
7. Clark, T., Jones, R.: Organisational interoperability maturity model for C2. In: 1999 Command and Control Research Technology Symposium. United States Naval War College, Newport (1999)
8. De Soria, I.M., Alonso, J., Orue-Echevarria, L., Vergara, M.: Developing an enterprise collaboration maturity model: research challenges and future directions. In: 15th International Conference on Concurrent Enterprising, Leiden, Netherlands, 22–24 June 2009
9. Naudet, Y., Latour, T., Chen, D.: A systemic approach to interoperability formalization. In: Proceedings of the 17th World Congress IFAC, International Federation of Automatic Control, Seoul, Korea, 6–11 July 2008
10. DoD, Systems Engineering Fundamentals. Defence Acquisition University Press (2001). http://www.dau.mil/pubscats/PubsCats/SEFGuide2001-01.pdf. Accessed 7 July 2012
11. AFIS, CT AIS, Interfaces techniques et architectures du système, fiche N°2 (2006) (in French)
12. Le Moigne, C.: La théorie du système général: théorie de la modélisation (1994) (in French)
13. Jean-Michel, P.: La modélisation par les systèmes en situations complexes. Thèse de Doctorat, Université de Paris Sud, France (1997) (in French)

14. Féliot, C.: Toward a formal theory of systems, Colloque d'Automne du LIX 2007 - CAL07 Complex Systems: Modelling, Verification and Optimization, Paris, Carré des Sciences, 3rd and 4th October 2007, http://www.lix.polytechnique.fr/ ~ liberti/cal07/presentations/. Accessed 11 July 2012
15. INCOSE, System Engineering (SE) Handbook, A Guide For System Life Cycle Processes And Activities Version 3.2.2, INCOSE TP 2003 002 03.2.2 (2011)
16. BKCASE Editorial Board. The Guide to the Systems Engineering Body of Knowledge (SEBoK), v. 1.3. R.D. Adcock (EIC). Hoboken, NJ: The Trustees of the Stevens Institute of Technology (2014). http://www.sebokwiki.org/. Accessed 17 July 2014
17. Blanchard, B.S., Fabricky, W.J.: Systems Engineering and Analysis. Prentice Hall International Series in industrial and systems engineering, 5th edn. Pearson College, London (2011)
18. Charlotte Seidner, Vérification des EFFBDs : Model checking en Ingénierie Système, Ph.D. Nantes University, 3 November 2009 (in French)
19. OMG, Business Process Modelling Notation 2.0. http://www.omg.org/spec/BPMN/2.0/PDF/. Accessed 16 March 2015
20. System Modeling Language SysML. http://www.sysml.org/. Accessed 16 July 2014
21. Mann, D.: Hands on Systemic Innovation. CREAX Press, Belgium (2002)
22. Altshuller, G.: The TRIZ method: numerous references and a presentation of TRIZ principles. http://www.altshuller.ru/world/eng/index.asp. Accessed 17 July 2012
23. Oxford creativity, Effects data base. http://wbam2244.dns-systems.net//EDB_Welcome.php. Accessed 27 November 2012
24. de Weck, O.L., Ross, A.M., Rhodes, D.H.: Investigating relationships and semantic sets amongst system lifecycle properties (Ilities). In: Third International Engineering Systems Symposium CESUN 2012, Delft University of Technology, 18–20 June 2012
25. INCOSE, Survey of Model-Based Systems Engineering (MBSE) Methodologies, INCOSE-TD-2007-003-01, Version/Revision: B, 10 June 2008
26. Nuseibeh, B., Easterbrook, S.: Requirements engineering: a roadmap. In: ICSE 2000, Proceedings, Conference on the Future of Software Engineering, New York (2000)
27. Mallek, S., Daclin, N., Chapurlat, V.: An approach for interoperability requirements specification and verification. In: van Sinderen, M., Johnson, P. (eds.) IWEI 2011. LNBIP, vol. 76, pp. 89–102. Springer, Heidelberg (2011)
28. Hollnagel, E., Paries, J., Woods, D., Wreathall, J. (eds.): Resilience Engineering in Practice: A Guidebook. ASHGATE Publishing Company, Farnham (2011). ISBN: 978-0-4094-1035-5
29. Thimbleby, H., Blandford, A., Cairns, P., Curzon, P., Jones, M.: User interface design as systems design. In: Faulkner, X., Finlay, J., Detienne, F. (eds.) People and Computers XVI-Memorable Yet Invisible, Proceedings of HCI 2002. Springer (2002). ISBN: 1852336595
30. Gruhn, P.: Human machine interface (HMI) design: the good, the bad, and the ugly (and what makes them so). In: 66th Annual Instrumentation Symposium for the Process Industries, 27–29 January 2011
31. Chapurlat, V., Daclin, N.: Proposition of a guide for investigating, modeling and analyzing system operating modes: OMAG. In: International Conference on Complex System Design and Management CSDM 2013, Paris, December 2013
32. Bérard, B., Bidoit, M., Finkel, A., Laroussinie, F., Petit, A., Petrucci, L., Schnoebelen, P., McKenzie, P.: Systems and Software Verification: Model Checking Techniques and Tools. Springer, Heidelberg (2001)
33. Nastov, B., Chapurlat, V., Dony, C., Pfister, F.: A verification approach from MDE applied to model based system engineering: xeFFBD dynamic semantic. In: Internation Conference on Complex System Design and Management CSDM 2014, Paris, France, December 2014

34. Formal verification tools overview web site. http://anna.fi.muni.cz/yahoda/. Accessed 10 April 2011
35. V&V Tools, RPG reference document (2006). http://vva.msco.mil/Ref_Docs/VVTools/vvtools-pr.PDF. Accessed 10 April 2011
36. Bilal, M., Daclin, N., Chapurlat, V.: System of systems design verification: problematic, trends and opportunities. In: Mertins, K., Bénaben, F., Poler, R., Bourrières, J.-P. (eds.) Enterprise Interoperability VI, pp. 405–415. Springer International Publishing, Switzerland (2014)
37. Ferris, T.L.J.: It Depends: Systems of systems engineering requires new methods if you are talking about new kinds of systems of systems, INCOSE (2006)

Author Index

Printed in the United States
By Bookmasters

Printed in the United States
By Bookmasters